Wide Open

D.M. DITSON

Wide Open

D.M. DITSON

COTEAU BOOKS

Edited by Janice A. Zawerbny
Designed by Jamie Olson
Typeset by Susan Buck

ISBN Hardcover: 978-1-7777199-3-7
ISBN Paperback: 978-1-7777199-2-0
ISBN Electronic: 978-1-7777199-0-6

Printed in the United States of America.

D.M. Ditson
www.dmditson.ca

Coteau Books

For Wendy,

whose words made space for mine.

Praise for Wide Open

"This incredibly brave and powerful memoir is written in prose both luminous and stark. I read it in one gulp, in awe of the author's willingness to surrender to her experience of trauma and of her generosity in sharing her journey with her readers. *Wide Open* will take you to the farthest reaches of what it means to be human."
> – Alison Pick, author of the memoir *Between Gods* and the novels *Strangers With The Same Dream, Far To Go* and *The Sweet Edge*

"D. M. Ditson's book is a courageous and powerful exploration of the insidiousness of sexual assault and rape. Approximately 460,000 girls and women are sexually assaulted in Canada every year. This book is an important glimpse into the world of one survivor of sexual assault. It has the potential to help us support survivors and reduce sexual violence."
> – Pamela Cross, feminist lawyer and co-chair of the Ontario Violence Against Women Roundtable

"In light of the worldwide #metoo movement as well as growing efforts to address post-traumatic stress disorder and its effects on people, D. M. Ditson's *Wide Open* is a timely, important and necessary read."
> – Dr. Vianne Timmons, President and Vice-Chancellor, University of Regina

"The narrator of this gripping memoir is on a journey to self-understanding. Why does she pick men who mistreat her? Why does she sometimes attack the men she loves? Why are her attitudes towards sex so confusing even to herself? She—and the reader—need to understand. Delving into her past, she examines the legacy of her family's fundamentalism and comes to recognize the ways in which her early experiences may have compromised her judgement, blighted her sense of boundaries, and coloured her responses to a horrific sexual assault suffered in young adulthood…In the last few years, Canadians have finally begun to acknowledge the pervasiveness of rape culture, but seldom has this problem been addressed from the point of view of someone who was raised as a conservative Christian. Written in vivid scenes, rich in dialogue and drama, and unfailingly honest, *Wide Open* tackles a significant subject in a voice that has rarely been heard."
> – Susan Olding, a juror for the 2017 John V. Hicks prize awarded to *Wide Open* before it was published

AUTHOR'S NOTE

This is the story of my life as seen through my eyes. Consequently, it is distorted through the lens of trauma. Others may have conflicting and equally-true versions of the events shared in these pages. My beloveds have already paid dearly for my wounds, and I regret any further pain my words may cause.

Some names and identifying details have been changed.

The past is never dead. It's not even past.

— William Faulkner, *Requiem for a Nun*

Of course it is happening inside your head, Harry, but why on earth should that mean that it is not real?

— J. K. Rowling, *Harry Potter and the Deathly Hallows*

Prologue

Now

Ian and I are on the couch watching one of his food shows. I slide my arm around his back, my fingers hovering above his waist. He doesn't suspect a thing. I tickle him.

He jumps and somehow I'm on the floor. He's kneeling on my shoulders and leaning over me. He clamps onto my nipples, pinching and laughing like a fiend.

I try to writhe away. "Stop," I say but there's no escape. His fingers are chewing at me. "Stop," I yell.

The pinches get harder.

Fuck you. I'm boiling, frothing. I fling my leg back, kicking over my head. My toe smashes something hard.

The pinching stops. I'm free. I won.

Ian's on the floor holding his face.

Right, it was Ian. The man I love. "Where did I get you?" I ask.

He doesn't answer. He's running his tongue along his teeth.

"Are you okay?"

"No," he slurs. "You kicked me in the face. You broke my fucking tooth."

I cover my mouth. Holy shit. I'm a lunatic. I'm as cold as I was on the minus-forty day I felt my eyeball freeze.

Ian's in the bathroom checking the damage. He spits and comes back. "It's chipped," he says. "What the fuck?"

I'm still on the floor, hiding my face. My head is shaking back and forth.

"Come here," Ian says.

I can't.

He sits beside me. "I'm sorry for getting mad. I'm fine. It's nothing a dentist can't fix."

"I'm sorry," I whisper.

"It's okay. It was an accident. I know you didn't mean it."

But I did. I wanted to hurt him. His face goes blurry behind the tears that are trapped in my eyes. My god, I didn't mean to mean it.

Later

"Why did all these bad things happen to me?" I ask my therapist, Nicole, a year into our work together. "I mean why didn't I learn? Why didn't I stop putting myself into such risky situations?"

Nicole's eyes remain as soft and steady as ever. "You didn't have the capacity to deal with what happened, so your subconscious took over and tried to resolve it for you," she says.

"I don't understand."

"We see a similar response in traumatized children," she says. "They'll often use their dolls to replay an upsetting incident over and over again until they can create a better ending."

My body shudders. A twitch of recognition. "Is that why I was obsessed about wrestling with Ian?"

She nods but she needn't have. I feel the answer all through me, the urgency and fire, the fury and desire.

Faith

1

HALLELUJAH

Now

I fly home from Belize to Regina on Easter Sunday, and it's like hallelujah, she is risen indeed. I spent two months deep in the jungle mending a broken heart, but now that I'm back on Saskatchewan soil my insides reflect the spring that's busting up through the dirt.

I try online dating and get a message from a hair-gelled engineer named Ian who is into science and nature documentaries.

"What do you like about science?" I ask when we meet for a walk.

"There are so many mysteries out there that we can understand when we look closely enough. One discovery builds on another and teaches us more about the entire world."

"So you're an atheist?"

"Ninety-nine per cent. I don't believe in God but I'm not closed to the possibility. How about you?"

"I believe in something. Maybe it's God or kindness or people being good to each other."

We go for dessert. Candlelight flickers across his hazel eyes as he tells me he's going to Africa on a volunteer trip this summer, and I get what Grandpa meant when he said he saw Grandma across the room and knew he would love her forever.

Later Ian and I go for a walk around Wascana Lake and he comes close when we get to a lookout point. Too close. My heart races and I dart away.

We keep going and climb a hill. At the top, he sweeps in and presses his lips against mine. Whoa, he likes me! My nerves quiet down and I wrap my arms around him and imagine how great it would be if I never had to let go.

Ian holds the ladder for me while I clean my eavestroughs. I throw handfuls of dirt and leaves to the ground, but some of the mess hits him in the face. I stare down at him with giant eyes. "I'm so sorry."

He spits out the clump that got into his mouth. "It's nothing," he says. "Keep going. There's lots of eavestrough left to go."

I tell Mom and my missionary sister Tenille about The Ladder Incident. "He must really like you to put up with that," Tenille says.

"Maybe," Mom says. "But D doesn't like anyone who likes her back. The instant she catches someone liking her, she runs away."

I pretend to laugh. It's better if that's what Mom thinks. The truth is that no one has ever wanted to stay.

I like Ian more each day. He bench-presses me and picks me up by my armpits to toss me in the air, like adults do to make kids laugh. We have water-balloon fights. He lets me give him a piggyback and jumps off my back in time to catch me when I topple over.

The only things I don't like about him are that he's into zombies and obscene TV shows like *The Sopranos* and has an awful photo above his couch – a woman drowning in dark waters. Her pastel skirt billows around her as she flounders, hopeless, suspended in death.

"Don't like it?" Ian asks when he sees me frowning at her.

"Sorry. It's super creepy."

He laughs. "Then don't look at it."

We're in my room kissing when I pull away. Shit, what if I don't mean anything to him? What if he just wants to get me into bed?

"What's wrong?" he asks.

"Do you want to be exclusive?" The words shoot straight out before I can catch them.

Ian looks startled.

"I'm sorry. I didn't mean to make things awkward. Oh god. I just… I don't want to fool around with someone who is dating other people." I'm biting my lip. I wish I could take it back.

"That's fair," he says, leaning against the pillows. "Let's try it."

"Really?"

My new boyfriend nods and kisses me again.

We're having dinner on a patio when I ask if Ian wants to get married or have a family someday. "I don't think so," he says. "It's not something I need. I don't even know if I'm capable of love."

"Oh," I say and push my hopes back down. I've been counting our days together and then our weeks, adding them up and wondering how long he'll stay.

We go back to his place. We're kissing and his body presses against mine and his hands are all over my long green skirt. I want him to stop but it's like I'm an empty tube of toothpaste and nothing will squeeze out. I concentrate hard and finally a "no" whispers forth.

Ian stops, but I'm crying in his arms.

"I need to take things really slowly," I say. "Some bad things happened to me a long time ago."

He wipes at my tears and new ones replace them. "Do you want to tell me about it?"

I shake my head.

"Okay. No problem. That's totally fine," he says. "Is there anything I can do to help?"

"Can you ask 'Is this okay?' any time you touch me? And can you only date me if you really mean it?"

"Of course," Ian says. "I want to be with you."

He pulls me closer. "Oops. Is this okay?"

I nod.

Other times when I shake my head, he makes us popcorn or gets me a glass of water.

I say yes now, some of the time, and it's glorious in the warmth of his arms.

"Have you dated much?" I ask Ian one day when we meet up after work.

"Not really. I've had a bunch of first dates but nothing that's lasted more than five or six dates. Women seem to find me obnoxious," he says with a grin.

"Why do you say that?"

"Because I don't hold back. One woman said it's gross to take baths, that it's like stewing in your own filth. So I said to her, 'I don't know about you, but I'm not filthy to start with.'"

"That's not very nice."

"Sure, but it was worth it," he says. "Did I tell you my friends made me promise not to play any racket sports with you?"

"Why's that?"

"They thought I'd get dumped again. I don't let anyone win. Not even my little cousins. You have to earn your victory or it doesn't mean anything."

Sure enough, when I finally convince him to play ping pong, he wins by like a hundred points. I ask him to cut me some slack but he says, "Not a chance. You knew what you were getting into."

I laugh but he means it so we stop keeping score.

Ian's holding his laptop when he opens the door to his apartment. "You have to watch this," he says. "My friends and I have been emailing about this video all day. You have to see it to know why my comment is so great."

He hits play. A woman in a bikini lies on a table in a medical office while a man draws on her skin with black marker.

"Creepy," I say.

"Yeah. Totally. It's about Satanic rituals. So now you're ready for my joke." He opens his email and reads his words back to me: "Hot. I added it to my masturbatory library."

"I don't think that's funny," I say.

Ian insists it is.

My stomach closes in on itself. I feel like I did when he said he once lived near a strip club or like I do when topless women prance across the screen during the shows we watch on his couch.

Is he a good guy or a perv? I'm so nervous I think I'll die but I have to know. "Do you watch porn?" I ask. Please say no. Please be the man I want you to be.

"Almost never," he says. "I could take it or leave it."

Okay. That's not so bad. I bet that's like once or twice a year. Maybe I can live with that.

I ask Ian why he chose to message me out of all the women online.

"I was casting a wide net," he replies. "You have better odds that way."

"Oh."

"It's nothing against you. It's simple math."

I must not look reassured because he continues: "You have nothing to worry about. I've only slept with two women."

Shit. The numbers conversation.

"You don't need to tell me about your past," he says after a silence that lasts a hundred years. "It doesn't matter to me."

Good, because I'll never tell him. It's impossible for someone to know and still like me.

2

SEE JANE TRI

Now

I'm doing a mini-triathlon called See Jane Tri in a few days, and Ian says he wants to cheer me on. "It will be boring," I say. "I won't be any good. I've barely trained."

When he won't be dissuaded, I try the real reason I don't want him there: "My parents are coming to watch."

"That's fine. I'm happy to meet them."

"Are you sure? It will be awkward. They're pretty devout Christians. I wouldn't be surprised if Dad shows up in a Rapture t-shirt."

"I'm not worried about it," Ian says. "I'll keep to myself when you start the race."

My gut clenches as I park my bike in the transition area and tuck my ponytail into my pink swim cap. I hope he doesn't hate my family. Also, I hope I don't finish last. Everyone else looks like they know what they're doing.

Ian walks over in a shirt so dark that it emphasizes his white headphone cords. Good, at least he has something to listen to other than my parents.

Mom and Dad arrive with my thirteen-year-old sister, Holly. I have four sisters – Bethany, Tenille, Jenna and Holly – but Holly is the only one who still lives at home.

I introduce Ian and cringe as my parents shake his hand. Please don't say anything awful, I beg my parents silently.

"Good weather for a race," Dad says, and they talk about my swim cap and if they'll be able to pick me out from the others in the pool. The conversation is restrained, dull, like a new hire getting toured through an office, but I wish I could drag them apart. It's going to go badly the second one of them mentions God, science, TV, politics or practically anything else.

I get called to line up at the pool and don't see Ian or my parents again until I'm running my laps at the end. He and my parents are on opposite sides of the crowd, waving at me. Phew, they haven't scared him away.

Childhood

It's crowded at the Calgary Zoo, way busier than usual. Mommy says everyone is here to see the giant pandas that came from China. It's a long time before we get to see the huge teddy bears eating bamboo.

They're so cuddly. I put my hand on the glass and wish I could reach through. There's a sticker on the glass above my head. It's a black bird, a stop sign so the birds don't bonk their heads. Nobody can get close to the pandas, not even if they have wings.

"Mommy, can we go see the butterflies?"

"Be patient. This is special."

I squirm as I wait.

"Ants in your pants?" Mommy would say if she noticed.

When she's ready, she pushes Tenille and Jenna in the stroller while Bethany and I run ahead to the building with insides that look like we're still outside. There are trees and leaves and a pokey cactus that's taller than me.

The air is hot on my skin as I push through the plastic strips that hang in the doorway to the butterfly room. Mommy says the plastic helps the butterflies stay inside. Why would they leave? This is the best place in the world.

Painted wings flit everywhere. Blue, red, black, yellow, orange, white and pink. I try to catch them but the butterflies are too fast.

"Look," Bethany whispers. Her Disney-princess eyes are bigger than ever. Whoa, a butterfly is standing on her arm.

I put my arms up and try to hold still like Bethany. I want a butterfly to pick me too. The butterflies dance like fancy figure-skater ladies in their sparkly dresses but don't come close.

"Time to go," Mommy says.

I drag behind. I wish I was perfect like Bethany and good enough for a butterfly.

"Right now, D," Mommy calls from the other side of the plastic.

I lean my head through the plastic strips. They slide closed behind me, locking the butterflies in.

Mommy takes us swimming and we have the whole pool to ourselves. I'm at the edge, ready to jump. Bethany dips her toes in. "Need go potty," Tenille says.

Mommy sighs. "Why didn't you tell me earlier?" She sends Bethany and me to a bench by the bathroom door. "Sit with your backs against the wall," she says, giving me The Look. Mommy carries baby Jenna as she leads Tenille by the hand. "Don't you dare move a muscle until I come back."

I bounce my favourite little pony and try to think about anything other than the pool. Cotton Candy has pink hair. Mommy says Bethany and Tenille have blond hair. Jenna's is brown. Mine is called carrots but it just tastes like hair.

I squirm on the bench.

"Sit still," Bethany says.

I try.

I can't go in. But Cotton Candy can!

I throw my pony into the pool. She makes a big splash.

I miss her. She's too far away. What if she sinks?

I run to the water and jump in. I splash around next to Cotton Candy and grin big.

Bethany stays on the bench. She's leaning forward as far as she can while keeping her bum smooshed against the wall. "Mommy, come now! D isn't obeying!" she yells.

Mommy yanks me to the side of the pool. Her fingers are tight, ouchy around my arm. "Why couldn't you sit on the bench for one single minute? You could have drowned!"

"I'm sorry," I whisper, chin quivering. "I wanted to go in the water."

"I know," Mommy sighs, kissing the top of my head. "But you were in the deep end. I need you to obey. I need you to stay alive."

I'm making a present for Mommy at Sunday school. I take a basket the size of my hand and stuff it full of cotton balls. Then I glue two fuzzy teddies on top. I hide the basket behind my back when Mommy comes to get me. It's not good enough yet.

In the car Bethany opens a brand-new pack of gum. It's light blue and smells like toothpaste but yummy. "Please, please, can I have a piece?" I whisper.

"No."

"Please, it's for Mommy. For this." I hold out the basket. Bethany shakes her head.

The next day she goes to school, leaving the gum on the dresser. She said no. But Mommy would love it. But I'm not allowed. But it's not taking if it's giving.

I sneak over to the dresser and open the pack. There are lots of pieces. I take one. Aw, it's wrapped like a present.

I put it in the basket next to the bears and run to find Mommy. "I have a surprise for you!" I say, bouncing up and down.

"Oh thank you," Mommy says. "Wait, isn't this Bethany's gum? Did she give it to you?" She stares down at me.

"Well, no, but I took it for you."

"You know better than that! That's stealing. You have to tell Bethany what you did."

When we hear Bethany's bus drive up, Mommy tells me to stand by the door.

Bethany comes in and puts her backpack on the floor. I can't look at her.

"D has something to tell you," Mommy says.

"I took a piece of your gum. I'm sorry." The words hurt coming out. They burn like throw-up.

Bethany's voice is quiet. "I'm disappointed in you."

I look up at her serious big-sister eyes, then down again.

"I'd even decided to give you a stick of gum tonight," she says gently.

I'm as chewed up as the old gum she spits in the garbage.

Daddy is lying on the couch in his usual spot, catching forty winks. Is he asleep? He's still but his breathing is quiet, not the bear snore that comes at night.

I stalk over to the flowery couch and pause by his feet. I watch his eyelids. They don't flicker. He doesn't know I'm here.

I crouch. Then pounce. I land in the gap between his knees and the back of the couch. His eyes stay closed.

I wedge myself in. I'm leaning against the couch, my feet against his legs. I push as hard as I can. Daddy is big like Goliath. He's big enough to see over the fridge and strong enough to open the Cheez Whiz. But I'm going to get him.

He budges, maybe an inch or two. He grunts as I shove and kick against him. He slides over, closer to the edge. His eyes stay shut. I push again, and Daddy crashes to the floor. Legs first, head last.

"Whoa, what happened?" he asks, looking up at me.

I shake with giggles, love.

Daddy gets back on the couch and shuts his eyes.

I stare at his eyelids. Please open!

They don't.

I find Tenille and Jenna in the playroom. "Come here," I whisper, and they huddle around me. "Help me knock Daddy off the couch!"

"Won't he get mad?" Tenille asks.

"It's a game. It's okay."

Tenille and Jenna look at each other. They're best friends. They look back at me.

"It will be fun. I promise."

The girls follow me. One after another we leap onto the couch, me behind Daddy's shoulders, Tenille at his back and Jenna by his legs. We push, shove, push. It's harder this time. We keep pushing. It's taking forever.

Daddy rolls close to the edge. Then thuds onto the carpet.

The girls and I laugh until my tummy hurts. "You got me," Daddy says. Then, "That's enough."

After that Daddy starts napping in his room but we follow him there too, pushing at him until we make him open his eyes.

Now

I go to the airport with Ian when he leaves for Africa on his volunteer trip. He's going to spend the summer in the Sahara working on an irrigation project.

We hug, and I wave goodbye forever as Ian disappears through security. He's going to forget me.

My phone is beeping when I get home. It's a message from Ian: "I was happy that you came to the airport with me and sad to see you leave. I'm sure I'll miss you while I'm away."

I save the message and play it over and over again, like a mantra.

The summer passes while I water Ian's plants and bring in his mail, and five weeks later he calls me from the Sahara. "I can't wait to see you," he says.

When he comes home, he scoops me up in his arms and reads me his journal, even the part about talking to me. "D has an interview for a communications job at city hall," he reads. "I'm sure she will get it."

"I did," I say, "and thanks for the vote of confidence."

We crawl into bed and squeeze against each other, and I'm so happy that tears leak onto my pillow, the one he bought so I'd be more comfortable at his place.

Ian is looking for a new job too. He has been since we met. He moved to Regina because it was the only place he could find a decent engineering job, but he wants to get a position in Toronto near his family. "Don't worry," he says when I chew on my lip. "It won't happen for a long time and we'll figure things out."

Ian and I go to my parents' place while they're away and spend a day on the trampoline and bounce until he hurts his back. I run a bath for him and give him a massage. When we tuck in for the night, he kisses my neck. "I thought you were tired, Mr. Sore Back," I say.

"Not yet," he says, running his fingertips over my skin. He kisses my stomach. "Is this okay?"

"Yes."

"And this?"

"Yes."

3

BIBLE SCATTEGORIES

Now

We're hanging out with my family and playing Bible Scattegories when Ian writes an obscene answer about the Sodomites.

Dad asks everyone for their scores. While they're counting, I grab Ian's sheet and scribble over his answer, greying it out. Ian chuckles. Mom and Tenille smile at me. They think he's having a good time. He's not. He's asked me like five times already if we could leave.

"You have to know that your family is nuts," he says when we're pulling out of the driveway.

"They're not so bad."

"Yes they are. Fucking fundamentalists. I'm impressed that you turned out normal when you grew up in that. I can't fathom what you get from being around them."

Childhood

Mommy and I are the only ones in the kitchen. Tenille and Jenna are napping, and I don't know where Bethany is. I pull the bag of marshmallows out of the cupboard.

"Please can we?"

"Aren't they better toasted?" she teases.

"They're better in my tum!"

She smiles and gets two forks. "Come here," she says and pops me onto the counter next to the stove. I hold still while she turns on the burner.

She spears a marshmallow onto each fork and passes one to me. "Hold it carefully, back from the element like this."

Mommy's marshmallow is turning golden brown. Mine is white on top. I put it closer to the burner. Uh oh, smoke! I pull it away but it's too late. My marshmallow is black.

Black like the first page of the construction-paper book I made in

Sunday school. When we are on that page we sing, "My heart was black with sin until the Saviour came in."

I remember a picture of Jesus I have in my room. He's glowing like a lightning bug. He's in a garden, knocking on a heart door.

I feel thuds inside. In my heart. Jesus?!

He knocks harder. Faster.

"Mommy, is Jesus in my heart?"

She takes my burned marshmallow and puts it down. "He will be if you invite Him in. Do you want me to pray with you? We can do that right now."

I nod and bow my head.

"Okay, repeat the words after me," she says. "Dear Jesus. Please forgive me for my sins. I need You. Please come into my heart and guide me all the days of my life. I love You. Amen!"

Mommy hugs me. Then she gives me her perfect marshmallow. It's yum, all warm and gooey inside.

We don't live anywhere any more. Mommy says it's too hard in Calgary right now so we're going to stay with Grandma and Grandpa.

It's late when we get to Medicine Hat but Grandma and Grandpa, Mommy's parents, are waiting on the front steps. Grandma is in her fuzzy housecoat. She smells like soap and cookies when she pulls me close.

Tenille and I get to sleep in the doll room so I nest into my blankets and look up at the shelves of Grandma's favourite dolls. They're everywhere, like stars.

Grandma rescues all the dolls she can find. She buys them from garage sales, stores and doll magazines. Sometimes she buys bags of heads at a craft store and sews bodies for them. Mommy says she saves dolls from garbage cans too.

When Grandma brings her new babies home, she washes them and makes outfits for them. She puts bows in their hair, ties their shoelaces and brushes pink stuff onto their cheeks until they look pretty, ready for church.

I hear her ask Mommy, "Doesn't this one look like baby Lisa? And this one with the mischievous expression, does she remind you of one of your girls?"

We don't go to real school any more because Mommy decided to be our teacher, but I do math at the table while Grandma sews.

Thirty fabric hearts hang on the wall under a giant heart that says

GOD LOVES. The pink heart with white polka dots says my name in light blue thread. There are hearts for each of my sisters and the rest of the cousins. Grandma loves us so much it doesn't fit inside her so she had to make all these extra hearts.

Mommy peels a great stack of potatoes. She is going to miracle them into doughnuts.

"Why did Jesus turn water into wine when alcohol is a sin?" I ask.

"Seems like an error in judgment," Mommy says. She is wearing a flowered apron she sewed herself. She shoos the girls and me out of the kitchen.

"But I want to help," I say. By help I mean eat.

"You can all help when I'm ready. I'll ring the bell for you."

When she finally dings the bell – the one I sometimes get to shake before dinnertime – we thunder back down the hall. The kitchen table is sprinkled with flour and covered with hundreds of white doughy rings. She hands us brown paper bags and we fill the bottoms with icing sugar.

When the oil in our green pot is hot enough, she takes a ladle and lowers the first doughnut in. A bunch more follow. We wait, giddy, hovering as close to the stove as she'll allow.

The kitchen timer beeps and she flips the doughnuts over, perfect shiny tops facing up. "Dibs on the first one," I call.

Tenille and I squabble until Mommy reaches in with the ladle, pulls one out and drops it in my bag.

"Yes, I won," I cheer, closing the bag and shaking it, making sure to cover every bit of the doughnut with icing sugar before laying it on the platter she uses for serving Christmas turkey.

I wait as long as I can, then take a huge bite. It burns my mouth. I pant to cool off my tongue.

I try again. There, that's better. It's still hot, but so sweet and soft it tastes holy.

The girls and I shake icing sugar onto hundreds of doughnuts, the white powder dusting our hands, arms, faces.

Whenever Mommy isn't looking, I pop the doughnut holes into my mouth, sometimes gobbling two or three at a time. Tenille and Jenna sneak them too. We catch each other's eyes and giggle as we make them disappear.

These doughnuts are our own family miracle. Our water into wine.

Youth

Now that I'm in high school, I'm the captain of my Bible quizzing team and get to challenge any rulings I want. Dad, who is one of my coaches, thinks it's rude, but I get way more points when I argue for them. All the quizmaster knows is what's on his set of cards, but I know the entire Gospel.

My team is in a close match. We're crouched over our seats on these pads like Jeopardy buzzers that light up the scoreboard when we lift our butts.

A kid on the other team beats me on the jump. He stammers out all the right words. I know because I'm mouthing them along with him.

"You're incorrect," the quizmaster says.

Jesus carries me to the centre of the stage. "I'd like to make a challenge," He says in my voice. Dad grimaces like he's accidentally taken a bite of something spicy. I look back to the quizmaster. "He was right. He said everything you should have on the card."

The quizmaster checks again and adds twenty points for the other team.

"Why did you make that face?" I ask Dad after the quiz. "Were you embarrassed of me? Did you think I was trying to take points away from the other team?"

Dad's face goes red like I busted him and he won't meet my eyes. "You did the right thing," he says.

4

BLUE HEARTS

Now

Ian doesn't get it. Sure my parents were strict and maximum Christian, but what's wrong with that? My childhood was perfectly fine. Or at least good enough. Okay, fine. It wasn't all sunshine. But I hate that he's making me admit it.

Childhood

I take the yellow *Leave It To Beaver* book off the shelf and open it. Whoa, there's a Bad Word! I know because it's hiding under a thick black line. My heart beats fast. I wonder what it says. I put my eyeball next to the word, so close my eyelashes touch the page. I see a "g." I gasp. I remember Eve and the apple. I slam the book closed.

What to do with it? I'll throw it in the garbage. No, that's bad too. I should tell Mommy but I'm too scared. She would know I looked at the "g" on purpose. Evil is everywhere, even in our house. And in me.

I pull an armful of books off the shelf, and put the yellow book at the back in the empty space. Then I fill the gap with Bible stories. There, it's gone.

Later, Tenille, Jenna and I are playing Barbies when Tenille makes her bad lady say, "Holy smoke." The hallway thunders. Mommy stomps in, grabs Tenille and drags her away. "You aren't allowed to say that!" I hear through the walls. "Only God is holy."

"What happened?" I ask when Tenille gets back. She hangs her head. It takes forever for her to speak. "Mommy washed my mouth out with soap."

I sneak into the bathroom and lock the door. I pick up the white bar of soap, the sin eraser. I lick it. I gag and try to spit but it's too late. The bubbles are sliding down my throat.

Mommy fills the bathtub. Bethany, Tenille and I climb in while she adds the bubbles. Mommy lifts Jenna in. It's squishy with all of us in the tub but I like it. We splash around together and share a bag of tub toys.

Mommy goes to the kitchen. "Call if you need help," she says.

I'm making a bubble beard when Bethany shrieks and points. A poop the length of a finger floats past. I yell too.

Daddy hears us and comes running. When he sees the poop, he scoops it up with one of our toys and plops the poop into the toilet. It's still flushing when he turns to us. "Who did it?" he asks.

We all shake our heads. Daddy's voice is loud. "You can't lie to me! Whose stink was that?"

Nobody answers.

"Stand up and bend over," he says.

We obey, and he checks our bums one at a time.

It wasn't me, but I feel guilty as I lean forward. Water drips down my legs. Daddy pulls my bum cheeks apart. My ears ring, the sound the TV makes when it's all grey and wiggly. Now I know: this is why Adam and Eve covered their bad parts with leaves.

My cousins and I are playing doctor in Grandma's front yard. One of the girls finds a dirty blue cup with a crack down the side. She pinches me with it.

"It's a needle," I say, and we chase everyone to give them their shots.

I'm under the tree when the doctor catches me again. "It's a bum needle. Pull your pants down," she says.

I obey.

"Panties too," she says.

I stare at her and we giggle. I pull down my white unmentionables. They're covered in tiny blue hearts. A cold breeze hits my bum and then the needle pinches. I pull my pants back up.

My cousin and I flop on the grass laughing.

Mommy opens the screen door. "D," she yells. "Get in here right now!"

Mommy takes me to the basement. She doesn't have a wooden spoon. Maybe she didn't see. But why isn't she saying anything?

Mommy sits on a hard chair. "Pull your pants down," she says.

"Oh no no," I say.

"Pants down. Unmentionables too."

The blue hearts break when I push them down.

Mommy bends me over her knees. She spanks me. Again and again. I cry as the spanks echo through the basement. When she's done, it hurts to stand.

"I'll blister your bum if you ever do that again," she says.

I don't know why the doctor game was bad or why I had to pull my pants down to make up for having pulled them down before.

We're at my auntie's house when she sends me to a cousin's room to get a toy. I'm reaching into the toy box when my cousin comes in and closes the door. "I'll show you mine if you show me yours," he says.

"Huh?" I ask. "I didn't bring anything."

He unzips his jeans and tugs down his unmentionables.

I stare at his pale eyelashes, the freckles splattered across his nose, cheeks. I can't breathe. I didn't say no. That means I owe him.

What does he want? Whatever it is, I don't want to. It's stealing if I don't. But I'll get in trouble if I do.

Forever goes by. My cousin pulls his jeans back up. "Never mind," he says and walks out.

Still, I can't breathe. I don't tell anyone. I know I deserve a blistered bum. I don't know why I'm bad, just that I am.

Daddy goes on an airplane, and when he comes back he has a new job. Government something. Audit and integration, whatever that means. He says we're moving to Regina, Saskatchewan, but we can wait until after my birthday.

I wear my favourite dress the day I turn eight. It's covered in rainbow hearts. We have confetti cake at my auntie's house and pink ice cubes made of juice. When I blow out the candles I scrunch up my eyes and make a wish: Please don't make us leave.

The grownups grab my arms and legs. Birthday bumps!

I fly up over everyone's heads. My dress goes up too. My face boils but the grownups keep going. I don't know why they don't stop. They fly me and my dress up again and again.

I see Mommy reach for my dress, feel her grab on with a tug that means I'm covered.

Then I'm yanked away. My dress blows so high it's all I can see.

Now

I'm showing Ian my photo album when I flip past a picture from that day. Mom's hand reaches into the frame, straining and helpless as my dress billows up, panties exposed nearly to the white elastic around my waist. She didn't say a thing. Not a word as the camera flashed and the others counted, "Six, seven, eight!"

Instead she stood silent, a pillar of salt, her hand outstretched as I was torn from her grasp.

Childhood

Tenille and I can't agree about who owns the pink plastic piggy bank. "It's mine," I say, yanking it away from her.

"No, give it back."

I take a steak knife from the drawer.

"What are you doing?" she asks. Her mouth and eyes are circles.

"Duh, I'm giving you half." I saw the knife blade along the slot in the top of its head where the coins would go if we had any.

Daddy walks in. "D! Put that knife down."

I drop the knife on the counter beside the pink shavings. "I'm being like King Solomon. We can't agree who it belongs to so we each get half."

Daddy is shaking his head.

"But I'm doing the Bible!"

"You aren't allowed to cut your toys. I'm not going to spank you, but Tenille gets the piggy bank."

"I don't want him now that you wrecked him," Tenille says, shoving the piggy bank at me.

After Mommy tucks me in I hear her go downstairs and fill the kitchen sink. I listen to the dishes rattling. Her voice floats up to my room. "Why is D always so bad?"

Daddy says something I can't hear. Then Mommy says, "I don't know what to do with her any more."

I hug the jagged plastic pig so tight my tears drip down his cheeks.

We go camping the summer I'm going to turn eleven. Bethany isn't with us. She went to Florida for missionary training and now she's in Papua New Guinea with a bunch of other teenagers. She writes us letters about how she got to ride in a wheelbarrow because she hurt her ankle and about who won the Miss Piggy award for having the messiest tent.

Our tent is clean on Mommy and Daddy's side. It's just their two-person sleeping bag, air mattress and zipped-up bags. The side I share with Tenille and Jenna looks like it exploded. After Mommy tucks us in, she zips the white canvas wall between us.

I hear Daddy click off the flashlight and watch as the ring of light disappears. A few blinks later I can see Tenille and Jenna again. We look like pigs in a blanket, ready for Mommy to pop us into the toaster oven.

Mommy and Daddy are whispering to each other. Tenille is snoring. Mommy and Daddy's air mattress groans once, then again. They're still whispering. Their sleeping bag rustles.

A sloppy noise comes from the other side of the canvas wall. It sounds like when Daddy eats chunks of oranges at the breakfast table, like when he slurps the juice from the rind, rips the flesh from the peel and smacks his lips.

But we don't have oranges.

My skin crawls like dirt full of worms. I thrash around in my sleeping bag to make the noises stop. I kick and squirm until Mommy's voice hisses through the tent wall. "Lie still. Go to sleep."

I hold still even though I want to smash through the tent window and run off into the night.

The noises keep going. There's a terrible smell, like dirty laundry and gym shoes. I don't know what's happening, but it's scary and wrong, like a Really Bad Sin that not even married people should do.

I gag and try not to breathe. I pull my sleeping bag over my head. The noises continue, growing louder. I'm frozen with my hands clamped over my ears and with my mouth and eyes squeezed tight.

After forever the noises turn into whispers. There's more rustling. The air mattress creaks. Then it's quiet except for Tenille's snores.

Later Daddy snores too, but I keep my hands over my ears. My skin is slimy and cold, like the morning dew that forces itself onto my toes in the prickly grass.

The orange noises come back the next night. And the next.

I drag my sleeping bag out of the tent before bedtime and carry it to the van.

Mommy catches me spreading it on the back seat. "Put your sleeping bag back in the tent," she says. "You're not sleeping here."

I scramble out of the van and stand as tall as I can. "It's too smelly in the tent and it's scary and I can't sleep and I hate it."

Mommy frowns but I don't care if she spanks me. I'm not going back in the tent. "I'm sleeping here," I say.

"Fine, but you better be good," Mommy says.

I crawl into the back seat and curl up. I don't even mind the seatbelt buckle that jams into my side. I'll do anything to get away from the tent.

When I go to the outhouse, I find blood on the toilet paper. "Something's wrong with me," I whisper to Mommy back at the campsite.

"But you're only ten," she says like she's talking to herself. She reaches into the van's glove compartment and hands me a yellow plastic package. "Attach the sticky side to your undies."

I beg my parents for quarters for the shower, but even as I rinse blood drips down my legs. I'm filthy, unholy, like the smell in the tent.

When we stop at a motel on our way home, I claim the shower, unwrap the white bar of soap and wash camping and tents and blood off me.

My parents are on one bed, Jenna has a cot and I stretch out on the other bed next to Tenille. I yawn. "Now this is better than camping!"

But as soon as Mommy and Daddy turn off the lights, the terrible noises are back.

I know better than to say anything. I pull the blankets over my head, plug my ears and try not to breathe. It's not as scary when I hold my breath, and I feel myself slipping away like in a dream. Not like falling asleep but like floating, there but not there at all.

5

TENDER BUD

Now

It's October. Ian and I have been together for six months now. It's the first time I've been able to track a relationship by months instead of weeks, and he still wants to keep me.

I'm on his flannel sheet. He's above me, and I'm running my hands down the back of his neck and along his shoulders. "Do you want to have sex with me?" I ask and blush when his eyes pierce mine. If he wants to, it will be our first time.

Ian rolls away to the far side of the bed. "Are you sure?"

"Yes."

He rubs my arm. "Not today. We should wait, just a little while, to be sure you mean it."

I pause. "I appreciate that you're looking out for me but that's kind of patronizing. It's fine if you want to wait, but I'm ready right now."

Ian kisses me and he's back above me and his eyes are deep, kind oceans.

It's beautiful. Slow and gentle. Like oatmeal with raisins, like a cat licking her kittens clean, like a flower swaying in the summer breeze.

I'm wrapped tight in Ian's arms. He fell asleep that way and I'm trying to stay awake, to make time stop here in this perfect moment.

I've been wrong about sex; it is holy. It's a needle and thread weaving through a broken heart and stitching it back together.

Childhood

We're on the way home after my Sunday school class watched *The Princess Bride*. "How was the movie?" Mommy asks when my sisters and I are all buckled in.

"Bad. They kissed even though they weren't married!"

"Oh, that's just pretend," she says. Her eyes meet mine in the rearview mirror. "They use special effects so it looks like a kiss."

I replay the kiss in my head. It looks like they kissed lips. "Those moviemakers sure know how to trick people."

"Yes. It's not nice."

Youth

When I'm seventeen, I'm at the theatre watching Julia Roberts and Hugh Grant kiss, their faces movie-screen gigantic. When she pulls away her bottom lip catches on his before bouncing back. It looks legit. And how much effort would it take to create a CGI kiss when they could lean in for an awkward second and be done with it?

"Do you think they actually kissed?" I whisper to my friend who's holding the popcorn.

"You're kidding."

"Well, wouldn't it be easier if they just kissed?"

"Uh, yeah," she says. "That's what they do."

Childhood

Mommy pushes a hardcover book at me that looks like it would have been old when she was a kid. "Read chapter three," she says.

I take the book and Mommy disappears while I flip to the right chapter. There's a drawing of a boy and girl in their undies. Arrows point at all their parts.

A few years earlier I drew nipples on a girl bear and Mommy got so mad that I scribbled over the whole page with my ugliest brown crayon. Nipples are bad on a bear but they're worse on kids. I slam the book closed and dust gets in my eyes.

Mommy must have given me the wrong book. I try to erase the page from my head. I know how: close my eyes, stop breathing and fill my ears with static.

That's what I did the time Daddy changed his clothes with the bedroom door open, when I saw his… Stop it. Don't say that. Cancel, delete, gone.

At Pioneer Girls my teacher says, "Boys try to trick girls into having sex. But sex is like tape: if you stick it to more than one thing it's worthless."

Obviously sex is terrible. And totally gross. I'd never. But I flip through the dictionary at my piano teacher's house while I wait my turn.

I look for all the dirty words I've heard in church: "harlot," "fornicate" and "lewd." When the student in the other room stops playing, I slap the dictionary closed.

Later, I'm sitting at the table at Pioneer Girls club. "What do you want to be when you grow up?" one of the girls asks Jody.

"A wife and a mom," she says.

The girls talk about their perfect weddings. The dresses, colours and flowers they want.

My ears are ringing, that fuzzy TV noise. I wish the teacher was here. "What about you?" someone asks me.

My shoulders shrug high enough to swallow my neck. I can't say I want to get married in the butterfly room at the zoo, my favourite place in the world. I can't say it, can't even think it, because it won't happen. I can't get married because no one will love me. "I don't want to get married," I say.

Everyone stares at me. I imagine them all in veils and lace, lovely and loved.

"But how are you going to be a mom?"

I can't breathe. I'll never be good enough for a baby of my own. "I don't want that either."

My sisters and I have been in real school since we moved to Saskatchewan three years ago. But in the summer Mommy says Tenille and Jenna aren't going back when school starts again.

"Why?" I ask.

"I'm going to home-school them again," she says. "They're having some problems with the other kids and this will be better for them."

"What problems?"

"That's not for you to know."

"But why?"

"Because that's what Daddy and I decided. You can be home-schooled too if you'd prefer."

I like my school, but I remember going to playgrounds and swimming pools and libraries with my sisters while the Medicine Hat kids were in class. I'd rather do fun stuff than sit at a desk. So Mommy buys me a bunch of textbooks and I stay home too.

Now

Twenty years later my parents and their foster baby come to my house for lunch after their church service. Mom is wearing an ankle-length skirt and a t-shirt that says, "Pray for peace in the Middle East."

"Why did you pull Tenille and Jenna out of school?" I ask. I spit the question out fast so it doesn't get wedged in my throat.

Dad's nostrils flare like a horse about to charge. "Some kids asked if they liked boys or girls!"

"Oh," I say. "And?"

"Kids shouldn't be talking like that. That's unacceptable."

"So that's why you took the girls out?"

"Yes," Mom says, scooping the baby up. "And you need to stop questioning everything we do."

My parents look old, like strangers, as they hurry to the car, Mom hunching over to shelter the baby from the wind.

Youth

I've been in home-schooling for two years when I decide to go back to my old school for real grade eight. Mom agrees but makes me wear a bra every day.

The boys follow me down the hall at school when I'm wearing a stiff hand-me-down bra that leaves red marks on my skin.

"Hey, pointy boobs," Dylan says.

I switch to my training bra the next day, but the boys keep pointing at me. I don't know why until I catch my reflection in the bathroom mirror. Gross, nipple dots are sticking right through my shirt!

I layer my bras after that, the pointy one underneath and the training bra on top to flatten it down.

Before recess Dylan comes to my desk and drops down to one knee like a marriage proposal. "You are so beautiful to me," he sings.

What, he likes me? Oh. No. It's sarcasm. I scramble out of my desk and rush to the door. I'm sure my face is as fiery as my hair.

Dylan follows me, scooting on his knee and singing louder as the other kids smirk.

I run to the bathroom. As I'm closing the stall, I accidentally see my reflection: a billion zits, nerdy glasses and stupid two-bra boobs. Dylan is right. I'm so ugly it's a joke.

After the final bell of the day, I go home, take my bras off and run up and down the basement stairs, desperate to bounce my boobs off.

One of the youth-group leaders is driving a few of us back to church. Another kid is in the front by the driver, I'm behind them and James, the weirdo who likes me, is in the back.

James reaches for me and paws at my shirt. I squirm away. He grabs my bra and snaps it. "Stop!" I say. "Leave me alone."

James keeps fumbling, trying to unhook my bra. "Quit it," I say. The guys in the front don't notice or don't care. I lean forward, my chest on my lap, hoping to scrunch down out of his reach.

James grabs at me again. I slap his hand. "Don't!"

He unhooks my bra. I reach back to do it up. While I'm struggling, he yanks on my bra strap so hard it rips off.

I cross my arms tight. Why isn't anyone helping me?

Back at church, I find Jody by her big laugh. She's my best friend but I'm not hers. I wave her over to the Sunday school supplies cabinet and she helps me dig out a stapler.

"What's going on?" another leader asks when she sees us in the washroom.

"James wouldn't stop bugging me. He broke my bra. Can you help?" I lift the back of my white shirt up to my shoulders and watch in the mirror as she staples my bra.

"You kids," she says, shaking her head.

"Maybe I shouldn't have leaned forward," I say. "If I had shoved back against the seat he couldn't have reached."

"Yeah, that would have been better." She shoots another staple into my bra. "There, now you're back together," she says brightly.

I tug my shirt into place and keep my arms wrapped tight around me all night.

Dad frowns at me when I come for breakfast in a striped t-shirt.

"Go get a sweater," he says.

"I'm not cold."

Dad's voice is. "You are not allowed to cause men to stumble. Go change."

"Guys are only interested in one thing," Dad says later. "Trust me, I know." He just came back from Promise Keepers, a men's conference that seems like it's all about sex, like it's for creepy men who can't obey God on their own.

I want to ask, How do you know? How bad were you before you and Mom got married? How bad *are* you? Why do you even notice if my shirts are too tight, my skirts too short?

Now

I watch the early spring buds on my elm tree being whipped in the wind. I can't bear it. They're so small and fragile, helpless against the cold blasts.

I call Ian. "I need to talk to you."

"Sure, what's up?"

"Can you come over?"

Five minutes later Ian is hurrying up the sidewalk.

My stomach is full of concrete, the quick-dry kind I used to plug a hole in my basement as rainwater flooded in.

Ian sits on the far side of Grandma's old floral couch looking like I'm about to punch him.

"Maybe we should end things now," I say. "I can feel love growing inside like a tiny plant and I'm so scared." A fat tear rolls down my cheek. "If you're not going to want to keep me, we should stop now. Otherwise it will hurt me way too much."

"Oh," Ian says. "Is that all? You're safe with me. I promise. I want to be in this relationship. I want to be with you."

"Aren't you worried that we don't have anything in common?" I ask. "We don't like doing the same things and you don't like anyone I care about."

"Yeah," Ian says. "I've thought about that too. But it doesn't matter because we are both interested in everything and we have good conversations."

"Are you sure?" I ask, wishing for him to be right.

"Yes," Ian says, and I let him kiss my fears away.

And so it continues. The wind stops bashing the branches. The baby leaves emerge from their buds. And I step off the edge and tumble madly and deeply into Ian's arms.

"I love you," I tell him a billion times, and one day he whispers it back. No, I must have misheard. "What?"

"I love you too," he says.

I'm falling. His embrace is all that's holding me up. "You do?" I ask through a waterfall. He leads me to the couch and we laugh at my tears and how happy we are.

Ian invites me to go to Toronto to meet his family and friends. I've never met a boyfriend's parents before. No one's ever liked me enough for that. What if his family can't stand me?

We go through the photos on his computer until I can recite everyone's names.

"I told my mom you're freaking out about the trip," he says.

"That's embarrassing."

"Not at all. She said it's good that you're nervous because it means you care."

"I guess, but now I feel even worse."

"It will be fine. Everyone will like you. The only thing to worry about is whether or not you will like them."

A few days before the trip, I bolt up in bed. "There's not going to be a separate room for me, is there? Where am I supposed to sleep?"

"We're sharing the guest room."

"We can't do that. I'll sleep on the couch."

"Don't be ridiculous. They already know we're having sex."

"What?!"

"It's obvious. That's what couples do. The only thing that would weird them out would be you sleeping in the living room."

Over the week, we stay at his mom's condo, his aunt's place and his brother's house, and everyone knows we're sharing a bed. My gut is clenched so tight that I'm not surprised when I get sick and a giant cold sore erupts on my face. The only time I can relax is at his dad's glass condo, which we have to ourselves.

The telescope Ian gave his dad for Christmas is angled at the waterfront. But it could easily swing toward any of the neighbouring units.

I don't look through it. "The telescope is kind of pervy," I say. "With all the glass bedrooms and bathrooms around."

"Why?" he asks. "No one leaves their curtains open unless they want to be seen."

"That's not true. For instance, it didn't even occur to me that someone might be zooming in while I showered."

That night when Ian reaches for me, I send him back to the curtain to pull it closed as tight as it will go. There's still a gap of night sky. I pretend it's not there and shut my eyes.

6

Purple Monster

Now

We're in bed one night when Ian asks, "Do you believe there's a purple monster in your closet?"

I know what he's after. "No," I say, "but there could be. Let's not fight about what my family believes."

"But Christianity is for morons. Like does your dad really think Jesus got him a good parking spot, like Jesus would prioritize his walking distance over helping starving orphans?"

I shrug. Ian continues. "If you look at the facts, atheism is the only answer."

"But you're not an atheist," I say. "You're agnostic, like me. That's what you said on our first date – that you didn't know for sure whether or not God exists."

"Sure, but that's only a technicality. Any open-minded person has to leave room to be proven wrong when more facts come in. Otherwise you cross the realm into fundamentalism. But you have to be a lunatic to think that someone died and rose again."

I'm stunned. I knew Ian leaned toward atheism, but there's a vast, cold chasm between a maybe and a no.

"Let's talk about Santa instead," I say. "I believe in him at least in that I don't disbelieve in him. You can't prove he's not real and it's fun to imagine that he is."

"You don't believe in Santa. You're not taking this seriously."

"Fine, most of the Bible is nonsense, but there are some nice parts too. Can you please stop trying to pluck the leftover bits of Christianity out of me?"

Ian sighs. "So you want to ban me from talking about religion."

"No, you can say what you want, but I don't have to agree."

Youth

When our Teen Missions International catalogue arrives in the mail, I run to my room and pore over the pages, memorizing them like my quizzing verses. The possibilities swirl in my head. Kilimanjaro. Nepal. Timbuktu. Puppet shows. Steel-toed boots. Orphanages, alligators, camels and lions.

"Can I please go on a missions trip this year?" I ask my parents.

"You don't even help Dad and I set up the tent when we go camping, so why should we believe you'll help your team?" Mom asks.

"I promise I'll do my best."

"We'll think about it."

I ask Mom again a few days later.

"Will you be good? Will you obey your leaders even when you don't want to?"

"Yes, I'll be perfect," I promise. "Please?"

Mom shakes her head but she's smiling. "Okay. You can go."

"What? Really?!" I shriek and bounce across the kitchen into Mom's arms.

I decide on Timbuktu. I'm going to build a church, swim in the Niger and give puppet shows.

My trip costs something like $4,500, and I need to get donors. I pass out prayer cards and sponsorship letters at church and school and mail them to all my aunts and uncles. Dad sends my letters around too.

Soon I'm getting tons of cheques in the mail. Even people I don't know are sending money.

Dad helps me add the numbers and track who sent what, but a few weeks before my trip I only have half the money I need. "How am I going to go?" I ask Dad.

"We'll figure it out," he says and writes me a cheque for the rest.

"You can't afford that," I say. My family has no money to spare. Anyone could tell from looking in our fridge. We're out of cheese, milk and eggs. Whenever Mom brings home groceries she says, "Settle down. This has to last until the end of the month."

"Maybe I can't go," I say. "Do I have to give all the money back?"

"It's fine," Dad says. "Missions are the Lord's work, so we'll make it happen."

"Woo hoo, I'm going to Timbuktu!"

My family waves as I climb onto an old school bus full of teens heading to Florida for training.

There's a really cute sandy-haired guy across the aisle. He's wearing a blue-and-white striped shirt and a necklace with a tooth on it. I dare myself to say hi.

"Hey," he says and smiles.

"Want to play I Spy?" I ask. What a babyish game. What was I thinking? A ferocious blush scalds my cheeks.

"Cool," he says. "Sure."

We spy trees, grain elevators and train cars. Later Scottie tells me he's going to India to help at an orphanage, and I fall in love.

We drive for three days. Late on the last night Scottie and I are at the back of the bus, poking each other with twigs. Our sticks snap and get shorter. He puts his in his mouth and pecks me in the arm. I laugh and peck back.

Our faces are close together. We drop our sticks. I stop blinking and breathing.

He leans closer and then his lips are on mine. He likes me! He really likes me!

I kiss him back. It's nothing like when I practiced on the mirror. It's warm and kind of slobbery, like puppy kisses, but it's perfect.

Something like hail hits my forehead. I ignore it and we keep kissing. Another fleck hits. Then another. Scottie tenses and straightens up.

"What's happening?" I whisper.

"I think they're pelting us with spitballs," he says.

The other kids have their backs to us, but I hear them snickering as Scottie goes to the front of the bus. I stay at the back, alone in the dark, twisting my chastity ring, a band of hollow gold hearts, around my finger. My first temptation and I failed. I couldn't even make it to the training camp without messing up.

When our bus pulls in, I find one of the leaders, a stern-looking woman in a ball cap. "I'm D. I'm on your team," I say. I stare at the dirt. "At least I hope I am. I made a mistake and kissed one of the guys on the India team. I understand if you have to send me home."

"It's fine," she says. "Just stay away from him."

I sigh out ten pounds. Thank you Jesus. I'm going to do better.

I write Scottie a note. "I'm sorry about that night on the bus. I shouldn't have got so carried away." I tap on his shoulder at lunchtime, slip him the note and dart away.

Scottie writes back the next day. His note says: "I'm sorry too."

We keep passing notes until his friend Raja, a stocky older guy, winks when he sees me handing off another one. "You can stay and hang out with us," he says. "I think someone would like that."

Raja has kind eyes, dark and deep. He walks with a limp because he has polio, but Scottie helps him.

One night before our teams will spread out around the world, the pastor invites anyone who wants to be a better servant of the Lord to rededicate themselves to God.

I go to the front of the room and kneel. Dear Jesus, help me be who You want me to be. Help me be more like You.

I pray until I feel God breathing through me, His breath rising and falling in my chest like when He filled Adam's lungs with air and brought him to life.

When I stand, I see that Raja is also getting up. His eyes shine and he looks holy, like an angel, when he leans in to hug me. I can see all the way through him, into the flame that flickers in his soul. It's in mine too and we're the same, twin fires burning for God.

"I'm proud of you, kid," he says. I shiver. I'm proud of us too. We're going to do big things for God.

The next evening my team marches off to board our bus to the airport. Scottie and I already said goodbye but I search the crowd for him. We lock eyes, and I slip out of line and into his arms. It's against the rules to hug for more than three seconds, but I'm not counting, just breathing.

"I love you," I say. It falls out by accident.

"I love you too," he says and folds his shark-tooth necklace into my hand.

I stare into his face and memorize him. Then I run to catch up with my team, my heart quivering.

As we fly over Mali, I look down on the golden Sahara. The mission field. Timbuktu looks like the desert; it is beige and gritty and rises from wind-blown dunes. We drive past sand mosques, sand roads and sand houses hidden behind thick sand fences, where glass shards, the barbed wire of the desert, poke up from the tops.

I help set up tents in the missionaries' compound, a giant, walled-off sandbox.

The first day we make bricks, I watch carefully and learn the steps. Three buckets of sand. Two of gravel. One of cement. Three, two, one. When the men are ready for water, the pile looks like grey cookie dough.

Our guides shovel brick moulds full of the cement mix. "Watch," one says as he smoothes the top with a board, flips the mould over and slams it against the dirt. He pulls the mould up and off the wet new brick. It looks easy, like making a sandcastle. He hands me the next mould full of cement. It's heavier than I thought. It almost pulls me down. I can't get the brick out, can't slam it hard enough against the dirt. I help with shovelling instead. I dig as hard and fast as I can. Sweat drips into my eyes. My arms ache. I think I'm getting a blister. This isn't fun at all. Actually, it sucks. I wish I was in India with Scottie instead. I miss him. I wonder if he's at the Taj Mahal or playing hopscotch with some sweet little orphans.

Midway through the summer our leaders call everyone together as we're getting ready for bed. We gather around and sit in a circle in the sand.

"I have bad news," one says and pauses. "There was an accident. A boy from the India team is dead."

I go cold. Not Scottie. Not anyone I know.

"His name was Raja," the leader continues. "He and some of the others were playing around on a train and Raja fell. He's dead, but he's with God now."

No, not Raja! Not his beautiful soul. When Raja hugged me, I'd felt life humming through him. He can't be gone, not forever. They must be wrong.

The leaders pray for Raja, for his family and for the rest of the India team. My head hurts as I try to block out their words.

Raja is dead. But he loved God. Didn't God love him back?

Sometimes God calls the best for Himself. No, that's not right.

Raja has polio. Had polio. How could he have lived then and died now? Why would God save him once but not again?

Who had I been joking with about the waiver our parents had to sign, the one that said it would be okay if we died? Was it Raja? I think it was. I gasp. Does that make it my fault?

I stay up all night and read my Bible with my flashlight. Tears run onto the pages as I remember the night Raja and I promised ourselves to God. I pray for Raja, Scottie and the rest of their team. I'm so sorry for them, for all of the world. What a sad, treacherous place where life can stop in an instant, where youth can end without age.

A few days later one of the girls sees me crying. "Why don't you hold your hand up and see if God takes your hand and offers His comfort?" she says.

I try it while I'm praying. Is that God or a breeze? Dear Jesus I want it to be You. I want You next to me. Still, all I feel is the soft desert wind. Or do I? Maybe it's God in the breeze.

I try to hold my tears back until bedtime. It's the hottest night yet so the other girls and I haul our air mattresses out onto the sand.

When their whispers turn to snores, I pray to my God who's as big as the African sky. Now that Raja is gone forever, I promise I'll love You enough for both of us.

Raja died young, but he really lived; he saw and knew and radiated God's love. Maybe he had the best death of all, slipping into eternity while in service to the Lord.

7

LOWERCASE GOD

Now

Ian and I are sitting on opposite sides of the couch with our legs stretched out, having what I call a triangle date because we look like two slices of pie nestled together in a Tupperware container.

"It's not a date if we're staying in," he says. "Stop calling it that."

Ian is reading *god is not Great*, and I can't pay attention to my own book. All I see is that yellow cover, that lowercase god, that blasphemy that reminds me of the time Grandma drove past waving when I was on a school field trip. I was jumping up when one of the boys asked, "Whose old biddy is that?" I ducked my head then, like Peter denying his Lord, until Grandma disappeared in the distance.

Ian loses his place or drops a snack and says: "Christ on the Cross."

I gasp.

"What, you've never heard that one before?"

"No! You can't gloat about someone dying!"

"What about 'tabernac'? Haven't heard that one either? That's the most offensive curse they have out east."

He keeps talking, but I see someone else before me – the man from Nazareth, nails piercing His flesh, blood running down His face like tears.

Youth

I'm so excited to go to church and give my friends the souvenirs I picked out for them in Timbuktu, but two of the girls don't want to talk to me. "Are you avoiding me?" I ask Mia.

"My parents said I can't hang out with you any more," she says. "They think you're a bad influence."

I can't understand why. I feel holy, like I'm just a skin in which God moves.

I follow Mom into her room when we get home. "Did Mia's mom say what happened? Apparently she isn't allowed to talk to me."

Mom's eyes darken. "That's what happens when you lie."

"What?"

"Don't pretend with me. I read your letters."

I had to send a letter to my family every week, and I slipped notes for Mia, Jody and all my church friends into the same envelopes, folded tight so the words would stay hidden. "Those were for you to hand out, not read," I say.

"I missed you and I can read whatever I want."

"That's not okay."

"What's not okay are all the lies you told."

"What are you talking about?"

"I read about that Scottie character. Making out on the bus. Saying he loves you. Like that happened." Her words are loud, bursting out like punches. "When I gave your notes to the girls' moms, I told them not to believe a word you wrote."

"I'm sorry you don't like what I did, but it's true. Look, I'm still wearing his necklace."

"No, you just wanted a good story for your friends."

"I feel bad about kissing Scottie," I say, "but that's what happened. And you had no right to read letters that weren't for you."

"You weren't saying much in your letters to the family."

"Well now you know why I don't talk to you."

I go to my room and cry. Dear Jesus please help me forgive her.

He does and I do. I get it. She'd rather have me be a liar than a whore. Anything but that.

In the fall I stand in front of my church on a special baptism Sunday. I'm wearing a white robe closed tight over my Mickey Mouse bathing suit as I tell the congregation about Raja and the love that burned through him, about his death and resurrection, his new life in heaven. "Raja inspired me to be a better person and to give my whole self to God," I say. Then I step down into the baptismal tank toward Pastor John, the youth pastor.

"I baptize you in the name of the Father, Son and Holy Ghost," he says before taking hold of my crossed arms and lowering me backwards into the water. My robe billows around me like angel wings.

As I rise up, dripping and new, the congregation cheers: "Amen."

I've been sending Scottie dozens of letters – a diary's worth of pages – and I shriek with excitement the winter day I finally get a response. It's short, only a page, but it's proof he remembers me. I sneak into my parents' room to call him. My stomach churns as the phone rings.

Scottie picks up. His voice comes out cold and quiet. "I was sad to hear about Raja," I tell him after a few minutes.

"You were sad? *You* were sad? You didn't even know him!" He sounds mad, like how dare I care.

"Yeah. But I liked him. I'm so sorry."

"A few of us were horsing around on the back of a train," Scottie says, his voice missing all the colours it used to hold. "We were doing pull-ups off the side. Everyone said not to but the train was going slow and it seemed fine. When Raja went down he was taking too long to come back up. I saw in his eyes that something was wrong. And then he was gone."

"I'm sorry," I say. "So sorry."

"Did you know the Indian police asked if I did it?" he asks.

"Oh no," I gasp. I cry until we hang up and more after that.

When I close my eyes I imagine Raja tumbling on the tracks. I open my eyes and try not to blink. All I can see is Raja losing his grip and falling to his death, his soul returning itself early to the God he loved.

Scottie's heart was so broken that I slipped out.

My cheeks are wet but my eyes are dry as I pull off his necklace. The shark tooth is piercing my heart. The leather cord is grainy, worn, full of sweat and sand, my old cells mixed with his, one.

He's gone and I can't help him, like I couldn't help Raja or even make a brick. I can't put Scottie back together, not even with all my prayers.

I write him one more letter. It's shorter this time, like a postcard: "I loved you and I hope God will give you peace."

I fold the necklace gently into the envelope, lick it closed and walk like I'm on death row over to the community mailboxes. I sniff back a million tears as I let go, as my last letter tumbles down deep inside.

8

THE CHAPEL DOOR

Now

Ian is dropping me off at Saturday night church when I see my parents' van. "My family is already here. Come say hi."

"No way. Their God would smite me with a lightning bolt if I dared darken those doors. You know you're too smart to be here."

"Okay, Sweetie," I say to avoid arguing and lean over to kiss him.

I hate church but I also miss it. Back when I was a believer, everything was simple. Everything was God's will and all the answers boiled down to: Obey.

Now there are no answers.

I stay in the sanctuary for the singing, but even that is super offensive – all 'God is great and please forgive us lowly humans for existing.' I shut my lips in silent protest.

When the drummer goes back to his seat, I take Bethany's kids – my nephews and niece – to run around in the gym. That's why I'm here: to entertain the kids until the adults are done prostrating themselves.

This is the part that feels like church, the love and laughter and sweaty kids playing freeze tag, waiting for someone to save them.

Youth

The summer before grade eleven, Pastor John takes my youth group on a missions trip to Seattle where I get paired with Mark, a guy from California with floppy blond hair. We hold hands to pray, and he presses my fingers apart and slips his fingers between mine.

Halfway through the week, Pastor John calls me aside. "You need to choose between God and Mark," he says.

"Why? Why can't I have both?"

He scowls. "Careful. All you're doing is proving that your faith is weak. Which one do you choose?"

There's a long pause. A standoff. "Of course I pick God," I say.

Pastor John exhales but he doesn't seem any happier. "Finally." He stands and dusts himself off. "You better get your priorities straightened out."

Back at church, Pastor John announces he's making some "structural changes" to the youth group. Instead of everyone being welcome to help out on anything, he's going to arrange us into tiers.

The newest kids and non-believers won't have any responsibilities except stacking chairs. The best kids, the disciples, will be on a leadership team and do the serious spiritual planning. Everyone else will be in the middle and will help with the ordinary events.

I know what it means to be in the middle. Pastor John just gave a sermon about lukewarm Christians and how Jesus said they're worse than non-believers. He quoted from Revelation, "because you are lukewarm – neither hot nor cold – I am about to spit you out of my mouth."

"I want to be on the leadership team," I tell Pastor John.

He shakes his head. His mouth is pinched tight like he's grinding his teeth. "Your faith isn't strong enough. You'll be in the middle group."

The Jesus-spit group. "Please? I'm really trying."

"That's great," he says like it's not and turns away. "You're in the middle group."

All my friends – Jody, the other grade elevens and everyone else who went to Seattle – are invited into the special club. Everyone except me.

Over the year, my church friends get closer to each other and closer to God and further from me. When summer comes, they pile into a van for a missions trip to Calgary and I bet they don't even notice I'm not on board.

I go to the principal's office on my first day of grade twelve and arrange to cram all my classes into one semester so I can get on with the rest of my life.

Nothing happens when I graduate at seventeen. No ceremony, no cap and gown, no flowers or fancy dinner. Christmas holidays come and go. When school is back on, the only thing different is that I don't go.

I get a filing job and get fired for being too slow. Then I get a job at Tim Hortons and get fired again.

I was planning to skip a church youth retreat at a lodge in Dundurn, Saskatchewan, but I sign up now that I have unlimited time.

I miss my old youth-group friends. Especially Jody. We haven't had a sleepover in like a year.

I miss God too, ache for Him. I don't know where He's been lately but I need to find Him.

I know everyone on the retreat, have for ages. We used to pray together, to share secrets and clothes. But I'm invisible now, my molecules spread so far apart that no one notices when I search the dining hall for a place to sit.

That's all right, I remind myself. Jesus is the only friend I need.

I go to the chapel. The hallway is long and dark, like a lonely night sky before the sun rushes in. I'm going to kneel at the altar, to beg God to take me back.

The wooden chapel door is closed. I turn the handle but it's locked. I pray for it to open. I yank the handle and crank on it some more. I fling myself against the door.

It won't open. It's locked and solid, refusing my pleas.

I know what this means: God doesn't want me. He doesn't love me any more. Maybe He never did. I collapse in a blubbering heap and lie pressed up against the door for ages.

A leader finds me. I'm sobbing so hard I can't answer her questions. She leaves and sends Pastor John down the hall toward me.

He's carrying a box of tissues, as though that could help when the God of Heaven and Earth turns His back on you.

"Come here," he says and leads me to a quiet room that's littered with chairs. "What's going on?"

"The door is locked," I say, words splatting out like grasshoppers hitting the windshield. "The chapel door. I wanted to go and pray but God is closed to me."

"You're being ridiculous," he says. "God is always here for you if you want Him."

I shake my head.

"Get up," he says and stands before me.

I weigh a million pounds but I pull myself up and cross my arms tight to keep my insides from spilling out.

"Stand on the couch," he says.

"Huh?"

"You heard me."

I step onto the faded couch and turn to face him. I'm so confused that my tears have stopped.

"Close your eyes," he says.

I do. I wobble and put my arms out to steady myself.

"Good. Now trust in God and jump off."

I stand perched on the edge, ready to take a leap of faith, but my feet are pressing hard into the cushions. Jump, I tell myself. I can't. I'm frozen like a statue. A pillar of salt.

Pastor John takes my hand, pulls a little and says, "I've got you. Step off the side." Then, irritated, "Just open your eyes and step down."

I open my eyes. It's nothing, only a foot down to the carpet. But even that is too far. I won't do it.

I stand quaking on the threadbare couch. Like God, like everyone else, eventually Pastor John gives up and leaves.

God isn't who He's supposed to be. Not my Heavenly Father or Best Friend or Beloved. He doesn't care to save me. He wouldn't even open the door to let me bow down before Him.

Jesus said, "A good tree cannot bear bad fruit, and a bad tree cannot bear good fruit." That's why I can't do anything right. All I am is rot, a tree to cut down and throw into the fire.

And if God is real, why isn't He always in my heart and everywhere else too?

I stand on the edge of that couch forever, until all my beliefs tumble down.

Now

"Whoa," Ian says with reverence when I tell him how God and I parted ways. "You're such an iconoclast. I admire that about you."

"What does that mean?"

"Iconoclasts question everything and only accept what they can confirm is true. I'm one too, but not to the same extent since I haven't had nearly as many beliefs to tear apart," Ian says. "It must have been hard to walk away from all you knew."

Youth

Bible quizzing is all I have left now that I don't believe anything any more. Sure I'm a fraud, but I have a shot at Internationals if I try really hard.

At the final quiz meet of the year – and of my life, if I don't make it to Internationals – I'm better than ever. I know every chapter, every verse.

"Not one," the quizmaster says, and I bound up to the microphone to finish the line: "Not one church shared with me in the matter of giving and receiving, except you only."

"You are correct," he says, and I take my seat as the audience cheers.

There's a tradition during the last church service every year when graduating quizzers recite their favourite verses as if they're a chapter of all the best lines. I ask if I can do it and get paired with a girl named Naomi.

During the service Naomi and I stand together on stage. She says a verse, then me, then her. These verses are my goodbye to everything I know: to quizzing, to church and to the missionary future I had imagined.

After today I'll have nothing, except maybe Internationals. But even if I make the team, by the end of the tournament I'll be too old to compete any more.

As I share my verses it's like I'm reciting a love story, like I'm tugging out my heart and sharing the last beats before it dies, like I'm Juliet alone in her room, saying: "Farewell! – God knows when we shall meet again."

Everyone claps like thunder when we're done. I feel it coming up through the floor like Helen Keller, who heard with her body instead of her ears.

I bow my head and leave the stage. "It is finished," Jesus said, when he surrendered himself.

The awards ceremony starts right after the service. I'll be lucky to be fifth and take the last spot on the team. I don't pray any more but I cross my fingers.

The quizmaster starts with first place. Then second. Third. Fourth. Is it me? No.

"And in fifth place," the quizmaster calls.

I'm holding my breath. Please. I need it so badly.

He reads someone else's name. I'm crying and can't make it stop. I'm not the runner-up either.

"And in seventh place," he says and calls my name. Seventh. I wish I hadn't tried. I'm dripping tears like maple syrup, like a tree full of holes, as I go to the stage and shake hands with the winners. I hug Naomi and try to say, "Great job, congrats."

I'm crying so hard I can't see my trophy when the quizmaster places it in my hands. Hundreds of people are watching my heart break. Everyone knows I lost something I wanted, something I wasn't good enough to get.

And this is it. The end.

Back in my seat, my tears are splashing onto my biggest trophy yet. Rust following everywhere.

"Now it's time for the role-model award," the quizmaster says. "For a quizzer who demonstrates strength of character and honour and who lives their faith each day."

I clap numbly when they call someone's name. Naomi's I'd bet if I cared.

"It's you," the girl beside me hisses.

"Huh?"

"You won. They called your name."

No one else is getting up. "Go on," she says.

I wait a minute. Other people are waving me up. I stand and walk slowly to the front of the room. It can't be me. I'm still crying, and it's going to be mortifying when they send me back to my seat.

People are clapping, cheering and whistling. I'm dizzy like I'm going to fall.

The quizmaster hugs me. "Congratulations, I'm so proud of you," he says.

You have the wrong person, I want to say. This is for Naomi, the good quizzer, the one who brought puff paints to Nationals so the girls could bond and paint sweet things on their clothes.

I'm the one who stole the coach's boxers, decorated them with ludicrous puff-paint hearts and hung them like a flag over his bag. The boys ran a bet about me and another girl, about who was going to get a boyfriend at Nationals. I got so mad when I heard about it that I dumped a bottle of perfume down one of their backs when we were driving. I didn't get in trouble, but we had to pull over to air out the van. If I'm a role model I'm the worst kind, an example of what not to do, who not to be.

The quizmaster puts a manila envelope in my hand. A scholarship for Bible school. Everyone claps. Someone yells, "I love you."

I'm invisible in front of all of these eyes. No one knows who I am, how black I am inside.

Secrets

9

JIMMY IN RHINESTONES

Now

Ian and I are playing Tell Me Something I Don't Know About You when I say, "Once I came pretty close to moving in with a pimp."
He gawks at me so I give him the whole story. It's the only one I can tell, the only one that's not too shameful to share.

Eighteen

I'm on the bus to Regina from Portage la Prairie. I spent the last two months selling magazine subscriptions across the Prairies, but I quit. Sort of. I didn't make a single sale yesterday so I pulled the plug before my boss could do it for me.
We've been driving an hour or so when the driver makes a stop in Brandon. I leave my backpack on the window seat and go to find a vending machine.
When I get back on the half-empty bus, I pause, confused. Why is that guy in my row?
He sees me frowning. I dart my eyes away.
"Hi," he says. "You in here?"
I nod and he stands, looming over me. He's huge, a head taller than I am, older and black. I squeeze past to the window seat.
"Sorry," I mumble when I brush his sleeve.
"I'm Jimmy," he says. "Just like on my hat."
I look up. Sure enough, his white ball cap proclaims his name in rhinestones.
"Mind if I sit here?" he asks after we're settled in.
"It's all right," I say. But it's not. His thigh is over the dividing line, threatening to touch mine. I skooch away.
"So you're going to Regina?" he asks as the bus pulls onto the highway.
I nod.

"What's there for you?"

"Home," I shrug. "I don't have any plans."

"Well a smart, pretty girl like you must have a lot of options."

I blush. I guess I don't mind sharing my seat. "Do you live in Brandon?" I ask.

Jimmy nods, holding my gaze until I have to look away. Holy, is he intense.

"I like Brandon," I blurt, filling the unbearable silence. "I was there a few weeks ago. Selling magazines door to door. Did you know there's a bar where they scan your ID to see if it's legit? Luckily I could use my real ID since the drinking age is eighteen here."

"Which bar is that?" Jimmy asks.

"I dunno. It had blue lights."

"That's not much to go on. Did I tell you I'm a nightclub promoter? If you get me the name, I can get you a job there."

"Really?"

"Sure, and you could live with me," Jimmy says as though he's offering a piece of gum. "No rent or anything."

"What, are you my fairy godmother?"

"I can read people. I already know you're good."

"You do?"

"I do." A slow smile spreads across his face.

I search his eyes. They smile. He really does know me. "But no rent? That's weird."

Jimmy laughs. "I guess it is, huh? But it would be nice to have some company. I don't really need the cash."

"What's a rich guy doing on the bus?"

"I'm not into driving alone. I like meeting people."

The prairies race by. Is this creepy or awesome? "I dunno," I say.

"Your choice. You'd have your own room and everything," Jimmy says. "Maybe it sounds crazy but I like helping people."

"I'd want to pay something."

"See, I knew you were a sweetheart. How's a hundred bucks a month?"

"Maybe," I say softly. A job. A place. A saviour. It would be so easy.

"Hey, look," he whispers a moment later, his breath warm in my ear. The girls I sold magazines with were right. That is kind of nice.

Jimmy gestures to a couple across from us. "I could go for some of that."

They have a blanket over their laps. The blanket is moving. Are they hiding a puppy?

Oh. No. Definitely not.

I gasp and whip my face back to the window. I don't know what they're doing but I wish it would stop. I'm hot and cold. Shivery. I feel gross, as if I haven't brushed my teeth in weeks. As if I'm covered in bug spray and camping sweat. I imagine an Etch A Sketch. Wipe it clean. Take a breath.

"What kind of ice cream do you like?" Jimmy asks.

"Huh?" I'd forgotten he was there.

"What's your favourite kind of ice cream?"

"Chocolate," I say, facing him again. "I like chocolate everything."

"Interesting," he replies smoothly. "I'm into vanilla."

"Vanilla? That's so boring!"

Jimmy runs his thumb across my cheek. His touch is a surprise, but it's so tender, so warm that I melt right into it. He laughs. "It's what I like. You're what I like."

My head tilts toward him, a stalk of wheat in the breeze.

We're already in Regina, almost at the bus station, almost back at my empty old life. "Do you really mean it? About me moving in?" I ask.

"Absolutely."

The bus pulls into the station. Mom and Dad are standing next to the old grey van, kangaroos waiting to shove me back into the pouch. "Those are my parents."

"Wish I could meet them but I gotta run," Jimmy says as he gathers his things. He passes me a black business card. "Call me when you decide."

He weaves his way to the front of the bus before it stops rolling. He's first in line. The moment the door opens, he disappears.

Mom tries to hug me but I pull away. "Welcome back," she says. "I'm glad you're home."

Dad backs out of the parking lot and a hymn erupts from the speakers and shatters my eardrums. No it doesn't. Don't be so moody. Okay fine, but it's giving me a headache.

Mom turns toward me. "So how was the ride?"

"Fine. Long."

She blinks but her eyes take forever to open. She shifts back to face the highway.

Stop being such a jerk, I tell myself. "I sat next to this really nice guy on the bus. We talked the whole way. He said he could get me a job in Brandon if I want."

"Sounds like a pimp," Dad blurts from the driver's seat.

I close my eyes and roll them hard beneath my eyelids. Typical Dad. He winced when I licked honey off a butter knife when I was a kid. "Stop it! You'll slice your tongue open!" he yelled across the kitchen. I put the knife down. When he wasn't looking I ran my finger over the blade, pressed it hard into my skin and sawed my finger against it. I didn't bleed. Not one precious red drop.

Dad doesn't know anything. Neither does Mom. "No, you can't go to the mall," she would say when my church friends invited me out. "The pimps are waiting there to steal girls like you. Stay home and read a book."

Childhood

When I'm eleven, Mommy lets us stay up way past bedtime on Canada Day. We walk through the crowd that gathered for the fireworks and look for the best place to sit.

"Oooh. Ahhh," my uncle cheers as we wait for the fireworks. "Say it with me."

"Oooh. Ahhh," my sisters and I say.

Boom. A majestic flash of white and gold fills the sky, bursting against the blackness. "Oooh." Red sparks fly. "Ahhh." The booms and colours come so fast they cover the ooohs and ahhhs. The sky is full of sparkling thunder.

When it's over, Mommy folds our blanket. She catches my eye. "Stay close so you don't get kidnapped."

Oooh. Ahhh. Wouldn't that be fun? That would be way better than getting into the van.

I hang back a few steps as we walk. I raise my arms to make them easy for someone to grab.

I imagine being a prisoner in a cabin in the mountains. A handsome kidnapper. A crackling fireplace. A whole new life.

My body is tingling, electric, as dozens of strangers brush past me. I keep my face aimed straight ahead and ping my eyeballs back and forth like a grandfather clock. Who will it be?

Maybe we'll live on a boat. Maybe there will be other kids.

The crowd is thinning, spreading out into the streets.

It's not too late. Someone could still steal me. I slow down, staying further back from my family.

Daddy reaches the van. He unlocks the doors.

I look behind me. No strangers. I climb into the back seat and cross my arms. Why didn't anyone want me? What did I do wrong?

Now

"I thought Jimmy was a good guy," I tell Ian. "I trusted him. I even convinced my friend Ann to take me to Brandon to see him."

"Crazy. How'd that go?" Ian asks.

"It was fun. Jimmy was charming. I was going to let him kiss me, but luckily Ann walked in and interrupted us," I say. "She interrupted all my plans. I would have stayed but she needed to get back. She was drunk, so I had to drive her home."

Eighteen

Ann's parents kick her out the second we get back from Jimmy's place. They say she lied, but she didn't. Not really. I know because I told her what to say.

"Just tell them you're staying with me," I'd said. It worked with Mom. It was true and that was all she needed to know.

Ann's parents keep yelling and don't change their minds, not even when I tell them that the trip was my fault and beg them to let her stay.

Ann can't move to Brandon with me because she's in university, so I go apartment hunting with her. By the time we get to the third place, I feel so guilty that I offer to move in with her.

"What about Jimmy?" she asks.

I try not to think about everything I'm losing, the future I won't get to have. "It's okay," I say. Ann can't afford a place on her own, and I owe it to her to make sure she has somewhere to live.

Now

"Was that it for Jimmy?" Ian asks.

"Not quite. He was coming to see me at my new apartment when he said I was still welcome to live with him. He said I wouldn't have to worry about ditching Ann because his friend in Edmonton liked girls who looked like her and would give her a free place to stay if she moved there. That's when I clued in that Jimmy was bad news."

Ian shakes his head and pulls me into his arms.

Early twenties

I'm in my third year of university when I decide to tell Mom about Jimmy. "Remember when I was thinking about moving in with Jimmy, the guy I met on the bus?"

She nods.

"I think he was a pimp."

"Yes he was," she says, like yes he was black or yes he was tall.

"You don't know that."

"The police said so."

"What?"

"Dad called them."

"Again, what?"

"When you called the magazine girls and told them about Jimmy, they were worried. They told your old boss so he called Dad and Dad called the police."

Ha, of course he did. That's so over-the-top. So fucking Dad.

"The police knew exactly who he was talking about," Mom says. "They'd been watching Jimmy for a long time."

"No way."

"Yes way. They told Dad to do whatever he could to keep you away from Jimmy. They said they couldn't protect you until he did something to hurt you, and by then it would be too late."

"Why?"

"They said girls kept meeting up with Jimmy and disappearing, never to be seen again. They thought he was leading a human-trafficking operation and shipping girls across the border into the States."

"When did Dad talk to them?"

"Before you and Ann went on your trip."

What the fuck? You warn me about the mall but don't say anything when I'm going to move in with a goddamn real-life pimp?

A girl from our church who was older than Bethany had moved to Victoria and hooked up with a pimp. The cops found her dead. Murdered. I didn't know her but I knew all about her, how it was her fault for going astray. That's what happens to sinners. Option 1: God. Option

2: Burn.

"Why didn't you tell me?" I ask, clamping my fury down, trying not to burst into flame.

"We didn't think you'd listen."

So you didn't fucking care to bother?!

Now

"Sounds about right from what I know about your parents," Ian says. "Turn your back on God and his flock will leave you for the wolves."

I need to build a fence but Ian is busy this weekend. I ask Dad to help me instead.

I bought a cheap house on a murder street a few years ago – it was all I could afford – and I'm sick of drunk strangers cutting through my yard.

Dad is on his way over when my jaw clenches hard enough to give me a raging headache. I'm so mad I'm shaking. Why didn't Dad tell me about Jimmy? I would have believed the goddamn police.

We've been working in the yard for an hour or so when I take a few deep breaths and hoark it out. "Remember when I was thinking about moving to Brandon?" I ask. "Did the police tell you Jimmy was a pimp?"

He stops shovelling. "Yeah."

"Why didn't you tell me?"

"We did everything we could." His voice is tight. Controlled but underlined with rage, like how dare I question him.

"Wouldn't 'everything' include telling me?"

"I was managing it," he says.

"How?" I ask. I'm trying my best to sound calm, respectful, but my teeth are grinding, hungry for blood. "What did you do?"

"We prayed," he says.

Holy fucking shit.

"And?" I ask but I already know the answer. And nothing.

I grab the shovel from him and force my fury into the ground.

"Remind me why you like me?" I ask Ian for the thousandth time. I know I'm being annoying, but I can't help it. I can't process why he wants to be with me.

"You're beautiful, fun, smart and spontaneous," he answers like always. "And you never get mad."

"I don't?"

"No," he says. "You might be the most easygoing person I've ever met."

It doesn't sound like me. But now that I think about it, we've never had an argument, not one single fight. We're perfect. Almost too good to be true.

Youth

In grade seven one of my church friends calls me over to where she's sitting in the hall. "Brent was talking about you," she says.

He noticed me?!

"He said, 'The only reasons anyone will ever like her are two round reasons.'"

I can't see. Everything burns. I scurry away but her voice follows me. "It's a compliment, don't you know? I think he likes you."

I don't answer. I lock myself in the bathroom until it's time to go home. Then I go straight to my room and flop face down across my bed, right onto my stupid round reasons.

A boy from church broke his hand punching a wall. Now he has a thick cast that looks like it would be awesome for punching.

I want to break a wall or a hand too, but I'm not allowed to wreck things, especially things that aren't mine.

Well the night table is mine. I bought it and my dresser with money from Grandpa.

I grip the edge of the night table, the lip that hangs over. I drop to my knees and clamp my teeth into the wood. I bite down, clenching and grinding. I grunt and spit comes out. My jaw aches. I bite harder.

When I let go, a set of grooves shows through the paint. I run my finger over the dents, my secrets chomped deep into the wood.

10

BLUE KOOL-AID

Now

Halloween arrives. I'm twenty-eight now, so it's the tenth anniversary of when I lost my virginity. It's kind of a funny story, if I'm careful to tell it right.

"Want to know about my first time?" I ask Ian. He rolls onto his elbow and waits for me to continue.

I take a breath. I have to tell him about my past, have to let him see more of me.

"It was on Halloween," I say. "This guy and I were playing Truth or Dare and I impulse-dared him to sleep with me. It only lasted half a second because I started crying. Then he cried too and we ate all the peanut-butter cups. The end."

Ian doesn't laugh, but I need him to. "Funny, right?" I ask.

"Sure," he says. "Truth or Dare, huh?"

Okay, fine, I want to yell. You're right. It's not funny. Thanks for reminding me that my whole life was shit.

But it's not Ian's fault I made so many mistakes, that I racked up all these secrets too black to tell.

Eighteen

After she gets kicked out of her parents' place, Ann and I find a basement suite and move in on Halloween. My parents help empty my room at home and load it into the van. I wish I didn't need them for anything but I guess they can carry the furniture. Not like I want to.

At the apartment, Mom finds a cloth and wipes the kitchen counter. "It's fine," I say. "Leave it."

"But it's filthy."

My new place is not fucking filthy. It's perfect and mine and she has to go. "I can do it. Bye." I herd my parents out.

Dad goes quietly. He's pathetic: the Tin Man, the Scarecrow and the

Cowardly Lion all in one.

Mom tries to force a hug but I don't let her. "You need groceries," she says. It sounds like begging. "Can I take you shopping?"

"Whatever."

"Okay, I'll pick you up in the morning."

I unpack and arrange my room. Ann and I don't have curtains yet so at night we shut the lights off and worry about bad guys and trick-or-treaters.

Someone bangs on our windows and makes us jump. We're shaking in the dark. "Why didn't we wait until after Halloween to move in?" I ask.

The banging comes again. And laughing. It's Steve, the pothead I'm kind of seeing, and the guy Ann likes.

"You jerks," I say when I open the door. "No Halloween candy for you!"

Steve and I drag my blankets into the pantry because it's the only room that doesn't have any windows. I light candles and put them on the shelves. We snuggle and play Truth or Dare. We trade secrets and he tells me one about a ghost. Then he dares me to take off my clothes. I do but I'm under the blanket so it doesn't matter.

Steve picks a dare. I look at him lying next to me, candlelight flicking across his face. "I dare you to have sex with me," I say. I bite my lip. I feel shy, embarrassed. "I mean if you want."

"Hell yeah," Steve says.

Once he'd seen me in a skirt and said he wanted to kiss me everywhere, starting at my feet.

"What's stopping you?" I'd asked, half curious, half revolted, and he'd taken me to his mattress on the floor, where he peeled my tights off and licked my toes. They must have tasted awful. I'd been standing all day and my feet were sweaty.

I flinched as he slobbered on my ankles, my calves. It felt like a dog giving a-million-too-many kisses. I wished he'd stop but I'd already agreed.

His penis was gross too. I saw it by accident when it popped out of his boxers as he dragged it over my hip. It reminded me of a hideous bullfrog. He caught me wincing and put it away.

I don't want to do any of that slobbery stuff again, but sex will be different. It's supposed to be amazing, all *Cosmo* talks about. Plus I'm bored to death now that I had to sacrifice my new life with Jimmy. I'm going to grab any adventure I can get.

Steve kisses me and crawls onto me. "Ready?" he asks.

I nod. Am I ever.

He pushes against me, tries to shove that disgusting giant frog inside me. It hurts. It's like he's punching, smashing his way in. Gaston bashing at the Beast's castle door.

I'm on the ceiling looking down. "Oww, stop!" yelps a tiny voice from below. Mine.

Steve pulls out and I tumble back into myself.

I go to the bathroom. Then I grab a handful of peanut-butter cups and slump down the wall in the pantry. I eat half a dozen, the wrappers crinkling at my side.

Steve goes to the bathroom. Or leaves. Whatever.

He comes back and sits next to me, wrapping himself in the afghan Grandma gave me for Christmas an eternity ago. There's no way to clean my blanket now. Or me. The sex only lasted a second, a fraction of an inch, but I'm ruined forever.

Everyone said sex was supposed to be fun, that people did it because they liked it. It's a lie. Sex is a sin you pay for from the start, a sin that splits you out of yourself. Thirty worthless pieces of silver to fling on the temple floor.

Steve is crying. I don't know why.

I didn't notice but I guess I'm crying too. I fall against him and sob. It's a scream-cry that sounds like ripping, like a wolf gnawing my heart out, like my last shred of goodness being torn away.

Youth

A theatre group puts on a play after one of my Bible-quizzing tournaments. The play opens with a couple in a tent. I see their silhouettes as they kiss and touch each other all over. The girl moans. Her ungodly noises echo through the sanctuary.

If it was a movie, Dad would harrumph and turn it off. I would too.

Soon after the tent scene the girl finds out she is pregnant and her boyfriend tries to kill himself. I get the point: Their sin ruined their lives.

When the lights come up, the actors switch to preaching. "As you just saw, the pressures of the world are strong," the suicide guy says. "Tonight we're asking you to promise God you won't have sex outside of marriage."

The actors pass pens and cards to everyone in the audience.

I sign my form even though there's no need. Of course I'm going to do what God wants. Also sex is gross, duh. Only boys want to do it.

I catch Dad watching from the back of the sanctuary as I hand in my vow. My skin crawls. This is private. He shouldn't be here.

Later Dad takes my sisters and me to a jewellery store. "You can each pick a ring from the catalogue," he says. "Choose one that's really special."

When the rings arrive and we pick them up, Dad says, "These are chastity rings to keep your hearts pure." Dad made it seem like my ring was a gift, but as he puts the box in my hands I know it's a trick, that the ring is a trade.

Mom buys all our gifts, so Dad has only given me two presents in my life: a cardboard lemonade stand when I was already way too old for it, and, for my last birthday, a present he hyped like it was going to be a candy store or a makeover but turned out to be a plastic cup of pudding with gummy worms on top.

"It's worms and dirt," he said when I didn't laugh. "Don't you get it?"

Back in the van my sisters oooh and ahhh as they open their blue boxes and show off their rings.

I glare down at my band of hollow gold hearts. If I'd known it was a chastity ring I wouldn't have taken one. Everyone knows they're basically advertisements: Hey boy, marry me and you can do all your pervy things! How mortifying. Especially since no one will ever like me, not anyone decent anyway.

Also, a proper chastity ring should have a single heart, not a dozen slutty ones you can see through.

"What do you say, D?" Mom asks.

"Thanks, Dad," I mutter and shove the ring on.

"Where's your chastity ring?" Dad asks a few years later when he gets home from work.

I look down at my hand. The hollow gold hearts are gone. "Oh, I must have lost it."

"Where's the last place you saw your ring?" Dad asks.

"I don't know. I had it this morning. The bathroom maybe. Or at school or on the bus."

Dad hauls his toolbox upstairs and lies down under the sink in the bathroom my sisters and I share. He grunts as he pries the pipes apart and stares into the dark tubes for a glint of gold.

He searches forever – like the shepherd who left ninety-nine sheep behind to rescue the one that had gone astray.

"You can stop," I say. "It's gone."

I didn't think my ring was that expensive, but Dad's eyes are rimmed with red. He looks like he did years earlier when Tenille and I went tubing and he thought the river carried her away. He raced through pastures, mud and bees, chasing the river and disappearing into the horizon.

At dusk when he stumbled back to the bridge where she and I were waiting, he was bloody and heartbroken, dripping with sweat that smelled like fear.

Dad closes his toolbox. "I tried everything," he says.

Eighteen

Steve is long gone by the time I take out a student loan and register for a major in English. He agreed to meet me at a coffee shop but didn't show up and didn't even bother to call.

On Friday night a group of new guys shows up at the apartment. One of them finishes off the jug of blue Kool-Aid I made.

"Not my Kool-Aid," I kid. "You better get me another packet."

I'm throwing up Crown Royal when Lance follows me into the bathroom. "Here, let me hold your hair," he says and sits on the side of the tub. When I'm done puking, he says, "Get up. Let's fool around."

"I don't want to."

"Is it because you like Dave more?" he asks.

I nod. I do like Kool-Aid Dave better, but he has a girlfriend and I just want to go to bed.

"No problem," he says. "I'm into Ann too so we can trade."

He leaves the bathroom and Dave comes in. They really did just swap us.

"Good night," I say and drag myself to bed alone as the others keep drinking.

The next afternoon when Ann's at work, Dave buzzes the apartment door. I let him in. Maybe he forgot something.

"Come on," he says. "We're going to get your Kool-Aid."

"Huh?"

"I finished your drink. Remember? I'm paying you back. Let's go."
I don't even want the Kool-Aid but I don't know how to say no.
He's being so pushy. Demanding. He should be with his girlfriend, not
coaxing me into his truck.

At Safeway I decide I'll just buy it myself. That will make him stop
acting so weird. I put my hand in my pocket. Shit, no wallet. "It's okay, I
don't really want it," I say.

"We're already here. I'm getting it for you."

Dave isn't touching me but it feels like he's dragging me down the
aisle. Everything is wrong.

"Here, it's this packet," I say, but he grabs a full-size container, four
dollars or so. In his hands the happy Kool-Aid smile looks like a lie.

"No, just the little one," I say, but he takes the big container to the
till. It's too much, way more than he drank.

Wait. Is he buying me?

My skin crawls and my stomach pulls in, turning hard like marble.
Oh my god. I follow him to the till, eyes darting everywhere looking for
help. What to say? Save me, he won't stop buying me Kool-Aid?

You're crazy. Settle down. It's just Kool-Aid.

Dave and I don't speak in the parking lot or back in his truck or
when he pushes my apartment door open.

I shudder and follow him in.

He slams the Kool-Aid on the kitchen counter and grabs my hand.
"We're going to have sex now," he says.

Fuck. Shit. No. I don't know what to do. I didn't say no to the Kool-
Aid. Do I owe him? I can't breathe. I'm screaming inside: You should
have said no. You stupid fucking idiot.

I don't say anything, don't do anything. Even my blood is cold.

Dave strips, pushes me onto my bed and yanks my pants off. Still I
say nothing. My head feels woozy, like my brain is floating away.

He shoves my legs apart and rams into me. It hurts as I lie there
staring at the ceiling and trying not to cry.

"Why does it hurt so bad?" I ask. My voice sounds spaced out, de-
tached, like it's coming from a robot. "And what does your girlfriend
think about it?"

"It's your hymen breaking," he says.

It's not. It's my soul. I feel like a zombie as he smashes into me over
and over again.

When Dave finally finishes he peels the condom off and throws it in the trash. It reminds me of a drawing I saw at church of a girl who was left in a Dumpster after having sex. The condom and I are the same: total garbage.

I can't get up, can't get dressed, can't say goodbye when he leaves. I weigh a thousand pounds, but my head is empty, light as a balloon. Dave slams the apartment door, and I spring out of bed. I run to the door, bodycheck it and flip the deadbolt into place.

I turn the kitchen tap on, open the Kool-Aid and dump all the pale crystals into the sink. They darken in the water and slide down the drain. I wish I could follow them out and away.

Ann and I have a big fight. She thinks I'm too slutty even though she slept with like four guys and keeps coming home with *Something-About-Mary* hair.

When I hear that Brit, a girl from high school, needs a roommate until the end of February, I beg her to let me move in.

Dad helps me take my stuff to the other apartment. He keeps trying stupid small talk but I answer like he used to respond to me: Yeah. No. Hmm. Fine.

We're tracking a ton of snow into the apartment and it's melting in the stairwell as we empty the van. All that's left is my dresser. I grab my half and go. Dad thinks we should turn around, that he should be the one to go backwards down the stairs. As if. I can do it myself.

I'm fine the first few steps but then it's like he's shoving the dresser at me. I slip and fall. The dresser smashes against my knees and I thunder the rest of the way down the stairs. My legs are killing me, and I can feel evidence of bruises yet to come.

Dad says he's sorry, that he should have been more careful. I know it was an accident, but I don't forgive him. Not for this or anything.

When we were at a gym for a Bible-quizzing party years ago, Dad asked me to help him try the rock wall. He climbed while I spotted him and kept the rope secure. When he wanted to come down, I gave him some slack but he took my entire line, jerking me into the air, throwing me to the floor and crashing down on top of me.

Our instructor ran over. "You're more than twice her weight," he scolded Dad. "Why didn't you at least have her anchor in?"

Gross negligence is why. I wouldn't even be talking to Dad if I didn't need someone to carry my things. When the dresser is in my room, I say,

"Done. You can go now."

He stands like a lump in the doorway but I keep my back to him, organizing until he lets himself out.

Brit and I are drinking at a lounge where they don't check ID when a cute guy walks past. I stick out my foot. He trips and catches himself on the table. "Hey, that wasn't nice," he says, but he's not mad.

He sits beside me. We're kissing. Frenching. I should be embarrassed but I'm so drunk that I don't care. He buys me more drinks.

Brit drives me and the guy to the apartment. He sits in the front seat and reaches back to hold my hand. I lean against the window and close my eyes.

The guy yanks my arm like he's playing tug-of-war. "Wake up," he says.

I groan and try to get my arm back from him, to sleep in peace. He keeps pulling, his grip tight like the blood-pressure monitor at the pharmacy that squeezes until I'm convinced my bicep is going to pop.

We make it to the apartment and I slump onto the couch. The guy's beside me, then on me. We're kissing, the slobber-string kind.

"Let's go to your room," he says.

"I can't make it."

"I'll carry you," he says, and does.

I close my eyes, just for a second. I dream I'm in an earthquake but it feels real, like my falling dreams that leave me covered in sweat. I'm stuck under something. Pinned. I open my eyes. Holy fuck, there's a stranger above me. In me.

I scrunch my eyes but he's still there. "Stop," I say.

He does but doesn't pull out.

Who is this guy? From the bar. Right.

He watches my eyes dart around. "Hi," he says.

"Uh hi."

"Did you just realize you don't know my name?" he asks, laughing down at me.

I nod.

"It's Roger."

I nod again.

He goes back to fucking me. Whatever. It's too late to take it back. It doesn't even hurt this time. I'm not sure but I might like it.

When he finishes he collapses beside me and puts his sweaty arm around me. "Tell me about you," he says.

I tell him about William Blake and his poem that goes, "Tiger, tiger, burning bright in the forests of the night... in what distant deeps or skies burnt the fire of thine eyes?"

Roger walks to the gas station to get more condoms and we keep going as the sun rises and crosses the sky and turns to dusk at the edges of my blinds. My body aches but I won't stop. He's leaving tomorrow for wherever he's from, so I'm gorging on him like when I ate a tub of cinnamon hearts, devouring every last one until my tongue was seared through.

Roger leaves after the fifth time he falls against me, spent. I miss him already but he didn't leave his number and I didn't have one to give. I don't know where I'll be living after Brit's lease runs out. Also it doesn't work that way. The cow and the milk and everything.

11

THE TERRIBLE NIGHT

Now

One morning when Ian's breathing slows, I say, "I once interviewed a symphony conductor and asked how music changed his life. He said there was nothing before music, that everything before was black and white, like he'd been living in a dark and musty cave. When he came out, all the colours were waiting for him and the whole world was new."

I'm crying into the pillow Ian bought for me. "I didn't get it then. But I can see it now."

"That's sweet," he says and kisses my face.

Later Ian says, "I want us to have some platonic dates. That way we can make sure our relationship keeps its substance."

"Okay. Seems wise."

After a few chaste dates, I want sex but am too embarrassed to admit it. Instead, I buy a purple nightie and slip it on before bed when I stay at his place.

"Wow, don't you look good," Ian says, but he must not mean it because he doesn't reach for me.

There's nothing to worry about, I remind myself as my tears drip quietly onto my lace. He must have a low sex drive. It's probably a good thing. It means I'm extra safe with him.

Eighteen

In my first semester of university, my theatre prof puts me in a group with the older girls who sit a few seats over. Tonya, who is twenty-two, has curly dark hair and a loud laugh. Amber, who is twenty-three, has super-straight blond hair. She's so beautiful it almost hurts my eyes.

Tonya and Amber met in a class that's just called University. It's like a welcome-to-university program for students who've been out of school for a while. "Mature students," they are called. The girls are taking the 100 and 110 levels of the course this semester.

I tag along when Amber, Tonya and a bunch of their older friends go to the Owl. I order orange juice so the bartender won't ask for ID. I'm sure I look like one of those puzzles for kids where you're supposed to circle the object that doesn't belong.

An old creep pulls up a chair. Gary. I recognize him from the mature-student computer lab where I meet up with Amber and Tonya when their classes are over.

Gary is forty and married and obnoxious as hell. He's foghorn loud and slamming back pints. "Nice shirt," he calls across the table and leers at my boobs, his voice dripping hostility like venom from a fang.

What a letch. I glare at him.

He laughs, raises his beer as if he's cheersing me and takes a loud glug.

"Why are you friends with him?" I ask Amber later.

"He's part of the group. Take it or leave it."

Gary makes my skin crawl but I'll just ignore him. No way am I giving up my only friends.

I'm sick of looking like a kid compared to my mature-student friends. I book myself in for a haircut and watch as the hairdresser chops off a foot of my hair. It used to go down to my armpits, but now my hair stops above my chin. I'm not sorry to see it drop to the floor, my old self with it.

I remember when Ann took me to get my belly button pierced and held my hand as my flesh gave way to steel. The hole pussed and oozed and crusted over but it's worth it to have a new body, one that's mine, not God's.

Amber and Tonya are sitting with the mature-student club when I walk into the Owl. I order a pop and take a seat, sliding my backpack under the table.

Old Gary is talking over everyone, as always, and slopping his beer. I'm glad he's across the table and a few seats over, but even that's not far enough away.

He looks at me, lips curling like a grizzly full of hate. "That haircut was a big mistake. You look like shit." He turns to the rest of the table. "Why do girls always sabotage their looks like that?"

The others laugh while I grind my teeth. Gary's a fucking troll with his beer gut and frizzed-out reddish-brown waves. I want to say: You're way uglier than me. You're the one bruising everyone's fucking eyeballs. And by the way stop leering, you creepy old pedo.

I don't say anything, just gulp my Coke and sit in silence, rubbing my thumb hard over my knuckle and waiting for enough time to pass so I can slip away.

March first is the worst day of my life. Brit's lease is up so we have to leave the apartment, but I have nowhere to go. Nowhere except back to my parents' place.

I unpack my bags in my old room but this place isn't home any more and the people who live here aren't my family. They're my judges, my jailors.

Holly is the only one I like. She's three, all giggles and chubby knees. Mom lurks over my shoulders as I play with her. "Stop calling her Bum," she says.

"Hey little Bug," I say to Holly and she laughs.

"No," Mom says. "You can't call her that either. Use her name."

I roll my eyes and go back to my room. I hide out there, the door closed on my parents and the billion condescending prayers they shoot up into the sky on my behalf.

Once Tenille had a sign on her door that said Keep Out. Mom found it too aggressive. She should see the goddamn sign I'd hang now.

Amber invites Tonya and me over for drinks and a sleepover.

"Sure," I say, trying not to look too excited. I can't believe they like me. This is going to be a blast.

It's a cold Friday night in March when Dad drops me off with my backpack. "If you want a ride, you have to call before ten," he says. "And you're on your own if you've been drinking."

"Fine," I say and slam the door. Fuck you too.

It's freezing as I run across the icy parking lot, past snowbanks that reach up to my thighs, and climb the steps to Amber's townhouse.

Amber and Tonya are already drinking so I crack one of the four-pack of pink coolers I brought. "Where should we go?" Amber asks Tonya, and they list off half-a-dozen bars.

"I thought we were staying in," I say. "I'm only eighteen."

Amber scowls.

"Should I go home?" I ask. I want to stay but I don't want to make the girls mad.

"Whatever," Amber says. "I guess we can invite the guys over."

Tonya nods. "That'll be fun. You have a nice place."

Amber calls Teron, her sort-of boyfriend, and Tonya invites another guy. I don't call anyone since the girls are my only friends. Amber strips down to her black bra and panties. Holy gorgeous. I keep my head angled away from her so I won't stare.

"Come here," she says and goes into her room. "This is where I'm going to seduce Teron tonight." She gestures to her four-poster bed.

I sit in the hallway while Tonya and Amber vie for mirror space in the bathroom. I didn't bring any makeup. I'm in jeans and my favourite t-shirt that's red with a line of rhinestones along the seams. I found it on a road trip with Tonya. I thought my shirt was awesome until tonight. Now it seems stale, juvenile.

I don't feel much older than Amber's daughter, a toddler who lives with Amber's mom. The little one is as invisible as I am. There are no toys here, no crayon drawings or photos on the fridge.

Tonya and Amber are talking about sex, about how it's been too long. I take another sip of my cooler. It's too sweet, too kiddish, too obviously not beer. "Yeah, I need to get laid too," I say.

Amber turns toward me. Her eyes glint like polished rocks. "Tonya's boring friend is coming tonight. I don't know if he'd be into you, but I'll ask. I bet you could fuck him."

"What? No!" I say. "I didn't mean tonight. I just mean I'd like to have sex again sometime. With someone I like."

Amber finally gets dressed, and Tonya's friend shows up. "I'll ask him for you," Amber whispers.

"No! Oh my god! Don't you dare."

Then Teron arrives and Amber forgets about setting me up. I sit in the corner, quiet, and crack open my second cooler. Amber's in charge of the conversation. She's charming and perfect and I wish I could be her.

Then someone bangs at the living-room door instead of the kitchen door. Weird. It's way further to get to the living-room door from the parking lot since you have to do a loop around the building.

The door flies open and someone barges in. Old-man Gary.

I check the time. Shit, it's too late to ask for a ride home. I'm stuck.

I pull my arms and knees in tight. I shouldn't have worn red, a flag to tempt a bull. My god I wish I could get out of here.

Gary leaves his jacket at the door next to his green case of beer. Pilsner, maybe. Then he saunters in like he's welcome here, like he's the king of the goddamn world. He's in a white t-shirt that's tucked into his stonewashed-denim jeans. I hate everything about him, even his white sport socks.

Someone suggests drinking games so I slip out of my seat, join the circle on the floor and keep trying to be invisible. I'm directly across from Gary, as far away as possible but still in his sights. I pretend he isn't here.

I take another swig of my pink cooler and choke it down. It's grotesquely sweet. I abandon it and go for half a glass of Amber's Long Island iced tea.

I don't feel right and don't know why. I can normally drink twice as much before getting buzzed. I'm way too drunk for how little I've had.

I'm floating away but also falling down. My bones are melting. Bones? Ha. Did I ever have any? I can't keep my eyes open. Nancy Drew and the sweet-smelling rag in her face. The room spins. So tired. I flop face down on the living-room floor.

I wake up. Rustling or footsteps or something. Where am I? On the floor. It's dark, late.

Someone comes up behind me. Presses up against my back. A thick arm wraps around me.

Fuck. Gary. "Stop it," I say. "Leave me alone."

Gary laughs.

I push his hand but it won't budge. "I'm sleeping. Go away." I try to free my right arm. It's pinned shoulder-to-elbow beneath me. Useless.

Gary rubs my stomach. I'm shoving him as hard as I can with my stupid, weak left arm and it's doing nothing. He's too strong. He grabs at my boobs through my shirt. "Stop!" I say, smacking his hand. "No!"

"You know you want it," he says and his filthy old-man hands touch me everywhere, his fingers the fangs of a hundred rattlesnakes.

"No! Stop."

He grabs at my crotch.

"Stop it. You're forty and married," I say, struggling against him.

"So?"

"I'm just a kid."

He fiddles with the button on my jeans, forces it open.

"No! Don't!" I push at his hands and keep failing. He shoves my zipper down and forces his fat finger into my inner sanctum.

"Stop. You have to stop."

He doesn't. "You're too wet to mean it," he laughs.

"Please stop," I beg.

He pulls his finger out and rubs it around and slams it back in.

"Ah," a sharp burst of air slips out from my lungs and betrays me, marks me for the slaughter.

Gary laughs again. "See, I knew you wanted it."

"No! Stop!" I shove against his wrist that's angled down into my jeans. I strain and sweat but he keeps on laughing. Oh villain, villain, smiling, damned villain.

I can't get his fingers off me. Out of me. I struggle as much as I can, tense my shoulder, gather all my might and try to force his hand away. It doesn't do a thing.

My shoulder collapses and drops in on itself, and the world goes dark.

12

Lot's Wife

Now

I'm lying on the couch with my eyes closed when something hits my throat. I scream and clutch at the spot and my body convulses like Old-Testament demon possession.

Ian's holding a pair of folded black socks. "I saw a vulnerability and flicked my socks at you."

I'm shrieking and laughing and crying. I can't stop shaking.

"I'm sorry," Ian says when I don't calm down. He pulls me into his arms, presses his lips against my hair and says a hundred times, "You're okay. You're safe."

Half an hour passes before I know it's true.

I have so many weird things like that wrong with me. I can't pinpoint when they started, but it hasn't always been this way.

In high school I had a choker, a pretty black-velvet necklace that I'd wrap tight around my throat, but now the thought of it freaks me out, makes me cry, convinces me I can't breathe.

I have a twitch, a jolt in my left shoulder that shudders through me when I'm cold or afraid and even when nothing's wrong.

I panic in elevators when the doors close and I hear other people breathing. I take the stairs instead, even fourteen flights up, because I'm afraid I won't be able to keep from screaming.

And I sometimes still do that thing in my sleep. Ian is bound to pick up on it sooner or later if he hasn't already. I should warn him.

"I have to tell you an embarrassing thing," I say, barely meeting his eyes. "I don't sleepwalk, but something else happens when I'm asleep."

"What's that?"

"Sometimes I touch myself in my sleep."

"That's not so bad," he says.

I don't respond.

"No, really. It's fine. Not a problem at all. What do you want me to do if that happens? Should I wake you up or ignore it?"

I'm so shocked that he isn't shocked that I joke, "I don't know. I guess we could have sex. Not like I'd know!"

Later I want to take it back, to tell him he can only touch me when I'm awake, but I can't make the words come out.

Eighteen

I wake up on the floor in Amber's office, lying on her white carpet with the morning light forcing its way through the blinds. I'm cold. And wet. Wet? My hair and shirt are damp. What happened? Oh. Gary. That fucker.

I feel disgusting, covered in sin and slime. My whole body aches. I'm stiff and sore and my mouth tastes like bile. Gary. His hands. I shudder. Don't think about that.

I dart up and go to Amber's phone to call for a ride home. I'm woozy, so weak I have to lean against the table as the phone rings. "I'm ready to go," I say when Dad answers. "Come get me?"

"I don't know what the plan is. I'll be there in a while."

"Soon? I don't feel good." I need my bed, need to sleep for a month.

"We'll see."

I change and shove my vile red shirt and dirty undies to the bottom of my backpack. I brush my teeth and still feel filthy, like death.

Everyone's gone except Tonya and Amber. Amber glares at me but I don't have the energy to ask why. Tonya's messing with the TV as I sink into the couch. "Check this out," she says.

It's a video from last night after I conked out in the living room. I'm lying with my face mashed into the carpet, legs spread. I look like a dead hooker from a video game. Why the fuck couldn't I have kept my legs closed?

Teron and Gary are sitting on the couch behind me and leering. "Don't you just want to fuck her in the ass?" Teron asks. Amber's Teron. Shit. No wonder she's pissed.

"Yeah," Gary laughs. Goddamn perv.

Video D pulls herself to her feet and lurches away from them, into the kitchen and out of the frame. Good. Get away!

The tape ends. "We found you downstairs in the laundry room," Tonya says.

"Yeah, and you puked all over the floor," Amber says. "I was pissed so I threw a bucket of water on you. You better clean that shit up."

"I'm sorry," I say.

"I got the guys to carry you upstairs. They dropped you and banged your head," Tonya says.

Makes sense. My head is throbbing. All of me feels pretty smashed up. My throat burns like last time I had the flu and puked acid rain. Dad finally arrives. "Why did you take so long?" I ask as I'm buckling in. I'm freezing and then boiling. Even with my shoulder strap holding me in my seat it's hard not to slump forward, to flop down onto my own lap.

"Don't you mean 'thank you for picking me up?'"

"Yeah. Let's go home," I say.

"Not yet. I have some errands."

"Can't you do them later? I feel awful."

The kids at my high school used to line up against the wall in the art room to be choked until they passed out and fell limp into the others' arms. No one caught the big blond guy and he crashed face down against the concrete. That's how I feel. Slapped against stone.

Dad scowls. "You made your choices and now you have to live with the consequences."

Shame on me, he means. On his goddamn fucking heathen daughter. Mom used to say my heavenly Father was everything I wanted Dad to be, but both dads are shitty as hell.

Finally home, I go to my room and close the door. I bury myself in bed, hiding my horrible body in blankets. I'm just a head now. No, that's bad too. I pull the covers over my face.

I can't bear it. I'm rubbing my legs against each other and scraping my thumbs over my knuckles. Guard your mind, I'm screaming inside. Don't let yourself think about last night.

I can't be back in my bed like this, in this ordinary way like nothing happened. My old self and my today self don't get to share the same resting place. I move my pillow to the foot of the bed and lie with my body facing the wrong way like when Peter asked his crucifiers to hang his cross upside down when he felt unworthy to die in the same manner as his Lord.

Why was I in the laundry room? From the video it looked like I was trying to leave, to run to the kitchen and out the door. Oh, I opened the wrong door. I must have been trying to go home but I went down instead of out. Of all the shitty luck. But it was cold out, the kind of Saskatchewan evening when those who lie down to rest never wake up. I could have frozen to death. That would have been better. Quit it. I'm not sleeping but I'm not thinking either. I close my brain down. It goes to static like Tonya's video before she got it to play, the fuzzy grey dots buzzing between my ears. I make the static fill my head and turn it up loud.

When I tell Tonya about Gary touching me even though I kept telling him to stop, she shrugs. "Get used to it. That's just what happens."

Next time I see Amber in the hall she says, "Gary says hi." Her voice is cold and sharp, an icicle spear.

I frown and shake my head. Maybe she doesn't know.

She laughs ice shards. "Yeah, he thought you'd be like that." Then she's off, stalking down the hall.

The black of night is pressing down and suffocating me. I've always loved my triangle bedroom, the ceiling that comes down at a forty-five-degree angle, my bed tucked snug into the crease at the bottom. But now the wooden beams are heavy above me, too close to my face.

I don't remember Gary leaving. Why don't I remember him stopping? But he had to have stopped. I was dressed in the morning, the button on my jeans done up, the metal teeth of my zipper clenched tight like speak no evil, like nothing had happened. That means he left and that was the end. It's the only thing that makes sense.

I'll look again, like Lot's wife turning back to Sodom, and prove it.

I go through the night from the beginning. One-and-a-third pink coolers. Red shirt, beige bra, my best wide-leg jeans. Gary at the living-room door. Can't call home. Long Island iced tea, half or a third?

Slump over, legs spread, bent knee. On the couch behind me: "Don't you just want to fuck her in the ass?" Men laughing. Me getting up, escaping. Trying to go outside, to run away.

Then nothing. Nothing until I'm lying on my side and Gary's behind me, his body pushed up against me, his arm crushing me, pulling me tight against him. Eww. No.

Keep going through the night. He stops in a minute. You'll see.

His hands everywhere. Pushing him away. "No, stop, but you're forty and married. Stop!" My zipper. His fingers. Pushing at him. The sigh. "Stop!" His laugh forcing its way into my ears. "Stop. No!"

Shoving against his wrist that angles down into my underwear. Grunting and pushing and he won't budge and he's laughing in my ear, his filthy fat fingers thrusting inside.

I lose. My shoulder falls forward.

And then? It's black. I try to force the darkness open. I stare into it. He left. He had to have left. I need to know that was the end. Still all I see is black inside my eyelids. I squint into it, strain against it.

There's a rectangle. A door. It's black and open a crack. Beyond it is a white light, blinding and searing. See, a door. It's him leaving. So he must have stopped.

Phew. I exhale like a million air balloons deflating, like search and rescue found me in a canyon and let down a rope.

It was a mistake. That's all. He said, "You don't mean it" when I said no. Maybe it was a misunderstanding? I did sigh. No wonder he didn't believe me. I'm the worst kind of slut if even the creeps can't tell when I mean no.

I'm jarred awake. Someone's touching me hard, forcing himself on me. What, why is my fist in my underwear? I yank my hand away.

I feel bruised, like I was punishing myself for my sins. I go to pee and it burns like fire. What the fuck? My labia are torn and raw, with an inch-long gouge that looks like a scar. Of my own goddamn making.

I feel like a monster the next time I wake up clawing at the crack. I cover it in Vaseline but it doesn't heal. It can't because I keep ripping it open night after restless night. I try pinning my hands under my head, try falling asleep on them to hold them still. It doesn't work. Nothing does. Not even wrapping my arms together in a Tensor bandage. Even then I wake up ashamed, tearing open my wound.

13

FOUR AND NO MORE

Now

"There's a mouse," I tell Ian. "In my house. A mouse or a family of mice." I've been trying to ignore the little brown droppings in the cupboards under the sink. They could have been anything – pencil shavings, chocolate splatters – but I saw him today. He scuttled through the kitchen and hid under the stove.

Ian comes over and takes me to get catch-and-release traps. We nab the rodent, but what if his whole disgusting family lives in my walls?

"I need new cupboards," I tell Ian. "I have to rip out the kitchen and start over. I'll never get it clean again."

"Isn't that overkill?" he asks.

"Maybe, but it's so gross."

Ian takes me shopping for new cupboards and the cheapest option is a couple grand.

"I know you want new cupboards," he says. "That's fine, but could I try cleaning yours some day while you're out? Just as a test? It would make me feel better if I took a shot at fixing up your kitchen before you spend all that money."

"Okay," I say. "If you're sure you won't be upset if I still want new ones."

One Saturday morning when I'm heading out to work overtime, Ian comes over with a bucket of paint. "Thanks for trusting me with this," he says.

I come home at suppertime to find Ian covered in paint splotches and beaming. He makes me close my eyes as he leads me in and whoa, it's like a whole new kitchen. He emptied the cupboards, bleached them, painted them and added rubber mats along the bottoms so they would be easy to clean if something vile came along again. He even changed the black handles to chrome and polished everything to a shine.

I lean against Ian. I'm not steady on my feet.

"What do you think?" he asks. "Is it okay?"

"Thank you," I whisper. "Thank you and thank you."

Ian darts home to change so we can go for dinner. I'm supposed to be getting ready too, but I back against the kitchen wall and slip to the floor.

I'm crying. Wailing, actually.

How did I get so lucky?

"Do you want to know how I ended up living in Fernie?" I ask Ian.

"You told me. You went with some guy you were seeing and stayed when he left."

"Yeah. That's not the whole story, though. Cameron was a con. He ditched me when I ran out of money."

"Whoa," Ian says, and he looks so sorry that I stop talking.

It's best not to say more about Cameron or my time in Fernie. I have burned, buried and flushed my diaries. No good can come from resurrecting those long-erased words.

Eighteen

After The Terrible Night, Amber and Tonya flunk out of school and disappear. I barely drag myself through the semester before I drop out too.

In the spring I get so lonely that I call a chat line whenever my family leaves the house. I meet this gorgeous guy Cameron and everything is perfect, so Disney that I can hardly believe it.

"Want to come over and watch a movie?" Cameron asks when we're sitting in the park.

"Of course," I say.

"I should warn you it's a halfway house," he says. "I'm getting out in a week."

"Oh no! What happened?"

"A load of bullshit. These goofs were coming to rob me so I waited behind a door with a baseball bat. Self-defence and shit."

"Oh my god! Were you okay?"

"Yeah, I took care of them. I took them down hard and got locked up for defending myself. It's fucked."

"I'm sorry that happened to you."

"It's all right. I'm almost done my time. So you're coming over?"

I bounce my head yes, and we walk over hand in hand.

When Cameron gets out on parole and moves into an apartment, he invites me to go for beers to celebrate his freedom.

It sounds like a real date. Like something from a movie. Only how am I going to make it work?

"Weird question," I say, "but could I crash on your couch? Otherwise my parents will want to pick me up before it gets dark."

"No prob."

At the pub where they don't ask for ID, Cameron orders our drinks and even pays for mine. We take a booth. "Why so quiet?" he asks when I'm halfway through my beer.

I look into my glass and then up into his eyes. I'm nervous about staying at his apartment, about having given him the wrong idea. "You can't kiss me tonight," I blurt.

Cameron's eyes narrow into cold slits. He comes around the table. He slides in next to me on the vinyl bench, grabs my head and shoves his beery lips hard against mine.

I hold still, startled and frozen.

Cameron heads back to his side of the table. He raises his glass and takes another drink like nothing's changed, like the sky hasn't fallen. I feel dizzy. How rude of me to reject a kiss that hadn't even been offered. Of course he was offended.

I only have a couple drinks because I'm worried about later, but Cameron orders pints until his voice slurs and he dumps so much salt on our fries that we can't eat them even when I try to wipe them clean.

Back at his place Cameron goes to the kitchen. I stay dressed in my jeans and button-up, and tuck myself in on the couch, pulling a blanket up to my neck.

I hope he takes a long time. I don't know yet what I'm going to say when he sees me on the couch. What about I have a cold? No, he already kissed me. AIDS? Don't be crazy. I'm tired? I snore? Shit, I can't think of anything good that's also true.

"What's this?" Cameron asks when he comes into the living room. He sounds like he wants to punch a hole in the drywall.

"I'm sleeping out here. Good night," I say. My voice is shaking. So are my hands, which are clenching the blanket.

"Get out of there," he says.

"But it's so comfortable."

"Don't be ridiculous. You're sleeping in my room."

Wide-eyed and afraid, I move to his room and lie down, still dressed, and shroud myself in his comforter at the far side of his double bed.

Cameron strips down to his boxers. He gets into bed beside me and pulls at the comforter. I've circled it around me like the dough that envelopes a pig in a blanket to seal myself off from him. It doesn't work. The comforter yanks out from underneath me. Cold air from his side slips in.

I don't know what happened next because I wasn't there.

I shake my head and a thick cloud passes.

Cameron is inside me, rolling his hips in circles.

Fuck. I lie still, hating myself for being beneath him. I shouldn't have stayed over. That was stupid, and I have only myself to blame.

But it's too late to change anything. I have nothing left to lose.

I raise my lips to his and join him in my desecration.

Nineteen

Cameron moves and disappears, and I fill my diary with more secrets I will have to burn. Cameron's the fourth guy I've slept with, after Steve, Kool-Aid Dave and Roger. Four is too many. Even stretched over my whole future, my number is too high. Cameron is the end. Four and no more.

Cameron's been gone more than a month when the phone finally rings. He did a B&E the other night and has to get out of the province. "Come with me. Please," he says.

He calls every day for a week until I agree. Cameron needs me, and I can afford to go. I have thirteen hundred bucks saved from my summer jobs – or thirteen hundred minus eighteen hundred if you count my student loan, but who cares about that.

I'm lugging my suitcase out the door to catch a ride to the bus depot. Dad follows me outside and stands at the top of the front steps. "I really wish you wouldn't go," he says. His eyes are glistening.

"Too late," I say. I don't know why he looks like his heart is breaking. Not like he gives a shit about me, not like I could ever be good enough for him. He must have caught an eyeful of sun.

Cameron and I get off the bus in Fernie, find a hostel and get an entire room of bunk beds to ourselves. He takes a top bunk and I settle in beneath him. When the sun comes in through our window, Cameron climbs down and joins me on my bunk. "Morning," he says and kisses me.
"Can you believe we woke up in the mountains?" I ask.
"Yeah," he says and shoves his tongue into my mouth.
"Wait," I say, pulling away. "I need to brush my teeth."
Cameron holds me still and kisses me again. "It's fine."
I don't want to fool around. I'm gross with my morning breath and messy hair. Plus my period isn't done yet. "We should go for breakfast," I say.
"Not yet," he says and runs his hands over me.
"Let's go outside. See the mountains."
"Later."
Okay, fine. Whatever. We can have sex. I just have to get rid of my tampon. "Just a second. I need to go to the washroom first."
Cameron doesn't let me go and I don't ask again. It hurts when the tampon bangs against my insides but I close my eyes and hold still.
I go to the washroom when he's done. When I come out I tell him my tampon is stuck, that I can't find the string. Cameron laughs. "That was a tampon? It felt like you had a two-by-four in there."
"Yeah," I say. It did.
Sitting in the waiting room at the doctor's office I replay what happened. Why didn't I take my tampon out? I have no willpower if I can't wait one goddamn second before having sex.

The hostel owner kicks us out. She says Cameron is stealing from the guests. We need somewhere to go, so I find us an apartment and pay our rent.
One day Cameron invites me to tag along on a camping trip with a hostel guy, his wife and their toddler. A few hours into the drive, we come across a car accident and pull over. A blue car slid partway down the mountain, and there's broken glass and pandemonium everywhere. Cameron and the couple burst out of the van and race to the rescue.

I wish I could help but I don't know what to do. I stay with their son and carry him back and forth, pacing on the shoulder of the road.

It takes forever for the paramedics to arrive. When they show up Cameron helps them load a thirteen-year-old girl onto a stretcher. He'd gotten too hot helping and stripped off his shirt and now he looks like a hero, like a god, like a man I could love, as he and the paramedics climb back up the mountainside cradling the girl's stretcher in their arms. They carry her to the ambulance and tuck her inside.

That night Cameron comes toward me in our tent. He kisses me and I'm happier than I've ever been. I see him again glistening in the sun as he rescues that little girl.

"Did you know she was wearing blue toenail polish?" he asks. "How cute is that?"

"Aww," I say. He's the sweetest.

We're peeling my clothes off when he says, "Turn around. Get on your knees."

"What's this?" I ask, trying to look back at him. I've only ever been the bottom missionary, and now I can't see him, don't know what he's doing.

He turns my head away, grabs my neck and holds it still. "Quit moving," he says. Then he rams hard into me in a way I didn't even know was a way.

Holy shit. It feels like fire and bullets and grenades. I grunt and fall forward onto my face.

"Get up," he says and does it again.

I bite back a scream and collapse on my pillow.

"Get back here," he says and his nails dig into my hips. "Hold still."

I try to obey. He bashes into me over and over again. It's awful. I'm grunting like a football player who's lifting a weight that's a billion times too heavy.

"Shut up," he says.

"I'm trying." I force my lips closed but the grunts are coming from deep inside. My brain is foggy. I don't get what's happening. I wanted to sleep with him – I'm the one who ripped off my shirt – but this doesn't seem right.

But I didn't say no and that's the same as yes. And how would he know that I didn't know what he meant? It's not his fault I don't know anything.

"Is this okay?" he asks after forever.

"Yeah," I say. Whatever he's doing isn't hurting as badly any more, and he's back on the mountain with sunlight shining off his chest as he carries that little girl with the painted blue toenails back to safety.

I've been buying Cameron everything he wants and am down to eleven dollars. I got a job at a coffee shop but it will be weeks before I get my first cheque. I need to get us more money and now.

I call Mom from a payphone. "I'm out of money," I say. "Can you send cash?"

"No," she says. "But we'd send you a bus ticket. We want you to come home."

"I can't eat a bus ticket," I say.

"I'm sorry but that's all we can do. We love you."

"You sure have a funny way of showing it," I say and hang up.

We're out one night when Cameron says he forgot his key and asks to borrow mine.

When I go home he won't let me in. "You don't live here any more," Cameron says through the door. "Your things are in garbage bags on the lawn."

"Please? I don't have anywhere else to go."

"Not my problem," Cameron says and flicks off the lights.

Now

Ian keeps leaving for work conferences and networking events. He doesn't have a job offer or anything but it's only a matter of time before he will be gone for good.

"Do you want to move in?" I ask. "I know it's early but this could help us make a good decision about our future when you get offered a better job in Toronto."

Ian agrees and we decide to wait a few months to give my parents time to accept the news.

I sign up for an adult swim class with Dad. I hate putting my face in the water but I heard being on good terms with your parents is one of the best predictors of whether a person can have a healthy relationship, and I'll do anything to bump up my chances with Ian.

Dad's driving me home after class when he says, "Don't let Ian move in with you. He's not a Christian. That means he's not good enough."

"Careful," I warn. "By your same logic, neither am I."

"That's right," he says. "You're not good enough either."

"Take it back," I say, my voice hard.

"No, I'm going by what the Bible has to say."

"Stop the car," I demand. I open my door. I jump out before he stops. Fuck him. We're done being family.

"I shouldn't have said that," Dad says. "Can you please get in?"

"Fine," I say quietly, sliding back onto the seat.

We drive the next few blocks in silence, my heart too broken for words.

He doesn't take it back. He can't because he'd be betraying his God. I'm his Isaac on the altar, the bloody sacrifice his Lord demands.

Ian comes over and I cry in his arms. My hair, still wet from the pool, soaks his sweater.

"What's wrong with him?" Ian asks. "That's the worst thing a parent could say. I'm going to tell him he can't treat you like that."

"Please don't. He can't help it," I say. "Not really."

"He's such a dick. You should be angry. I don't understand why you keep making excuses for him."

"He doesn't know how to love me any better than this," I say.

Dad asks me to arrange a private conversation between himself and Ian.

"No way," Ian says when I bring it up. "You know that's going to go really badly."

"Could you please humour him?"

"Okay, if you need me to," Ian says. "But if he gets to share his mind, so do I."

"Fine. But go easy on him."

Dad and Ian head to the family room the next time everyone gets together.

After an hour or two I go to rescue Ian. When we're back in his SUV I pelt him with questions. "What did he say? How did it go?"

Ian recounts the conversation: "He asked how I felt about helping you to break the chastity pledge you made as a young teen. He said he had all his daughters promise – in writing, I think – that they wouldn't have sex before getting married. He thought it was morally questionable of me to help you break your pledge.

"I told him you were a grown woman who could make her own decisions, and it's not my place to enforce his rules on you. The most offensive thing in the whole conversation was how he continually denied your agency in making decisions, suggesting that I should help save you from yourself."

We're still going over the conversation when we're back at my place. "He asked, 'What about what you're stealing from her future husband?' and I said, 'I don't care about that guy!'"

I laugh. "I bet he wasn't crazy about that."

"Nope," Ian says. "He even asked me to imagine if you'd had sex with a dozen people and asked if I would want to be with someone so promiscuous."

"He asked if I was too slutty for you?!"

"It doesn't matter. I don't give a fuck what your jerk of a dad thinks."

"Now I have to tell you everything."

"No, you don't. People are the sum of the lives they've lived. I wouldn't begrudge you anything that contributed to you being exactly who you are."

"Thank you," I say. "But he's forcing me."

I stare down at the hardwood and count on my fingers. I mess up. I'm shaking. "It's hard to quantify because I didn't want some of the things and I have trouble figuring out which ones were my fault."

"Stop," Ian says, petting my hair. "You don't need to say anything."

But I do. What if Dad's right? What if I'm too awful for him? Ian deserves to know so he can choose to leave.

I count the guys again – one hand for yeses and the other for ones I didn't want.

"It's ten," I say finally. Almost as bad as the worst number Dad could imagine.

"I didn't agree to five of them. And with three more I might have been too drunk to consent. But maybe the guys were too. And then there was The Terrible Night, where I don't really know what happened."

I swallow hard. "There were only two that started with a real and sober yes: my first and now you."

I can't meet Ian's eyes as I wait for him to tell me I'm not good enough. I should give him and Dad a pile of stones and kneel in a field. "Oh, D," he says and his voice cracks. "I'm so sorry to hear about the bad things that happened to you. You shouldn't be ashamed. It's not your fault."

"You're not leaving me?"

"Not a chance. I love you." He holds me close. "How can such a remarkable woman have such a dud for a father?"

I laugh through my tears. "I can't wait for you to move in."

14

MR. NEW YEAR

Now

Ian doesn't drink. He's never even had a sip. It barely registered before because I don't drink much these days, but tonight – on our anniversary – I ask him about it after I order a glass of wine and he goes for a pop.

"I have an addictive personality," Ian says. "I know myself too well to risk a drink. But you go ahead."

I'm buzzed after two glasses of wine and can't stop giggling.

"You're funny when you drink," he says.

Maybe after a glass or two. Any more and I turn full-on psycho.

Nineteen

This Christian hippie, Katie, finds me wandering the streets of Fernie with my garbage bags after Cameron kicked me out. I move in with her and her friend. I don't know why they let me, but they insist that it's fine, that I can pay when I'm able.

My roommates and I go to the pub. I get so drunk I lay my head on the table. The girls are shaking me to sit up but my neck is too tired to lift my whole brain.

That's all I remember, but Katie tells me the rest in the morning. "You slid under the table. We couldn't get you to come out so we got the bartender to help. You made a huge scene."

"No way," I say. How embarrassing.

"Yeah," Katie says. "You kept yelling for him to stop touching you but it's not like he could just leave you down there. You were going nuts – crying and hitting him and everything."

Oh god. I cover my face with my hands.

"When we got you to the car you seemed like a newborn kitten, all helpless and afraid."

One day I check to make sure that my roommates are out before calling an old high-school friend who turned bad like me. I have to confess my sins, and she's the only person I know who won't be horrified. "Just think," she says. "You slept with four guys in less than a year. If you keep going at that rate you'll be at eight when you turn twenty and like fifty by the time you're thirty."

"Oh my god!"

She laughs. "I know, right? And my number is even worse than yours."

"Can I tell you something?" I ask.

"Sure."

I drop my voice to a whisper and tell her about Gary and my jeans, about how I told him to stop and how he wouldn't listen.

"That's brutal," she says.

Then she tells me about being raped when she was just a girl, barely old enough for double-digit candles on her birthday cake.

"Oh shit," I say. "I'm so sorry."

I can't even imagine. Gary was nothing. I shouldn't have complained.

On New Year's Eve my roommates and I get dressed up and go to a church party across Fernie. I'd rather be at a bar, but whatever. At least I don't have to be on my own. There are a bunch of balloons hanging from the ceiling in a clear plastic sheet that will drop at the stroke of midnight.

The church band plays all my old favourites. The words are projected on the screen as everyone sings. The lyrics glowing above us are so awful that my lips clamp shut. No way I'm spending my New Year's singing about how I'm a hopeless wretch, about my pitch-black heart, about how it's a miracle I haven't been tossed into hell.

It's not even eleven but I'm out of here, balloon drop be dammed. I grab my coat and start walking.

Halfway home I see some people in the distance. Guys. I catch their laughter on the cold breeze. I'm about to pass them on the other side of the street when one yells, "Hey, Happy New Year!"

"Thanks," I say and cross over toward them. Maybe the night isn't over yet.

"We're in from Calgary and looking for a place to get a drink," says

a guy with a toque and twinkly eyes. "You know anywhere good?"
"Yeah, I was heading home but I can show you. It's on my way."
"You can't go home before the countdown," he says. "Hang out
with us instead."

I laugh and Mr. New Year passes me a can of beer and loops his
arm around me. We're drinking as we walk. We're almost at the pub when
we see flashing lights in the distance. "Cops," someone yells and the guys
run off in a dozen directions, leaving Mr. New Year and me alone on the
street. We wait at the pub for a bit but it's dead and none of his friends
show up.

"Looks like you've been abandoned," I say. "Want to come to my
place?"

When we're inside, Mr. New Year unzips his backpack. "Good thing
the guys left me in charge of the champagne," he says, popping the cork.
We drink straight from the bottle, watch the first few minutes of *Mission
Impossible* and leave a trail of clothes on the way to my room. We're about
to tumble into bed when I pull away from him.

"What's wrong?" he asks.

"Nothing, but I have to say something."

He waits.

I open my mouth but can't get the words out. I try again. "I'm okay
with anything except sex," I make myself say. It's my new rule. Anything
but the big bad sin. It was awkward to say it out loud but I'm proud that
I did, that I drew the line with a thick black Sharpie.

"That's cool," he says. "Hey, it's almost the countdown."

"Three, two, one!" we say together as midnight strikes. Then we
kiss and swig more champagne.

Mr. New Year is crawling up after going down on me when all of
a sudden he's inside me.

I scream but it's silent. A puff of air. A tiny hamster yell.

Somehow he hears it. Or maybe he sees me crying. Tears are pouring
down my cheeks, so many it's like I'm in the shower. But no, I said no.

He stops. "It's okay, babe," he says. He's petting my hair, which is
saltwater damp. "You're okay."

I'm freezing and shivering like it's minus forty and I'm locked out
in the snow.

He pulls me against him. "I'm sorry," he says. "I got carried away
for a second. It was just the tip."

I don't say anything, just keep shivering.

"You're okay," he says again. "You didn't do anything wrong."

"No?" I ask. I must have.

"No."

I burrow my face into his chest like a gopher digging a home. In the morning I stay tucked in bed while he lets himself out. My body is heavy, like a dozen bodies all in one. He said he knew it wasn't okay, but I'm the one who brought a total stranger home. Maybe I should have stayed at church and sung those fucking songs asking God to light me on fire and burn the darkness out of me.

"How did you even find a guy to bring back here?" Katie asks. "I was home an hour and a half after you left."

I shrug. "Charm and luck."

Katie doesn't laugh. "What are you doing today?" she asks.

"Nothing. Just going to the clinic." Mr. New Year stopped after a second, but I'm not taking any chances. I'm not on the Pill any more. I started taking it after Kool-Aid Dave – because a *Cosmo* girl should always be prepared – but quit after Cameron when I made my botched-up promise to stop being a slut.

"You didn't even use a condom?"

"So what?"

"That was pretty stupid."

I know. I couldn't help it, I want to say. "It was New Year's Eve."

"And now you're going to kill a baby. Another great choice."

"Well, who wants a souvenir from a one-night stand?"

"I'm adopted," she says and storms off.

I go to the clinic and the doctor thinks I'm a moron too. Like I don't know about diseases and shit. I swallow the murder pill. Happy fucking New Year.

Mr. New Year calls a few weeks later. He's drunk or stoned. "It was an accident," he slurs, "just a little mistake. It sure felt good though."

He doesn't say anything else. The phone is still connected but I think he passed out. I hold the receiver close and listen to him breathe.

Later I catch a ride to Calgary. I have Mr. New Year's number but I'm not going to call. No way. But when I see a payphone I run over and punch the numbers in fast.

"Hello?"

Shit, it's him.

"Hello?" he asks again.

Twenty minutes later I'm buzzing his apartment and freaking out. What am I doing here?

He takes me for a tour. One couch. One plant. One mattress on the floor.

I interrupt the tour to kiss him hard. I shove my hands under his shirt. I am powerful, made of steel. I'm going to make him fuck me.

My necklace snags as he tears off my sweater. The chain breaks as he yanks at it, beads scattering on the floor like ashes, like shards of who I used to be.

I shake my head. Get it together.

I rip his shirt off too and push him onto his mattress. He added himself to my list of sins, so he better fucking make it worth it.

I get so wasted that I keep falling down and end up in bed with another guy. I don't bother to make any rules. I'm too drunk and so is he and who gives a shit.

It's still snowboarding season when Amanda, a girl who's always blow-drying her hair, moves in. She's just like me, all drunk and boy crazy.

Amanda and I go drinking one night. It's still dark when I wake up in my shirt and panties. No pants. I run all over the house yelling, "Where are my pants? Wake up! Where are my pants?"

Amanda stumbles out of her room rubbing her eyes. "What's the problem?"

"Where are my pants?"

"I don't know. You had them on when we put you to bed," she says.

"We?"

"The girls and me and the guy I brought home."

"Where is he? Did he take them?"

She glares at me. "No, he's been kind of busy making out with me all night."

"You're sure he didn't do anything?"

"Yeah, and that's pretty rude."

"I'm sorry. But where are my pants?"

"I don't know, but can you keep it down?"

My body aches like after sex, and all my secret parts are sore. I can't find my pants even though I keep searching.

Amanda's guy didn't creep into my room, did he? No, she's way prettier than me, he was already getting laid and he would have risked waking everyone in the house. So it wasn't him. But what happened? A long time later I find my pants wadded into a ball at the back of my closet shelf. My ears ring. I have a splinter of a memory, a sepia-toned haze, of me putting them there myself. What the fuck is wrong with me?

15

THE SHOWER WALL

Now

"Let's wrestle," I say, flinging myself at Ian. He flips me on my back on the mattress and pins me in seconds. His arms are three times the size of mine and I can't move.

"Stop," I say, laughing as his pinchers get close. I'm thrashing like a fish that already knows it's over.

Ian pauses. His brow furrows. "It's not fair to call off the game before I launch my attack."

"But I'm losing!"

"Yeah, you have to get better at this."

"You need be less strong."

He lets me go. "I'm not wrestling if you're going to cheat your way out before I pinch you. That's like someone making off with your cake as soon as you pull it out of the oven."

"All right. You make a compelling argument, sir." I move to grab him but he catches my arm midflight. He cuffs my wrists in one hand and his other darts toward my orange sports bra.

I wince. Squirm. Yelp. Don't say stop.

He clamps down on my nipple.

I hold my breath. Don't say no.

He's pinching and releasing, pinching and releasing.

I'm in hysterics, shrieking and convulsing. I try to say stop but it sticks in my throat.

He pauses while he shifts his weight. I try again. "Stop." It's a whisper. A plea.

Ian rolls off me. "See, wasn't that more fun?"

I nod but I mean no.

Ian is pinching me again.

I say stop a hundred times.

He doesn't. He said before that we could only wrestle if I wouldn't tell him to stop unless I really meant it, and he doesn't think I do.

I lurch away, fall off the bed and land on my shoulder.

I'm crying. He doesn't know why. Neither do I.

"Let's stop wrestling," Ian says. "You get so upset that I don't think it's good for you."

Nineteen

In the spring Amanda and I are at the Northern getting liquored up. A gorgeous guy buys her a drink and wraps his arm around her waist. She laughs in his ear and they look like old Hollywood, like a black-and-white film.

The guy's musclehead friend leans toward me. "Hey," he says. "I'm Kyle."

I turn away from him and watch the dance floor. The guy moves with me and mocks the people who are dancing. "So you're the wingman too," he says. "Sucks to be us."

"I'm not her wingman. I'm her guard dog."

He laughs, even though I said it with spite, and brings me a drink. "Where are you from?" he asks.

"Regina. You?"

"I'm from here. I'm going to University of Calgary but I'm home for the summer."

Amanda pulls me aside and whispers in my ear. "We're invited to their cabin!" she says. "Want to come?"

"No. It's late and I'm tired and you got the good one."

"I did, didn't I?"

"Let's go home," I say.

"You can. I'm going with them."

"As if I'm sending you off with two strangers."

"Whatever," she says and rolls her eyes like I'm the lamest.

What a little shit. "Fine, we can go," I say.

Amanda squeals and gives me a hug. We get into Kyle's car and he drives a long way into the woods. Is there even a cabin? Are they serial killers?

So there is a cabin. That's a good sign.

Amanda disappears into the bedroom with the other guy and leaves me alone with Kyle.

"You want a beer or anything?"

"No thanks. Just a blanket. I assume we're here for the night?"

"Yeah, no way are they coming out until morning," he says.

I lie on the couch and he gets a beer and comes back. "Shove over," he says.

Fuck. Isn't there anywhere else for him to sleep? I wedge my back against the couch, pressing hard into it so he can fit without touching me.

He lies down and squeezes against me, all of him pushed up against all of me.

I can't breathe. My stomach feels tight. Like a junkyard car getting crushed. I smell the beer on his breath. It makes me shudder, reminds me of things I can't think about. Things that have to stay far, far away. I feel screams inside wanting to burst out.

I shove my face against his, banging his nose with mine. Then I'm kissing him like I'm a CPR doll, like I'm forcing his breath into me. I don't know why, but I'm starving for his beer lips, for his tongue in my mouth.

"That's a nice surprise," he says.

I don't let him talk any more, just cover his mouth in mine and writhe against him.

It's freezing in the cabin but he takes my clothes off anyway. He goes down on me and it's gross. I pull his hair to yank him up, to make him stop. It doesn't work. Fuck you, I tell him silently.

When he comes back up to kiss me I won't let him. "That's it. Go to sleep," I say like a cop with a Taser.

"But it's my turn now," he says.

"That was your turn," I say and glare at him until he shuts up and closes his fucking too-blue eyes. It takes eternity to fall asleep mashed between him and the back of the couch.

I hate him even more when I wake up. Fucking asshole. As if there isn't a single other place in the cabin he could have stayed.

What was I thinking?

I dig through the couch cushions looking for the underwear I lost in the night. I don't care if I wake him, if I throw him on the floor. My breath is coming out like fire. My fingers clench. My arms tremble. I want to break his goddamn porcelain face.

He opens his eyes.

I jump back and run to the washroom. I lock the door. I'm totally insane and sweating and panting. I wait in the bathroom until I hear Amanda and the other guy. "Great, you're up. Let's go," I say and practically bite everyone's ankles until we're back in the car.

At home I go straight to the shower and scour Kyle's dried saliva off me.

I see Kyle working at the bike shop but he just looks away. Fuck off. I'm the one who doesn't want you. But he's better looking than I remembered.

Next time I see him I'm playing soccer. Kyle's like the star of the opposite team. He's kind of hot. Weird that I missed that. I go up to him after the game when he's stretching on the grass. He won't look at me so I kick his foot. "Hi," I say.

"Hey," he says, and that's it.

I'm going to make him like me. I go back to the bike shop and keep asking for help until he invites me to a movie.

"Sure," I say with a shrug. "I guess I could."

"So what are we seeing?" I ask when he picks me up. "Did you say *Star Wars* or *Star Trek?* I can't keep them straight."

"Take it back or I'm not paying for your ticket," he says and drops the steering wheel to squeeze my knee.

Whenever I'm at his place, Kyle says I can sleep over, that his parents won't mind, but I walk home late and crawl into bed alone. I want to do things right this time.

Katie gives her notice and moves out. Amanda is leaving soon too. Kyle's all I have left, and even he's only here until the end of August when he'll leave for school.

One night Kyle takes me to a house party and ignores me while he plays cards. For like three hours. "I'm walking home," I say.

He puts his arm around me. "Aw, stay. I'll drive you home in a few minutes."

Another forever goes by and then Kyle takes me back to his parents' place. "What are we doing here?" I ask. "I want to go home."

"Yeah, but I really shouldn't be driving," he says.

I waited all night to go to my place, not here, but it's dark and late and I don't want to walk back by myself. I crawl into his bed and squeeze against the wall. I want to take things slow. Since the night at the cabin, we haven't even got to second base, and I think we might have a shot at a real relationship.

Kyle reaches for me but I ignore him. He presses up against my back. He runs his hands over me. I pretend I'm asleep and wish for him to stop. He doesn't. He lifts the bottom of my knee-length skirt and circles his fingers across my thigh. His hands keep roaming, touching me everywhere.

I'm ignoring him but then holy shit. My body is going crazy like a string tangled in a fan. I face Kyle and he covers my mouth with his and swallows my moans and I hear them reverberating in his throat.

Whoa. So that's never happened before.

When my body is back to normal I give him a goodnight kiss and snuggle up against him. I'm almost asleep when Kyle punches the bed and yells, "Why aren't we having sex?"

Shit.

"Can you turn on the light?" I ask. I sit up as he flicks on the lamp. I'm squinting as I look him straight in the eyes. I love him and he'll dump me for this but I have to say it. "Because I don't want to," I say. "It's a big deal for me and I'm not ready. I won't be before you go back to school next month. I really like you but I don't want to sleep with someone who is planning to leave."

Kyle mutters to himself and shuts off the lamp and rolls over, away from me. I follow him and lie close, curling my body around his. I kiss the back of his head. Please, I beg him silently.

He kisses me in the morning and we're happy again. Plus we've moved to a whole new level. He must really like me since he wants to be with me even though we aren't going to have sex.

Kyle and I keep having sleepovers, even naked ones, now that I'm safe behind such a big no, a no that he heard and hated but accepted.

And then one morning as we shower together at my place, as I'm laughing and rubbing a handful of soap over his chest and blinking against the spray that's getting in my eyes, Kyle kisses me and backs me against the shower wall.

I run my fingertips softly over his shoulders and down his biceps. My hands are rounded like I'm playing the piano, like I'm cradling a bubble in my palm, like my touch is a prayer: Please, please let me keep you.

He slides his hand between my legs, and I lift a foot onto the shower ledge, grin up at him and lean forward for a kiss.

He turns his face away. He rubs his dick against me. What's he doing? That's too close. Too much like sex. Relax. It's fine. He knows the line.

Then Kyle shoves something deep inside me. It hurts. How many fingers is that? But wait. His hands are gripping tight around my hips. He's fucking me. No, he can't be. He knows I said no. But he is. He's ramming into me over and over again. No! I scream. No! No! No! Nothing comes out. My voice is silent. My lips are still. I'm screaming and screaming and can't make a sound. I try to push him away. My hands won't listen either. They're limp against his chest. Useless. Dead. So am I.

I slump against him. I'd disappear down the drain but his G.I. Joe arms are in the way.

When he's finished, he gets out of the shower without a word. He dries himself off and tosses the wet towel at me.

I cover my shame, like Eve in the Garden. It takes every ounce of my strength to follow him out. I collapse in the hall.

He goes to my room, gets dressed and comes back past me. He's moving so fast it makes me woozy. He doesn't try to kiss me. Doesn't say anything. He won't even look at me crumpled on the floor.

He's racing to the door when I ask, "Why don't you like me any more?" My voice cracks as the words slip out, desperate and raw, the bleating of a lost little lamb.

"I have to go," Kyle says and leaves.

It's a long time before I can drag myself to my room. I can't sleep and I'm too withered up to cry. I'm a thousand years old, an ancient river that's gone dry, a forest after a fire, the ground around Regina the year it was cracked deep with thirst.

I dig out a puzzle. It's a horse-drawn carriage in a lamplit street. I work on it with bleary eyes, starting with the edges first. Why doesn't Kyle like me? Maybe he's pissed because I was such a slut that first night at the cabin. You can't fool around with someone and take it back, can't dangle sex like a cat toy, like Charlie Brown's football, only to whip it behind your back. I fucked up and I don't think I can fix us.

Just do the goddamn puzzle. There are so many dark sky pieces that I give up on them and switch to the purple ones. Some lady's long skirt.

What if I'm pregnant? Oh god. I fish out a pack of birth control from under my bed. The doctor gave it to me last time I needed the morning-after pill.

"If it happens again just take a couple of these," he said.

It did, so I do. Why does this keep happening to me? Shh. I go back to the puzzle. Where are the rest of the carriage pieces?

Katie comes over to show off a fat rock. Her boyfriend proposed. Of course he did. That's what happens for girls who are gorgeous and fun and perfect. For girls who are not me. "I'm happy for you," I say and I am, but I'm also devastated.

Why do I keep having all this sex I don't want? I count on my fingers: Kool-Aid Dave, Cameron, Mr. New Year and now Kyle. Four.

And then there was The Terrible Night.

Plus I didn't mean it with Roger, the stranger from the bar. I was blacked out when he started. But is that a no or just not a yes? I don't know.

All the girls I know have a story, one guy who pushed them. But not four. It's way too many to be a coincidence. I must be doing something wrong.

I give up. I can't do life on my own.

"I'll take that bus ticket," I say when Mom picks up the phone. "If you're still offering it, I mean. I'm ready to come home." I don't want to go back but at least at my parents' place it will be harder to keep fucking up.

"We'll pick you up this weekend," she says. "It will be good to have you back. We love you."

I sigh and hang up. You wouldn't if you knew.

Kyle finally returns my calls.

"I'm sorry I was so moody the other day," I say. "Wanna come over?"

He does and we go straight to my room and fuck. It's shitty and hurty and dry as a cactus. When he finishes we go to sleep facing opposite walls with miles and forever in between.

In the morning I reach over to the nightstand and crack open a pack of gum.

"Not again," he says when he hears the foil. "I'm beat."

"It's just gum," I say and try not to turn to ash. Doesn't he want anything more from me before we leave for our separate corners of the earth? Why did he fuck me in the shower if he doesn't even care?

Kyle gets into his shiny car without a backwards glance and leaves me for good. "I love you," I whisper through the window as he drives away.

I go back to packing and tidying the house. My parents will be here in a few hours.

I take last night's condom out to the garbage bag on the back porch. I reach into the trash and dig a hole, burying the condom deep in the refuse of my life.

Still, I do not cry.

16

Name on a Napkin

That's not all I haven't told Ian.

I wrote the next things that happened in my diary and freaked out seeing the words. I filled the bathroom sink, ripped the pages to pieces and dropped them into the water.

I went to a workshop once on how to make recycled paper, and that's what they did – just soaked the pages, mashed them together and let them dry. The teacher's paper came out new and better than ever, like how I was supposed to after I got baptized.

I left the scraps soaking until I was sure the ink had time to wash off, but I could still read them through the water. I panicked, grabbed the scraps and dumped them into the toilet. I flushed and the toilet made a sound like it was gagging. Like my words were too much for it. Like they were so much worse than shit.

Only a few scraps went down. The others swirled in languid circles like they were floating in a pool on a hot summer day. I flushed a second time. A third. A fourth.

I was sweating and boiling when I flushed again, when the last of my words disappeared, swallowed by the sewer.

That's where they have to stay.

Ian moves in while I'm at work, and when I come home the house looks like him.

"I want you to feel like you belong here," I had said so he swapped out my furniture for his and hung his art on the walls.

I pause in front of the black frame hanging over the couch. It's his photo of the pastel lady drowning in dark waters. It gives me chills. We should replace it with one of my drawings, something bright and cheery. "Sweetie, let's take the drowning lady down. She's too depressing for me."

"It's art," Ian says. "It's worth a lot. You need better taste."

I shake my head and the dying woman continues watching over us in her never-ending last exhale.

Except for the creepy picture, living with Ian is a fairy tale. When he comes home from work, I run to the door like a puppy and throw myself into his arms. Every day. I do it for months until he asks for some space, for me to be a little less enthusiastic. Then I hold back in the kitchen, counting the seconds until I can greet him.

I leave for work before he does, and so many times I get out of the shower and crawl back into bed next to him. We go for bike rides and toss a football in the park by our house – *our* house.

He makes dinner all the time, and he's really good at it. He doesn't like what I make so I stand over his shoulder for lessons. He tells me how to chop a tomato so it doesn't get all mashed up, how to make soup, what spices work together.

On Valentine's Day he comes home with so many velvety *Beauty and the Beast* roses that we have to put them in the pitcher. We have stay-at-home dates pretty much every night, and I'm happier than I've been, than I ever knew I could be.

He is too, he says. "Even my mom is noticing it. She says I'm less robotic and more communicative since we met."

I laugh and kiss my favourite robot, the one who just invited me to be his Costco spouse.

It's the closest I've come to being Chosen, to being loved forever. I beam as Ian fills in the paperwork and as the Costco girl takes my photo. For better or for worse until death do us part.

Early twenties

When I leave Fernie and move back into my old room at my parents' house, I give up sex and dating and everything. I go back to university and get accepted into the journalism program. I'm perfect now, a little automaton with no friends and no sins. I do homework and bake cookies on the weekends. The worst thing I do is sneak down to the basement to watch *Friends*.

Dad thumps down the stairs and stands behind me with his arms crossed. "Harrumph," he snorts after any sex jokes.

"You're welcome to stop watching," I say, but he keeps glaring at me, trying to force his shame in through my skin. I cringe as he stands guard but I refuse to turn off my favourite show.

Jenna is eighteen now although she seems more like twelve. She's working at A&W when one of her coworkers, Brad, invites her to a Halloween party.

She pulls me into her room and shuts the door. "Should I go?" she asks.

"Do you want to?"

She nods and blushes.

"Well that's your answer." I'm freaked out for her though. She's never seen a beer or pack of cigarettes. Other than me and Brad I don't think she's talked to a non-Christian in her life. "There's going to be alcohol at the party," I say.

She gasps. "You don't know that!"

"Yeah, I do. A hundred percent. And they're going to offer you a drink."

She looks spooked.

"You can say no, but if you take one make sure it's in a sealed bottle or can. If someone mixes a drink for you they might make it way too strong or put something bad in it."

She looks like she's memorizing my words like they're Bible verses so I continue. "Don't have more than one or two and drink slowly so you can pay attention to how it's affecting you."

An hour before her date Jenna is pacing the living room. "I'm going to barf," she says.

"You don't have to go," I say, "but it's normal to be nervous."

Jenna cancels her date but Brad becomes her boyfriend and later she tells me she tried drinking with him and coughed her way through a few cigarettes.

She's with him all the time and I bet abstinence is all she knows. "This is super awkward," I tell her when Mom and Dad are asleep, "but if you're going to have sex, you're going to need protection."

I pass her my biology textbook and open it to the birth-control pages. "You can borrow this. See what you think. Condoms and the Pill could be a good combination. Oh, and if you do have sex, you have to tell the doctor the next time you have an appointment."

Jenna doesn't tell me when she and Brad start having sex. Dad does. Jenna wrote an online journal to sort through her emotions and Dad found her blog while he was going over the computer history.

I get home before Jenna that cold Friday night. Dad is standing at the front door. Mom is a few steps behind him. "How dare you?" Dad yells. "You ruined Jenna's life."

"What are you talking about?" I ask. What an insane asylum. Why do I live here?

"We knew you were full of sin but we would never have welcomed you back if we knew you were going to destroy Jenna. You turned your sister away from God. You forced her to drink and smoke and have sex."

"Forced?"

"You told her that sex is fun and she should try it."

"No I didn't," I say. It comes out so quiet he can't hear me over his yelling. I'm trembling, a chopped tree standing tall for one last second before crashing to the ground.

I raise my voice and drown him out. "All I did was tell her how to be safe so she wouldn't get attacked like I did." I yank the door open and run into the night.

"You do not have permission to take our van," Mom yells after me as I get into the driver's seat. I peel away and drive all over the countryside before I realize I have nowhere to go, nowhere on earth that is home. I get out on a gravel road and kick at the wheat stubble, bending the fucking weak stalks to the ground.

I knew they thought I was bad but it's way worse than that. They hate me. They think I'm the worst person alive, that I'm as awful as the devil. I run as far as I can before my feet turn numb and my lungs ache from the cold.

I wish I hadn't yelled the thing about old-man Gary. What a stupid mistake. Now my parents are going to ask me about The Terrible Night, and I don't want to talk about it.

They don't deserve to know anything about me. Besides I already know what they'd say: We told you not to drink. That's what happens when you sin.

My tears turn to icicles and spike out from my coat.

I only meant to save Jenna. To be for her the helper I never had. But even when I'm being my best all anyone sees in me is darkness. I'm like Frankenstein's monster before the book goes to shit, before he cracks and shuts down all of his goodness.

I'm freezing. I get back in the van and crank the heat. It doesn't work. I stay in Park until I'm so cold my toes can hardly press the gas pedal.

I go back to Moses' desert, the land of the forty-year exile, and wait outside until all the lights are off. Then I slither to my room undetected. Like a fucking devil snake.

I work the night shift so everyone except Mom is gone when I finally leave my room. "I have cinnamon buns in the oven," she says.

For your evil daughter? "I didn't do any of that," I say.

"Dad was upset. It wasn't fair to take it all out on you."

"It sounded like he meant it, like he thinks I'm the worst person who ever lived."

"Well you need to forgive him."

"No way. Not unless he takes it back."

She scowls and I'm out of there. I'm not eating any of her forgiveness bribes, not even when they come out of the oven all sticky and sweet.

Mom talks to Dad and he shoves a card at me. I open it alone in my room. "I apologize for the incorrect linkage," it says. What a moron. He can't say anything that makes sense.

"What does this mean?" I ask him.

"That you didn't force her to have sex. She made her own choice, but you told her what to do."

"No I didn't." I'm Claire Danes in *Brokedown Place,* smashing the prison fence and yelling that I'm innocent.

"I get it," Dad says, his head bobbing earnestly. "It's the same as if you opened a Mars bar in front of her and took a bite and said, 'This is so nice and tasty. You should try it. Here, have some!'"

"I only told her how to be safe," I say, flinging my arms open like Christ on the cross, like Father forgive him for he's an ignorant ass.

"Look, it's not all your fault," he says like he wants to pat my shoulder. "I have to take some responsibility too. I haven't been the best father lately."

No fucking shit.

"I haven't made enough time for Jenna because I've been struggling with pornography," he says. "I've been addicted to the Sears catalogue. And God punishes the children for the sins of their parents."

Holy fuck, make him stop talking. I run for the bathroom, the only room with a lock, and hide out in the tub for hours, tears dripping into the water.

During the February break in my third year, a bunch of my journalism classmates and I drive to Saskatoon for the night. We rent a room and I drink way, way too much. I'm trashed before we get to the pool. We move to the hotel bar and I perch at a table trying not to fall off my stool. Everything goes foggy. Like I've lost my glasses and someone's smoking in my face. I have to get away.

I wake up gasping for air. My throat is collapsing. Shit, someone's in bed next to me. He shifts and the streetlight hits his face. Phew, nothing bad. Just a guy from school.

But my ears won't quit ringing. I taste blood in the back of my throat like when I ran hard in track and field and my breath cut like knives.

I shake the guy's shoulder until he opens his eyes. I put his hand onto my waist and tip my face toward him, all kiss me right now.

"I shouldn't," he says. "You were really drunk and I don't want to take advantage."

"I'm good now," I say and lean closer.

He kisses me and we fool around for a minute or two and he changes his mind. Whatever. At least my head is done buzzing and I can go back to sleep.

A few days later one of the girls pulls me aside at school. "What's up?" I ask.

"Not here," she says and takes me to an empty classroom. "Take a seat."

"What's with the spy tactics?"

She doesn't smile, just leans closer. "Have you told anyone else?" she asks.

"What?"

"Have you told anyone about when you were raped? Have you reported it?"

I haven't been raped. I don't even know which guy she's talking about. This is bullshit and I'm out of here.

"You told me about it when you were drunk," she says. "I know all about that old guy raping you and how you thought you were going to die."

I stare ahead until the room blurs away. It's like when I donated blood and the nurse pulled the needle out when my bag wasn't quite full. I stood up and so many nurses were running at me that they looked like a giant green sheet as they laid me down and pressed cold clothes on my forehead. My blood holds still. Like I can't give a single drop, can't risk any more falling out.

She reaches into her pocket, uncrumples a bar napkin and holds it out. "Gary," it says.

Fire alarms blare in my ears. I back away. I fall against the desk. Gary was shit but not like that. He stopped. He quit and left.

Splinters of memories poke against my skull. Me saying no and stop. But you're forty and married. Struggling. Failing. Giving up. I'm as cold as if a ghost is passing through me. As cold as if my brain is freezing to death.

She keeps talking. "You passed out under the pool table. You wouldn't let the guys help. I asked what was wrong, why you were so afraid, and you told me everything."

"Stop," I say and run from her.

I beg another classmate, one who doesn't know anything about The Terrible Night, to go out for ice cream. "It's an emergency," I tell her, trying not to crack open, not to shatter like glass dropped on the floor.

My classmate asks what's wrong after we've ordered, but I just shake my head. I can't taste my vanilla cone but it's numbing, like ice on a sore.

I tremble in my room as I get changed for bed. I hate my skin, this bare-naked flesh that's as raw as a plucked-bald chicken. I lie down and shoot straight out of bed. I can't sleep here. Not when everything is wrong, not when the world is upside down.

I pull my blankets onto the floor and lie there staring up at the ceiling. What happened that night? I see Gary walking into Amber's party carrying a case of beer. His t-shirt tucked into his stonewashed jeans. A black belt. Me lying on the carpet. Him behind me, his hands on my skin. A glimpse, sepia-toned, of...

I retch. Go back, I beg my ghost. Please. You can't be here.

I pad down the dark hall to the bathroom. When I pull my underwear down I have to slap my hands over my mouth to keep from yelling. I'm way too exposed. I'm shaking as I pee. When I wipe, my throat explodes in a billion silent screams.

Later, I wake in a panic. Someone's touching me. Hard and frantic. Fuck, it's me.

I slink through the door of the counseling place on campus. "I need to talk to someone," I whisper. "I think I'm crazy."

It's a week before I can get an appointment. I keep sleeping on the floor and catching myself in the act in the middle of the night. My labia are cracked and it burns when I pee.

"You know you want it," old-guy Gary had said. I didn't and I don't, but then why do I keep waking myself up like this?

I try to get off so I can go back to sleep. It doesn't work. None of my sexy stories seem right any more, not even the ones about Roger or Mr. New Year.

Finally I get in to see the therapist. Maddy's wearing all black with her blond hair slicked back in a ponytail. I'm afraid she'll laugh at me or say I'm way too fucked up, but she says I can tell her anything, that I'm safe with her.

I take a deep breath and exhale it along with why I think my brain is broken. "I lied to my friend when I blacked out," I say. "I told her I was raped. I wasn't but I don't know what happened on The Terrible Night."

I don't cry, just spit out facts about Gary like cherry pits. Pew, pew, pew.

I stop. She's not saying anything. Shit. I look up and catch her eyes. They're big and soft and look like a broken heart. "I'm so sorry to hear that," she says.

I don't say anything for a long time. Then I ask, "Was it my fault?"

"Absolutely not. It couldn't have been. There's no way it would be haunting you like this if you had given consent."

"But I was wearing a tight shirt," I say. "I was drunk. I shouldn't have been at the party. I should have been stronger. I should have pushed harder."

"It wasn't your fault," she says. "I promise."

"There's more." I hang my head. "I moaned for a second when I was pushing him away. He said it meant I didn't mean no."

"But you did," she says. "You said no and you meant it."

I nod and my eyes threaten to leak. I will not cry. I spread my eyes wide and hold them open until they burn. My eyes go dry, suctioning the moisture back inside.

"I've never seen that," Maddy says. "It took a lot of effort to hold your tears back, didn't it?"

I nod.

"Yeah. But it's okay to cry. You're allowed to feel."

Later in her office my eyes fill again and I'm too tired to fight it. I duck my head and a tear drops onto my lap. A flood follows. Tears and snot and sobs pour out, like glaciers melting and covering the world.

I tell Maddy about the black door and the light beyond. "I thought it meant he left."

"I don't think that's what it means," she says.

So I'm lying on my bedroom floor going over the night again. I get to the door, go up to it and pull it open a smidge. The light is blinding. In it is a stained and yellowed bird's eye image of me on my back. Of Gary between my knees.

I blank it out and run to the kitchen and bake chocolate-chip cookies. I concentrate hard. Sugar, butter, eggs, vanilla. Beat together. I eat half the dough before the first batch is ready to come out of the oven.

"Why did my blackout self lie to my friend?" I ask Maddy at our next appointment.

"Was it a lie or a truth you didn't want to see?"

I shudder. "How do we find out?"

"I do hypnosis therapy. We could try it and see what your subconscious has to say."

I think about it and then pretend she never said it. I don't want to know.

17

FUNK AND WAGNALLS

Now

I want way more sex than Ian does. I ask all the time but he's too full or too tired or wants to watch a show or has a headache. "Let's wait until morning," he says and turns me down again when he wakes up.

I buy balms and silky things but the body paint is too messy, the gel too tingly and my lacy top too scratchy. He doesn't like my ideas either. My exercise ball is too dangerous. The car is too hard to clean. The tub is too small.

"Do you want anything different?" I ask.

"No, I'm perfectly satisfied," he says.

I'm disappointed but it's a relief that he's at maximum capacity, that I'm giving him everything he wants.

One Saturday Ian wakes me by wrapping his arm around me and pressing himself against my back.

"Morning Sweetie," I say and go for a kiss but he won't let me face him.

"Let's try it like this," he says and pushes my sweats down.

"Not that way."

"Please? I really want to," he says.

I'm squashed under his arm. I'm numb and dizzy. I do want to, just not like this. "Okay," I say.

He kisses me at first but then I can't reach. I can't even see him.

"Hold still," he says.

I do and then I freeze in place. It's like we're not together, like I'm not even here.

Afterwards Ian washes off and lies next to me. He's talking but not making any sense. "What's wrong?" he asks.

"I don't know," I say. "I'm really sad all of a sudden."

"Can I do anything to help?"

"Will you pet my head and tell me you love me?"

He does.

"Can you please say it again and again and that everything is okay?"

Ian recites my words back to me, and I lie next to him, heavy and alone, the sounds ringing just outside my ears.

Early twenties

I'm standing on the grass in front of the university, waiting for Mom to pick me up. Maddy said I need to tell her about Gary. The grass is a fucking inappropriate shade of green. It should be darker or dried-out yellow, but it's giddy, nearly fluorescent. I kick it.

Mom pulls up and I get into the passenger seat. No one else is in the van.

We start driving. "Nice day," she says, and I disagree. It's the worst.

"I have to tell you something," I say when we're on Ring Road.

She glances over at me. Shit, now I have to say it.

I swallow hard, then spit it out. "I was sexually assaulted when I was eighteen," I say flatly. Like I'm reading from our Funk and Wagnalls encyclopedia. "An old guy came over the night I stayed at Amber's place."

Mom gasps and her fingers turn white as she grips the steering wheel. But she's weirdly silent. She doesn't ask about it. Doesn't ask if I'm okay.

Good, I decide. Whatever. I'd rather not talk about it anyway.

When she finally speaks Mom's voice sounds far away, eerie, like someone else crawled into her throat. "You were three," she says. "The babysitter called. She'd broken her leg and couldn't look after you and Bethany that night. She said: 'It's okay, my brother agreed to cover for me. He's fifteen so he's old enough. He does lots of babysitting.'"

Mom's creepy voice continues, "I had a bad feeling. I didn't know how to say no. The family went to our church, and they already knew we needed a babysitter. If I said no, they'd think I didn't trust their son."

Her words are picking up speed as they tumble out. "Dad wanted to go curling. Our friends were expecting us. Where could I find another babysitter? It would only be a few hours. It didn't seem right but the babysitter was waiting. I needed to answer. 'Okay,' I said.

"I was nervous when I hugged you and Bethany. I worried on the way to the curling match and while we played. Dad wanted to stay after the game but I said no. We rushed home and I was relieved to see you safe in your beds."

Mom pauses for a long while and then whispers. "But you were different when you woke up."

I wait. Nothing. Then I ask, irritated enough to scratch my skin off: "What do you mean?"

"You had a strange new walk like you were trying to keep your legs together," she says. "You asked how boys go the bathroom because 'doesn't that dangly thing get in the way?' You started noticing boys everywhere. 'There's a boy,' you'd say and bury your face in my shoulder. Remember your friend Andrew? When he tried to give you a Christmas present, you hid behind my skirt until he left."

I shake my head. "I don't remember any of that." Therefore it can't be true. That's Descartes. I smirk at my joke.

"I'm sorry. I'm so sorry," Mom says soft as rain as she drives.

"Stop it," I say angrily. Fuck her. "You don't even know if that means anything! Why would you tell me that?"

"Something happened to you," she insists. "I could feel it. I knew something bad happened the night you stayed at Amber's place too. So that's why you started showering in your sleep."

"What are you talking about?" I hiss.

"You were taking all these showers in the middle of the night," she says. "You were sleepwalking. I knew better than to wake you, but I always wondered if you were okay."

My body shudders. I'm cold even though the air conditioner is broken. Oh yeah? Then why didn't you fucking do anything?

It's like the time we were all on vacation when Mom and Dad sent Jenna, Tenille and me to our hotel in one taxi while they and Holly followed in another. I didn't know our driver was drunk, but my parents did and they watched our cab pull away, too afraid to speak, maybe even too fucking afraid to pray.

Fuck them.

Mom and I don't speak again the rest of the way home. There had already been too many words.

After I do her tell-your-mom assignment, Maddy asks if I want to talk to the police.

"No," I say. "I'll die."

"You won't die, but it's your choice and you can report Gary if you want. What he did to you was against the law, and you might be able to keep him from assaulting someone else."

Shit, so I have to. I can't let him hurt anyone else, not if I can help it. I go to the police station alone. I wait a long time and my hands are shaking when it's my turn to go up to the counter. The officer hands me a set of pages like a school exam booklet and asks me to write my statement.

I write everything I remember. Everything Tonya and Amber told me. Everything I saw in Tonya's video. And everything I told my classmate the night I was drunk. I cry while I'm writing and wipe my tears on my sleeve. It's hard to be here, to put my words on the record, but it matters.

Later a policeman calls me. "There are some holes in your statement," he says. "We need more information. Can you come and meet with us?"

The next day I wear a knee-length skirt and a cream sweater. I look like I'm going to church. I kind of am. Repent and be saved.

When I arrive, two gigantic policemen flank me. They take me down a narrow hallway lined with closed doors. I want to run, to make a break for it, but I bet they'd throw me to the floor.

The policemen direct me to a cold gray interrogation room that's like a prison cell. I can hardly breathe. They point me to a chair and sit between me and the door, barricading it, locking me in.

You're okay, I tell myself over and again. It's Maddy's voice in my head. You can do this. They're the good guys. They're here to help you.

"We read your statement but tell it to us again in your own words," one says.

Shit, I thought I wrote it so I wouldn't have to speak. I close my eyes, suck in a big breath and begin. "There was this old guy. He was forty and married. He came to a party at my friend Amber's place," I say.

They're looking at me, silent and stern, waiting for me to continue.

It's humiliating beyond belief but I keep going. I tell them I said no and stop and tried to push him away but he kept touching me. I tell them how I struggled to keep him from undoing my jeans, and that he laughed and kept going. I tell them how he shoved his finger inside and how he wouldn't listen when I tried to make him stop.

I'm back there again, in The Terrible Night, looking down on the stained-brown room. "That's where my real memories stop but I know he raped me," I say. My voice is far away. Outside my body, like water on skin that I'm flicking off. It's true and it has to be said but it wasn't this me that Gary hurt. It was that other me down on the floor. I know because I see her but not out of her eyes. I'm up here, by the ceiling, above the old guy and that poor dead girl.

Someone's firing off questions. I squeeze my eyes tight. Shake my head clear. Drag myself back.

"Were you drunk?" asks the scarier cop.

"Yeah," I say. "Blackout drunk but I don't know why. I only had two drinks. One and a half coolers and part of a Long Island iced tea."

"You said in your statement that you passed out and then woke up with this guy..." He flips through his notes, "...this Gary behind you."

"Yeah."

"That's not how passing out works. Once you're out, you're out."

"Oh," I say. I'm confused. "Maybe I wasn't passed out? I guess I could have just been sleeping. But I woke up when he was behind me."

"You said there were others in the house at the time?"

"Yeah."

"If you wanted him to stop, then why didn't you yell?"

My eyes dart from one cop to the other. I wish I could bolt, that they wouldn't shoot me if I took off down the long hall. It's like that night when I was trapped, pinned beneath Gary's arm. "I don't know," I say, hanging my head. "I didn't think about that." Does that make it my fault?

I'm bawling but I only brought two tissues and they're so full of snot and tears that they won't absorb any more. I wipe my cheeks with my sweater.

"If you think we're being too hard on you, imagine being in court in front of Gary's defense lawyer," says the other officer. He's nicer but still terrifying. "How do you expect to convince a judge of anything when you don't really remember what happened?" His voice sounds gentle but scolding, like he caught me stealing a loaf of bread but forgives me because I'm just skin and bone.

I can't do anything but shake my head. I can't breathe. I might die in this room, freeze to death in my shame.

"Your therapist couldn't possibly have thought you were ready to report this," the mean one says. "We'd need his name and something that links him to the party that night and even then it would still be your word against his."

"But can't you get his last name? Please? The university has it. I know a class he was in that semester."

"You haven't provided sufficient evidence to warrant reaching out to the school."

My eyes are raw like they've burnt out.

"Tell you what," says the nicer officer. "We'll close your file for now but you can come back when you remember the rest. Let's not wake the bear until we're ready to catch him."

It's up to me to find Gary. I go to one of the phone interview booths in the journalism school and call Campus Security. "I was sexually assaulted by a student and I need his last name so I can report him."

"That's personal information and I can't give it out," says the man's voice on the other end.

"Okay, then could you give it to the police? They need his last name or they won't be able to find him."

"I already told you I can't give out that information."

"Then what can I do?"

"Nothing without a warrant," he says and hangs up.

I go to see Maddy but our appointment is cancelled. She's gone. Like forever, the receptionist says. "Do you want to book in with someone else?" she asks.

I don't know if I answer. I'm running down the hall. I'm in a bathroom stall, crouched against the wall. It's like I've been punched in the heart, like the time Tenille got hit in the chest with a paintball and it rocked her off her feet.

I feel Gary next to me, his breath hot in my ear.

I don't know how to escape. I can't start over again.

"Don't wake the bear," the officer said. I wonder if I should settle for an eternal winter, for a hibernation that lasts the rest of my life.

I look Tonya up online and call her at her parent's place in Medicine Hat. When she answers, I force myself to say, "Remember that party at Amber's? Gary sexually assaulted me that night."

"Was that the old guy?" she asks.

"Yeah. Do you know his last name?"

"Sorry, no. That night is a blur. That was a long time ago."

"Yeah. Five years," I say. "You filmed a video that night. I was asleep on the floor and he was behind me acting creepy. It's on one of your little blue tapes. Any chance you still have it?"

"Yeah, I bet. I have a bunch of boxes in the basement. I'll check."

"Thank you. Could you mail it to the Regina police station for me? That way they'll be able to add it to my file."

"Sure," she says. I imagine Tonya finding the tape, slipping it into a manila envelope and the less-scary officer reopening my case.

I look for Amber too but no one with her last name lives in Regina. I call all the Saskatchewan numbers listed. The last woman says she knows Amber.

"Great," I say. "We were friends in university." Amber's going to be pissed that I'm tracking her down but I don't know how else to find Gary. "Do you know where she is?"

"Last I heard she moved back to the reserve."

The reserve? But Amber's white. So white I once tagged along to her fake tan appointment. "Can I get her number?"

"She doesn't have one. There's no way to reach her."

I leave a message with this lady, her aunt maybe, and wait for Amber or Tonya or the cops to call.

I've used up all my investigative reporting tricks and I don't know what else I can do. In my secret brain, the inner one where I used to allow wisps of the thoughts I didn't want God to hear, an idea floats past: I'm home free if no one calls. I've done everything I have to.

"You don't have to tell me anything that's too painful," Maddy's replacement, Leah, says later when I don't want to speak.

I don't tell her about Gary or The Terrible Night. Instead I tell her how I'm obsessed with drawing and how I've wallpapered my bedroom with pictures of trees.

"Interesting. Why don't you bring some of your pictures?"

Next time I show her a charcoal drawing. It's black and white, just a trunk and a hundred naked branches whipping in the wind.

"Is this you?" Leah asks.

"No. It's a tree." Obviously.

"But does it represent you? Sometimes people draw themselves into their pictures."

I go to my room and stare at my wall of dead trees, black scribbles and the browning acrylic tulip that droops to the ground under the weight of its bulb.

Leah's right. They are all me.

Together

18

THE SHAPE OF MY TEETH

Now

Ian bounds up the sidewalk carrying a pot of purple flowers. I open the door for him and he passes me the pot. A note is sticking up above the petals. Not a note, a cheque. For a grand.

"It's a loan so you can pay the mortgage off right now," Ian says.

He knows I've been obsessing about the mortgage. I only have one more payment until it will be gone, until the house will be mine instead of the bank's.

"I'm proud of how hard you've worked to pay off your house," he says.

"Our house," I say, mashing myself into his arms.

We're wrestling again. Ian went on strike for months, but I begged him for it so many times that he finally gave in. Wrestling is my favourite thing next to the sex we're barely having. I don't know why, but I need his body against mine.

He's lying across my stomach, his weight locking me in place. He pins my wrists and still has a rogue hand. "The python moves slowly," he narrates like Morgan Freeman. "His strategy is graceful in execution. He waits patiently for his victim to exhale, coils tighter and goes in for the kill."

I kick but can't reach him. I'm helpless.

His eyes are shiny with mischief. No. Malice.

He pinches me through my sports bra. Pinch. Release. Pinch.

My legs kick wildly but they can't reach anything. I nip at his bicep. No reaction. I dig my teeth in further.

He's pinching fast and hard and laughing like a five-year-old. "I'm going to pinch your nipple right off," he says.

Fuck you. I'm going to make you stop. I clench my jaw and bite down hard, imagining one of his bloody steaks. I grind my teeth deep in his muscle.

"Stop it!" he yells and lets me go. Tooth prints are gouged deep into his skin.

"I'm sorry," I say, hanging my head. "I thought you would give up when it started to hurt?"

"That was vicious," he says as he rubs his arm.

I know. "I'm sorry. I'm so sorry."

"It's okay," Ian says. "You just got carried away." He kisses my cheek and notices that it's wet. He sighs. "It's fine. It's not that bad."

When the dents finally smooth out, they don't go away. They turn blue. Then green. Then yellow. "I'm so sorry," I whisper each time I see them.

The next time we wrestle I bite his face.

I don't know why I'm being so crazy, why I keep making Ian bleed, why his arm is bruised in the shape of my teeth. Even when I dated the shittiest guys, I was still nice to them. Come to think of it, I never left any of them. They all walked away from me, everyone except Thomas.

Mid-twenties

When I graduate university, I land a freelance newspaper gig and interview a snowplow driver named Thomas. He's so hot I have to look at my notepad instead of him.

When I'm done with my questions, he has one. "Shot in the dark," he says, "but would you go out with me?"

Before our date I meet up with a Christian friend, a virgin who's had a bunch of boyfriends.

"How do you go out with someone without sleeping with him?" I ask.

She laughs.

"Seriously," I say.

She goes quiet. I shouldn't have asked. I must seem like a total nympho.

"I have a pants-on rule," she says. "Anything else is fine but no one gets to undo my pants until we're married."

"What if they don't get it?"

"What do you mean? It's pretty easy to understand."

I never wear belts but I borrow one from Mom's closet and cinch it up tight. The more to keep me done up the better. It's four and a half years since I quit having sex, and I'm not starting again any time soon. Maybe never. If I do, it will be because I've found someone I love, someone who is crazy about me.

Thomas grabs my butt on our first date and unzips my sweater on our second even though I tell him "no" and "that's not okay." Afterwards he disappears long enough for me to forgive and forget and to wish he would come back.

We're in my room kissing one day when my family is away. Thomas grabs my boobs over my shirt. My head is cloudy, like no but also like yes. He tries to undo my pants. "No," I say. "Not that. My pants are staying done up."

His hands slip beneath my shirt and I'm not into it but whatever. Pick your hill to die on, Dad used to say.

Thomas's fingers roam over my jeans, slinking lower. "You can't touch me there," I say and pull his hand away.

He kisses me and then he's running his thumb under my waistband. "No," I say. "Stop it." We're battling, me against him, and he isn't listening. "Quit it."

He doesn't. I try to pull his hand away from the danger zone. He won't budge. His fingers slink lower inside my jeans.

"No!" I shove against him but it doesn't do a thing. I'm losing. I don't know how to make him stop. My arms give up. They flop to the side, totally dead.

"No," I say. "Stop. I'm done."

He keeps going. He's clawing into my panties. His fingers rub against my spot.

I shudder. A whole body grimace. It happens on its own and is wild, like an earthquake, so violent it knocks his hand away.

I'm bawling. "I said no," I say. "That's not okay."

"You stopped pushing so I thought you changed your mind."

"I shouldn't have to push you away when I'm saying no!" I yell, fury erupting from somewhere deep inside.

"You're right. I'm sorry," he says.

"You have to go."

Even though I get a sweet communications contract with the provincial power company and move into a bachelor suite downtown, I can't stop thing about Thomas. Maybe I overreacted. I guess it was confusing when I stopped pushing. I should have been more clear.

I call and he comes over and I don't know how it happens but he gets his hand in my pants again and I give up. Boys will be boys. Another time he tugs my pants off and tells me to get on my knees beside my bed. I do. It reminds me of praying, and I clasp my hands tight. Thomas kneels behind and pushes his finger inside me. It's awkward that I can't see him, that he's making me hold still, but I guess it's all right.

He stops for a second and then it's not his finger any more.

"No, stop." It's a whisper but it's as loud as I can scream.

He doesn't.

I wait, silent, and try not to breathe.

After Thomas leaves, I go to the pharmacy for the morning-after pill. The woman at the counter asks, "Did you consent?" I nod but I'm a shit liar and my eyes pool with tears.

"It'll be a few minutes while I get that for you. You're welcome to wait in our privacy room if you'd like."

A few minutes later a cop opens the door.

"So you were raped?" she asks.

Fuck. I shake my head.

"What happened?"

"Nothing," I say and my voice is quaking.

"Then why did you have the pharmacy call us?"

"I didn't."

We stare each other down.

I didn't push Thomas away. I didn't yell. All I did was give one little no, and apparently that means fucking go ahead and help yourself. And what if he did stop before he got to the end? It took a long time for him to stop. But did he quit because he finished or because I asked him to? I don't know. I couldn't see his face and there was no condom, no semen bag, to tell me what happened.

Plus the Gary cops couldn't do anything for me so what's the difference now? If there's no scream, no witness, no blood stains under my nails, then there's no goddamn fucking crime.

"What's his name?" she asks.

I don't answer. As if I'm that stupid. Why can't she go after Gary instead? Lock up the real asshole, the one I'd never liked, not even for a second, the one who couldn't possibly be excused.

I hate this woman and the pharmacist who betrayed me and the cops who did fuck all about Gary. I'm so tired and I have a terrible headache and all I want is to swallow one fucking No Baby and get out of here.

"It was my fault," I tell the officer in a voice that sounds strangled, like it's coming out of a rock. "A misunderstanding."

She sighs heavily, like I'm the biggest villain she's seen all day, and goes to leave. She stops with her hand on the door and turns back to me. "Do us both a favour and get a better boyfriend, would you?"

I don't answer when Thomas calls, but he keeps on trying. He leaves me a message and asks, "What would it take for me to be your boyfriend?"

My boyfriend? I didn't think he liked me. Relationships are so confusing.

I call him back and he invites me over. "No thanks," I say.

"Please? I want to make you dinner and treat you to a movie."

Whoa, a real date. And he wants to be my boyfriend.

I cab over and Thomas plops an ear of corn on my plate. We eat on the couch as he flips through the channels. Kirsten Dunst and her upside-down *Spiderman* kiss flick by but he keeps going until he lands on a porno.

"How about *Spiderman*?" I ask and he goes back to it.

He offers me a beer and I say yes because I'm still hungry and we're out of food. I take a sip and set the bottle down. I forgot I shouldn't drink around him. Best to be sober so I can stick to my rules.

He forces a kiss. I pull away.

"You owe me," he says. "You had my beer."

"I do not!" I'm yelling and getting up to leave.

"I'm sorry. Of course you don't owe me anything," he says. "I just meant a kiss would be nice."

"Oh."

He kisses me again and I let him. "Drunk, huh?" he asks and laughs.

"Did you mean it when you said you wanted me to be your girlfriend?"

"I never said that. I said, 'What would it take for me to be your boyfriend?' See the difference? Good one, right?" He looks proud, like he wants a high five.

"Yeah," I say. "You got me."

He goes back to the porno and it's so zoomed in I don't know what's happening. "I want to do that," he says and whips my pants down and I don't have the energy to care any more.

We go to his room, and when he's done I grab my mound of clothes, lock myself in the bathroom and take a scalding bath. I'd cry but the fountain is dry and dead and Joan of Arc burned at the stake.

I get dressed but I'm missing my socks. They're my favourite pair, fuzzy ankle socks with blue and green stripes, but they'll have to fend for themselves.

I tiptoe down the dark hall and shove my bare feet into my shoes. "I'm leaving," I say when I'm a second from the door.

"Come on, stay," Thomas calls from the bedroom. "I'm not driving you."

"No."

"How are you getting home?"

"Walking."

"It's far. Come back to bed. I'll call you a cab in the morning."

"No." I take off into the cold night and walk forever, a million steps away from him.

I think about the lady cop. Did Thomas do anything wrong, like technically? I don't know. I fucked it up with all my giving in.

I take another university class so I can see Leah, the therapist who took me on after Maddy left. She is only allowed to help me if I'm a student. Back then I wouldn't talk, wouldn't tell her what was wrong.

Now I have no choice but to tell her about Thomas. "I don't know if I can stay away from him," I say. "I keep forgiving him and taking him back, and I'm afraid I'll do it again the second he says he misses me." I'm so lonely and pathetic that I fall for it every single time.

"Yeah. It might be a sex addiction," she says. "Don't talk to him and try going celibate for thirty days."

I don't think sex has anything to do with it since I don't want it and am trying my best not to have it, but I take Leah's advice. I give up solo sex and everything and cross the days off on my calendar. I keep picking up the phone and setting it back down.

19

THE DAY IAN FORGOT TO MAKE THE BED

Now

Ian joins a yoga class that doesn't fit my work schedule and I try not to worry about him being in a room of spandex ladies. When he goes on work trips and is too busy to call, I reassure myself that he's coming home to me. Some nights he's on his computer long after I've to gone bed and I lie awake reminding myself that he almost never watches porn. One day I laugh when I come home and see our rumpled duvet. We've been living together for six months, and he's made the bed every day and lectured me about it a bunch of times. I'll have to text him about how my sloppiness is rubbing off on him.

I go to straighten the duvet. Ian's iPad is lying on the sheet. I'm moving it to the night table but I don't put it down. Should I look? No. But I'm allowed to use his iPad so it isn't really wrong, is it? Why did he forget to make the bed?

I push the home button and the screen lights up. Skin. A brunette on her knees. Bare-naked everything. A penis swallowed up inside her.

Spam? A pop up? It's fifteen minutes into a video. Not an accident.

I want to smash the iPad but it's not mine. I set it down gingerly like a bomb. I need to break something, for something other than me to be destroyed. I hurl a plate to the floor and it shatters like a busted soul.

I text Ian. "I know why you forgot to make the bed."

"I'm coming home right now," he says.

Fuck you. I throw my phone on the bed and hide in the park across the street. I watch through the bushes as the stranger I once loved rushes inside. I seethe in the park until I'm shivering, until my rage freezes over.

Ian rushes to the door when I come home. I can't meet his eyes. "I love you," he says. It stabs me in the forehead. More fucking lies.

"You can't say that when it's not true!" I'm pacing, wild. "You can't love me and chose to watch porn instead of being with me. It doesn't work like that."

"I do love you. I prefer being with you, but I don't think there's anything wrong with liking porn too."

"How often do you watch it? More than almost never?"

"I don't know how often. It's not a replacement for you."

"Do you watch it more than almost never?"

Ian pauses.

I get louder. "Do you?"

"Yes."

"You said 'almost never.' You said you didn't care about it!"

"I'm sorry. I didn't want you to worry."

"So you made me believe a lie? You tricked me into loving you."

"I'm sorry you feel betrayed," he says.

I go to the basement and curl up into a ball on Grandma's old couch, the one I bought from her estate when she died. What's wrong with me? Why aren't I enough for Ian? What use am I now that he doesn't need me for anything, not even sex?

I cry when I'm stripping down to shower and accidentally catch a glimpse of myself in the mirror. Look at this body that isn't good enough. I'm hideous. No wonder my boyfriend would rather have imaginary sex than touch me. I yank the mirror off the wall.

I wince as the water touches me, as I run the soap over my fat belly, my floppy boobs.

I start changing in the bathroom so Ian won't have to look at me. I worry when he goes to the gym, when he's home without me and when he stays up late. When he reaches for his iPad I ask what he's reading.

"The news," he says.

"Oh yeah, what's the news?"

At Chapters Ian picks up the *Sports Illustrated* calendar and turns it over to look at all the swimsuit ladies. I can barely hold my tears back so I walk away.

"Seriously?" he calls after me. "It's a calendar."

I can't respond. All I have is this reservoir of salt water inside.

Ian takes my boots off for me when we get home. I'm too weak to do it myself.

We're still having sex once or twice a week, even though I've been asking for more, but I can't get out of bed afterwards. I lie there demanding my limbs to move but I'm buried in that thick spring-melt mud, the kind that refuses to let go.

Ian pulls me up. "Come on, let's get going," he says.

I slump back down. I want to get up but the gravity is way too strong.

I reach out to the City's HR department and someone emails back telling me I can have all the counseling I want: they'll pay for me to go on my own, with a partner or with any family members. "We want our employees to be well," the email says. "The healthier our staff are, the better they perform their jobs."

I see a new therapist, Brenda, but I'm mad about it. Ian should be in therapy, not me. He's the one who tricked me into dating him and sexing him and moving in together. He's been lying to me for two and a half fucking years.

Brenda is nice enough but she talks like a professor and her shoulders are stiff beneath her leather jacket, beneath two sets of skin. But she's free and god do I ever need help.

I convince Ian to see Brenda with me. In her office I tell him, "I don't want you to watch porn any more. Not more than 'almost never,' like you said in the beginning."

"You don't get to censor me," Ian says.

"That's fair," Brenda tells him. She turns to me, "You're entitled to set limits for yourself but you can't impose them on other people."

Ian's lying on the couch in his brown housecoat when I get out of the shower. "I'm sorry you feel betrayed," he says, pinching his forehead. "But you're going to have to decide if you can get past this."

"What do you mean?"

"You're going to have to figure out if you trust me. Otherwise you'll have to walk away."

I fall to my knees on the floor beside him and grasp his hands in mine like we're praying. "I won't leave you, not ever. I promise. We're going to figure this out. We're going to make it work."

I'm crying and his eyes are red but dry, and holy shit I have to fix us or he might actually leave.

"Let's take a trip," I beg. "Up north to Waskesiu, like we talked about. It will be beautiful this time of year."

I book us a room at the resort and we head up for Thanksgiving. It's snowing and cold, but we hike the trails anyway and Ian piggybacks me just like old times.

We have the paths all to ourselves, so I dare him to strip down for a wilderness-man picture. "Do it," I say, "It will look like you're part of that *Sigur Ros* album cover."

I was sure he would say no or don't be so ridiculous, but he drops his clothes, faces the lake and poses with his back to me, his hands on his hips and his feet apart. I'm laughing so hard I can barely get the shot. Then he's dressed and insisting it's my turn. "You're spontaneous like this," he says. "It's one of the things I like most about you. Come on."

I can't say no when I started it so I whip my things off, strike the same bare-bum pose and hurry back into my clothes.

The rest of our hike is perfect and just like before, and maybe we can be new again, fresh like the first autumn snow.

I flip through our photos in the car and the ones of him are brilliant, powerful and wild. Then I see mine and fall silent. I don't look right. It's too close up for starters. My butt is lumpy and the lighting is all wrong and I'm so obviously not the girl from his porno. Even I agree that I'm not good enough for him.

Ian takes my phone from me. "You look great," he says. "So cute. Please don't delete it." His voice cracks and I know he's begging, but I can't handle it. I erase ugly naked me.

That night we go for dinner at a sports bar and I keep turning around to see whatever he's watching over my head. It's just a bunch of guy sports, but I'm so afraid of what he could see, of everything I can't keep out of his eyes.

"Shoot me in the forehead with a tranquilizer dart," I beg Brenda but she thinks I can push through on my own. I'll try. I don't want to be so weak, to have to pump myself full of drugs just to survive.

I try hypnosis and meditation classes and read the horrific *Hite Report on Male Sexuality* where none of the men have a clue what love is.

Ian comes back to Brenda's office with me but she sides with him. "You could try watching porn together," she says. "Some couples like that."

We try once and it's awful. I don't want him to see that girl. I don't want to see her either. And how do we know she wants to do that? What if he thinks she's better than me? He must or he wouldn't be staring at her.

I don't look before I cross the street any more. I wish I could get run over, that there would be some tragic accident, that I could shuffle off this fucking unbearable mortal coil.

One day Brenda says I'm fine and that we should end our sessions. She couldn't possibly be more wrong: she's the only reason my skin is staying on.

I'll do anything for her to keep me. Even tell her about the bad things.

"Maybe my past is making this harder," I say. I tell her about Cameron the con and shower-wall Kyle. It's not enough to get her attention, to prove that I need help.

I tell her about The Terrible Night.

"I don't know what happened after my brain went black," I say as my stomach clenches tight. My head drops low and my words come out in a whisper, "Gary might have." I stop, then force myself to continue, "might have kept hurting me."

Brenda asks if I want to try a treatment where she repeats my memories about Gary back to me. "Sometimes our brains get stuck in difficult experiences, so this therapy is like a windshield wiper that could clear things up a bit for you."

The next time I go in she sits so close our knees are almost touching. "Follow my hand movements with your eyes," she says and moves her fingers across the reach of my peripheral vision. "Fighting over your zipper. Saying, 'But you're forty and married.' Saying 'no and stop.'"

She repeats everything from The Terrible Night like two thousand times. It's obscene and horrendous and I try to black it out.

When I finally escape, Ian asks how it went.

"It was stupid and awful," I say. It was like getting stabbed in the eye a hundred times, and I refuse to think about it for one more second.

When I go to bed that night, my legs spasm and kick on their own.

"Stop it," Ian says. "I'm trying to sleep."

I try to hold still but my legs keep thrashing like they're attached to someone else, someone who is being eaten alive.

20

Jungle Termites

Now

Ian and I are watching the Calgary Flames when they come to Regina for a preseason game. In the third period I get a text from Shane, the last guy I dated before I met Ian. "I see you," he says from across the arena.

Ian seems fine with me texting Shane, but when I ask if it's okay if Shane comes over, Ian stands and zips his jacket. "Let's get out of here so we don't get trapped in the parking lot."

I try to convince him to meet Shane or at least wait so we can see the final score, but he's set on leaving.

Ian has nothing to worry about when it comes to Shane. In fact, Shane is his biggest ally. The day I found Ian's porn, Shane was the one I called. Not to complain but to beg for advice. See, because Shane dated me, he knows what's wrong with me. He's coaching me on how to be less crazy, on how to keep Ian.

"You're never going to be able to date anyone if you can't get over this porn thing," Shane keeps telling me. "You need to be less sensitive."

Mid-twenties

Shane's soccer team is short on players, so I'm pitching in tonight. I've known Shane for years. We used to work together and have some friends in common.

Shane invites me over after the game. "Want to go out with me?" he asks, when we're sitting on his futon.

I hadn't thought of that before, but sure. Why not?

He kisses me and I like it at first and then I get dizzy. He stops. "Why are you crying?"

It takes a long time for my brain to form any words. "Sometimes it's hard for me to say no," I say. "Will you be careful with me?"

"Of course," he says and squeezes my arm.

When I agree to sleep over, my stomach caves in on itself as soon as we're in bed. "Everything is off limits unless you ask first," I say. "Should I go home?"

"That's all right," he says and his arm on me is warm and still.

We have a dozen sleepovers and fool around and he listens to my breathing and figures out exactly when to stop. He knows before I do, like he's some kind of shrink.

I'm happy but I'm crying all the time.

"What's wrong?" he asks.

I don't know. Maybe it's because he said he can't keep dating me if we don't get to the sex part soon.

On Friday night he shows up at my place three hours late because he had a dollar invested in an online poker game.

"Do you like me?" I ask, holding the tides back.

"I wouldn't be here if I didn't."

"That's a backwards way to say it. Can you just tell me that you like me?"

Shane's face hardens. He looks so different I don't recognize him and then he's gone, striding across the street.

I run after him and fling myself into his car. "I'm sorry," I say. "I take it back. I want to be with you."

"I can't give you what you want," he says, his voice colder than the February wind. "You're too emotional. I'm not your guy."

I sob for weeks and beg Shane to change his mind but it's not going to happen.

A neighbour takes me to a meditation group in some guy's living room and I cry there too. A dozen of us sit on chairs or cross-legged on burgundy cushions on the floor with our eyes closed.

"Pay attention to your breath," the leader says and falls silent for half an hour. I spend most of the time in imaginary conversations with Shane, but then I catch something deep in my belly: a hollowness, a turn-around, a fluttery kick like when Bethany put my hand on her baby bump. The kick comes and goes: my inhale flicking itself into an exhale.

I get invited to a house party with Shane's friends and I'd bet a grand on him being there. I find him playing crokinole in the basement, but he ignores me.

I get wasted and bummed and then I'm in his room saying, "Throw me on the bed."

"No way."

"Do it," I say and he does and we have sex for a second and everything goes black.

When I wake up beside him I'm so happy that it overshadows my sex shame. He likes me and we're back together. I kiss him but he turns away.

"I'm glad we're together again," I say.

"We're not. We were trashed and it was nothing."

My communications contract at the power company is ending in a few weeks, and I don't have any leads on a new job. I can't bear the thought of having no Shane *and* no job.

When Grandma died, my parents gave me a thousand dollars from their inheritance. I'd been saving it for something special so I book a ticket to the Philippines to visit my missionary sister Tenille and her husband.

As my trip gets closer I wonder if Shane would sleep with me again. If I can talk him into it, maybe he'll realize he wants to be with me.

Shane and I meet in the park downtown on our lunch break. "I have to ask you something," I say, working up my nerve. "Do you want to try having sex until I leave? No strings or anything."

I'm staring at the sidewalk and words keep shooting out. "It could be kind of like therapy and you could show me that it's not so scary, that I don't need to cry all the time. It might make it easier next time I date someone."

Oh god, what a stupid idea. And so transparent. He's going to say no.

"Sure. I'll come over tonight."

My gut clenches. I go back to work and worry all afternoon. How do I get out of it? Am I allowed to bail if it was my idea?

When I get home I'm too nervous to go inside so I rake and bag the leaves I'd left on the lawn all winter. My nails fill up with dirt. I should clean them before Shane gets here. No I should leave them so he thinks I'm gross and changes his mind.

A ladybug is struggling to climb out of the bag. I drop my armful of leaves, scoop her up and lower her to the ground. She's so timid she doesn't want to leave my fingertip. "You're safe," I tell her and slide her onto a blade of grass.

Shane drives up. Shit. What if I say I lost my house key? He bounds down the sidewalk and flashes a string of condoms at me.

Inside I sit on the far end of the couch and wrap my arms tight around myself. "I don't know," I say.

"We can just talk. You don't have to do anything," he says.

"Can we try kissing and have it be okay if I want to stop any time?"

"Sure," he says, and his lips taste like forever. Maybe I can do this.

I put Pachelbel's *Canon in D* on repeat. My teacher used to play it in the background of my high-school English class and I noticed back then that the song was playing me. One note as I inhaled, the next as I exhaled. I was breathing it, the sadness and the beauty, the loneliness and the love. It was like a meditation.

I breathe the notes as Shane pulls me into a hug.

"Are you sure?" he asks. "It's fine if you don't want to."

I need to. Even if he doesn't want me back. We're going to put me together again.

Afterwards, Shane doesn't care if he sees me. Even when he can have whatever he wants, I still can't get his attention. I can't wait to get out of here. To be an ocean away from my oozing heart.

Jenna decides to come to the Philippines with me, and it's dark and late when we meet up with Tenille at the Bible translation camp where she lives. We go white-water rafting and to the rice terraces and the night market, and it would be great except that I miss Shane like every second.

When I get home, Shane looks at me with soft eyes and asks, "Do you want to try again?" I cry and kiss him like a bachelorette who was sure she wouldn't get a rose.

I land another communications contract, but I keep all my evenings and weekends free for Shane. He doesn't have time to hang out though. We only get together like once a week because he's so busy with his friends and soccer and poker and laundry.

"Stop," I tell him when we're in bed. "That's as far as I want to go."

"Then why did we have sex before?" he asks.

"Our deal was like therapy. It was strategic, with a timeline and an end, and even then it was a big deal for me. I'm not ready to do it again."

"Sex is a requirement in a relationship," he says and dumps me again. "Besides if I wanted to be with you, I would have made time for you."

For Canada Day, Bethany invites Mom, Dad and Holly to join her family for a heritage celebration on a farm. I go too and cheer as the kids do their best in the potato-sack race. The grass is extra bright as I sit beside Bethany to watch my niece and nephews play. "I love your kids," I say. "I'd like to spend more time with them."

"No," she says and her voice is hard, way worse than when one of the kids refuses to obey. "I can't have them around you. Evil seeps out of you."

"What?"

"You encourage them to question my authority and you tell them things aren't how they seem."

"I don't think that's true," I say, trying to hold my voice steady. "Why do you say that?"

"Remember Noah's birthday? You gave him a box of candy and told him, 'Your mom won't like this.' You set me up to be the bad guy."

"I'm sorry. I only meant to be funny."

"That's not all. When we had pie you told the kids that sometimes people put meat in pies instead of fruit."

"Yeah, like chicken pot pie. What's wrong with that?"

"You're undermining everything I'm teaching them." She stands and dusts herself off and her four little ducklings follow her away.

I call Shane when I get home. I'm too upset not to. I'm telling him about Canada Day and somehow end up in his bed. "Want to have sex?" he asks.

"No. Want to be my boyfriend?"

"Standoff," he says and laughs.

We fool around whenever he gets bored but we don't have sex. I'm sure it would make me too sad. Even our sleepovers break my heart for months.

In the winter, when my latest communications contract is about to end, Shane invites me to join his friends at a pub.

"Okay," I say. "But that's it. No fooling around. We're just going to be friends now, right?"

"Sure," he says.

I walk over and down a pint of mead. I'm already wobbly and done because I hardly drink any more, but Shane dares me to chug a second. "Deal, but only if you call me a cab right now," I say.

He does and I slam the mead back like it's a giant shot. I get up to leave and am so messed up I don't notice when Shane gets into the cab with me.

He comes in, uninvited, and lies down on the couch. "What are you doing here?" I ask.

"Need somewhere to sleep."

I roll my eyes. "Fine, you can stay in my room."

We fall into bed and it's dark and somehow we're fucking. "I love you," I say.

He laughs. "You're wasted."

"But I do," I say. "I love you. And you love me too."

"Uh, no, I don't," he says and grabs his clothes and lets himself out.

I wake up and holy fuck am I ever embarrassed. I love him and I'm nothing to him and it's been this way for a year and a half.

I turn my computer on and find a farm in a jungle that won't charge much for me to stay. I'd been scrimping for months so I could make an extra payment on my mortgage, but I need to escape. I'll go to Belize and hide out until I'm over Shane for good.

I'm in a dory with a villager who is standing at the back of the boat and pulling us upstream. Maybe half an hour passes before he sends out a sharp whistle like a bird call. The jungle responds with a call of its own.

"You're here," the guy says. "Get out."

I stand in the dory. I'm not sure what to do. We're nowhere. The place he's leaving me isn't a dock. There isn't a path. There are no signs saying, "Yes, this is the farm and we're waiting for you." There's nothing but wildness. I step out.

"Go that way," he says, pointing into the dense jungle. Then he glides away down the river.

I walk into the bush. I make out what might be a faint trail. Hopefully not one created by jaguars. I follow it.

The whistle comes again, and a few minutes later a dreadlocked woman appears. What a relief. She takes me to a rustic wooden cabin and I settle in.

There are five of us staying at the farm: the owner, Dreadlocks, another worker and a second paying guest. We rise with the sun and bathe in river water.

Some days I work for an hour or two, pulling weeds or harvesting cocoa beans, but mostly I'm on the drying floor, the place where the sesame harvest is laid to rest. I meditate, do yoga and take warm naps there in the green light under the jungle canopy.

I cry every day and wonder if I'll ever dry out like the sesame. Shane never loved me. I miss him and I can't have him. That's all there is. I cry about snowplow Thomas too and about old-man Gary and about shower-wall Kyle and Cameron the con and Kool-Aid Dave. And everyone else who made me afraid, who made me need someone like Shane to pull me together.

As I bawl on the drying floor, my skin stings like the jungle termites are burrowing into my heart. Or digging their bloody way out.

Two months pass. I hike out of the jungle, catch a bus to town and get a room at a bed and breakfast. I go straight to the shower and groan under the stream of hot water, scrubbing a layer of jungle, of leftover self, off my skin.

21

CAPTIVE

Now

Brenda, our therapist, recommends Ian and I make a sex schedule. I pester Ian into booking a sexy time later that week and daydream about how great it's going to be.

"Remember what we're doing today?" I ask.

"What?"

"Our homework!"

"There's nothing sexy about an appointment," he says. "Hey, are you pouting?"

I'm trying not to. "Can we at least wrestle?"

We do and I'm losing.

"Stop," I say.

Of course he doesn't. Fucking men.

I forget everything. Except this blinding rage. I kick and bite and claw. Ian lurches away. He's clutching at his balls and his back is raked over like he's been mauled by a beast.

I shudder at the work of my own hands. "I'm so sorry," I say and my tears flood the world.

"What's happening with you?" he asks.

It's a long time before I can find the answer and longer before I can say it. "I don't feel safe with you."

He glares. "That's cold. It's not fair to say that after everything I do for you."

"I take it back," I say. "You're right. You do a great job taking care of me."

He stomps around the house and leaves.

I'll never say it again.

Brenda isn't fixing anything. She might even be making us worse.

I call the clinic and ask to try someone new. We get in with Nicole, a woman who has a grey bob and light eyes and who offers couples therapy.

I have a panic attack in our first session when Ian tells her he doesn't see anything wrong with porn. My back drips sweat and I'm boiling and Ian is rubbing my shoulder while this new lady tries to help me calm down. I can't say it. Not to anyone. I shouldn't even think it. But I feel it. There's a flashing light inside me: Danger.

"How am I supposed to go home with him?" I ask Nicole at the end of an awful therapy session.

"I don't know," she says. "But our time is up."

Ian and I argue the whole walk home. I don't want to go into the same house as him, don't trust anything about this man who insists it's his right to stare at all the vaginas he wants.

As we cross the street, he says, "Okay, fine. I won't watch porn any more."

"Never?"

"Not as long as we're together. I don't see anything wrong with porn, but I'll stop watching it for you."

"Good," I say. "You should have to be the person you pretended you were."

We've only been home a few minutes when he says, "To be clear, I won't look at it any more but I'm still going to watch it in my imagination. You don't get to police my thoughts."

There's a brick in my stomach. Who are all these women? I bet his office is loaded with pretty girls.

"Look, I'm choosing to be with you. That should be enough," he says.

It's not. I have no idea why he's with me. I'd ask but last time I did he said, "I've told you a hundred times. You should know by now."

I rush to the door and reach for the handle. My wrist won't work. I have to escape, even for a minute, but I can't get out.

"Please don't go," Ian says.

I fall to the floor.

"Come here," he says.

I can't. I can't move.

He lifts me up like a baby. "What can I do to cheer you up?"

"Only the things you said you won't do."

"Why does porn bother you so much?" Ian asks. "Have you watched it on your own?"

"Only a little. I tried but the men are such pervs, and I don't think the women want to do it. It looks like they get tricked into it."

"Yeah, there's definitely a lot of awful porn out there. But it's not all bad. Try searching for something female friendly. I bet you could find something you like."

I shake my head but decide later to give it a shot. If I could quit worrying about porn, it would fix everything with Ian.

When he's out in the evening, I do some Googling.

Fine, the female-friendly stuff is better. Hot even. I find one couple who look like they're having a good time, and bookmark the video. Maybe porn isn't so bad. Maybe it isn't always exploitative.

I read the girl's bio and find out that she was raped when she was a kid. At the bottom of the page are links to her other videos, ones with heinous titles like *Receptionists are never safe*.

I'm dizzy with shame. I wish I hadn't watched her video. Anyone who does is just as bad as the predator who raped her, is also profiting from the wounds inflicted on a child.

Healthy women don't do this, don't strip down and spread their legs for the perverts of the world. All porn does is steal from those who don't have the capacity to fight back.

Ian insists we watch *Rome* and *Game of Thrones* and pre-watches the episodes so he can warn me when to look away. That's the only way I'll agree to see any of his gruesome shows.

All these people are sitting around outside when a guy is suddenly missing his head.

I'm hyperventilating and clutching my throat.

Ian hits pause until I catch my breath. "I'm sorry. I forgot about that one," he says. "That was a pretty stealthy slice."

Ian doesn't warn me about the sex stuff – maybe because there is too much to avoid it all – but the rapey scenes burn into my mind. I don't know how to turn the images off so they fester and grow, playing on repeat for months.

Even sex crimes in the news are infecting my mind: A woman who was taken captive. A doctor who molested his patients. A young lady who was assaulted on the same street I walked earlier that day. As hard as I try, I can't stop replacing their faces with my own. I can't understand why each woman didn't just agree, didn't convince herself that she wanted it.

"You can't rape the willing," the boys at my elementary school used to joke. Turns out it was good advice. These women made their lives so much harder when they fought back.

"Spank me," I tell Ian when we're in bed.

He does.

"Harder. Way harder."

But no matter how loud his slaps ring out it's never ever enough to pay for the wrongs I commit behind my eyelids when I participate in these women's suffering, when I long to feel their pain.

I try to tell Ian, but he says: "There's nothing wrong with sex. It's ordinary. You've been taught that it's shameful and now you're trying to force your shame into me. It's not going to work."

I wonder how dark it must be inside the mind of a man who imagines tearing off a stranger's clothes and stealing what she would never give.

I sign up for all the meditation classes and retreats I can find. I need something that can help me calm down, that can undo the knots in my stomach.

I'd forgotten about meditation when I met Ian. I was so happy, so together, that I didn't need it any more.

But now I can't go a day without meditating. I go to our room half an hour before bedtime so I can lie still and breathe and let my tears fall in silence.

In the spring I go on an eight-day meditation retreat in Moose Jaw. Near the end I sit down in a field. My ankle is itchy. It's a tick! I jump up and flick it off and there's this screaming inside: There shouldn't be a tick on me!

I notice my panic, and a new voice answers with a chuckle: Of course there should be a tick on me. I'm in his home and he did exactly what ticks do.

In the meditation hall it occurs to me that maybe Ian is only doing what men do, is only being human, is not out to suck my blood.

A prayer rises up in my chest: May I accept love as it is when it is offered to me.

Ian and I curl up in bed as soon as I get home.

"I saw love," I tell him. "It was an outstretched palm, open wide, as a chickadee hopped around, nibbled some seeds and flew away."

"That's nice," he says, but I don't think I said it right, don't think there could ever be enough words to explain the kind of love I long to give.

Ian surprises me with a bucket of Jenga blocks and we build towers on the living room floor. My towers are single blocks that I stack eight or nine high before they come crashing down. Ian's are complicated creations with supporting beams and braces. Despite his engineering, he can't make his towers reach any higher than mine. We're locked in a tie when Ian goes to the kitchen to get our dinner.

I sneak over to his tower and stack mine on top of his. It's stable and tall, a tower of Babel that reaches maybe not to the gods but twice as high as either of us could get on our own.

I call Ian over. "Look," I say, "It's proof that we're better together, that we're a great team."

Ian laughs but I think he trusts the evidence too because he takes a picture of me with our peace tower.

We are chatting in bed when Ian grazes my throat with his thumb.

"Quit it," I say, swatting him away.

"Trust me," he says as he trails his thumb over my throat like a feather. I can't breathe.

"You're okay," he says and keeps petting my throat as tears stream down my face. His touch is as tender as love, as a kiss on a toddler's scraped knee. He continues stroking my throat until my tears fade, until I believe him when he whispers, "You're safe."

Ian and I sign up for yoga and I grin over at him when we're in downward dog. We go into pigeon pose and I bend my knee in front of me and lean forward. My thigh quivers. I straighten my arms and hold myself up but the shaking continues. I wait it out.

Is Ian looking at the other women? Fuck, I hate men. A rage-tear slips down my cheek and I swat it away.

"Time to switch legs," the instructor says and I hate her too as I sink low over my thigh. I hate this class and yoga and the guys behind me who are breathing so loud it's all I can hear.

Next class my face goes so red in pigeon pose that the instructor comes up beside me. "Are you okay?" she asks softly.

I nod, choking back sobs. When I lay down for meditation at the end of class, a tear slips from the corner of my eye. Fuck. Nothing is wrong. Can you please stop being crazy?

On Saturday morning Ian pulls my back against him and says, "Let's do it my way this time." I agree and we do but I hate it. He doesn't kiss me and doesn't want me to move. It's like my whole function is to be quiet and catch the mess.

I can't get out of bed afterward. I'm weighed down like I'm made of stone.

Ian pulls the blanket off me and puts my feet on the floor.

"I'm not ready," I say and the words take every bit of energy I have.

He puts on *Charlie Wilson's War* while he waits for me.

I'm still trying to make myself get up when I hear Tom Hanks in the hot tub with two strippers. Fury shoots me into the living room. "Must you?" I ask.

"It's not about the strippers," he says. "It's about how Charlie doesn't even notice them."

"But did you?"

Ian grabs his forehead hard.

"It doesn't seem like quitting porn means much since you're still watching naked women on screen every day. All you've done is substitute one kind of porn for another."

"I've given up enough," he says.

I close my eyes and imagine hanging myself from the beams in the basement. I feel relief as I imagine the life slipping out of me, my face going pale, my body limp.

Ian and I wrestle in my dreams. I'm stronger there. "I beat you last night," I say. "You'd be proud of my dream moves!"

Another night I bolt up in bed. I'm drenched in sweat. My heart is banging in my chest.

Ian is lying beside me. I can't look at him. Oh god, please don't be dead.

Please. I'm so sorry.

I'm shaking, grieving like a widow.

I love you. I'm sorry.

I'll report myself. I need to be locked up.

Ian shifts, and I jump.

He's breathing. He's alive. Oh my god.

"I'm sorry," I whisper. "I love you."

I don't dare touch him, I don't trust myself, but I stay up watching him sleep, watching his chest rise and fall.

"I had a crazy dream," I say in the morning.

"Oh yeah?" He looks up from his iPad.

Shit, I can't tell him. I shake my head, pretend it's the kind of dream that evaporates as soon as you try to think of it. "I don't remember," I say.

22

CHURCH CAMP

Now

"Going to get evangelized?" Ian asks with a laugh when I tell him Bethany invited me to church camp. I'm basically only invited to the church things Bethany does with the kids. "Doubtful," I say. "But is there any chance you'd go with me?" "You already know the answer," he says. "But I want to go, just not without you. There will be canoeing, rock climbing and horseback riding." "You might as well spend some time with your family. I should do some work this weekend anyway." So I go without him. Bethany said I can share a cabin with her family. Mom, Dad and Holly will be here too, but they're staying on their own. I am setting my pillow on my bunk in Bethany's cabin when my parents walk in with their double sleeping bag. My forehead sweats. "Aren't you guys staying in a different cabin?"

"We'd rather be with the rest of the family," Mom says, claiming the only big bed, the bunk where the counselor sleeps when kids' camp is in session.

I go outside and debate sleeping in the van for the weekend like I did when I was growing up. I hear my nephews and niece squealing as they play with the camp cats. I can't abandon them.

I catch up with Bethany. "Hey," I whisper. "Mom and Dad invited themselves to stay in our room. Will you go with me to ask them not to fool around in front of everyone?"

Bethany glares at me. "Absolutely not. I trust their judgment."

"But they don't have any," I call after her as she walks away.

I chase after Dad when I see him alone. "I wouldn't have come if I knew we were sharing a cabin," I say. "I need to know you aren't going to have sex in the same room as me and the kids."

"I'm a once-a-day kind of guy," he says. "I can't help it."

Fuck. Get some goddamn self-control. And who says shit like that to his kid. "You can so help it," I say. "It's not fair to force everyone to hear what you're doing."

"It's none of your business," he says, "but we've decided to practice sixty hours of abstinence this weekend."

"Good," I say, and race away. He's disgusting, the worst person I know. I go down to the lake and feed myself to the mosquitoes.

When everyone else is in chapel that evening, I call Ian.

"How's it going?" he asks.

"Brutal," I say. "I should have stayed home."

"What's happening?"

"Well there are the mandatory prayers before the meals, no vegetarian food – I had a hot dog bun with mustard for supper – and church services every night. That's where everyone is now. But the worst part is that my parents are sharing our cabin."

"What's wrong with that?"

"They brought their double sleeping bag."

"So?"

"I had to ask Dad not to have sex in front of me and the kids."

"What the fuck?" His voice is harder than I've ever heard it.

"It's okay. He agreed not to."

"Why did you ask him that?" His voice is softer now, but sounds manufactured, like he's trying not to yell. I must be way out of line.

"Because that's what they do. I don't care if it's normal, I can't be around it. I can't let them do that to the kids." I'm whispering now, pleading for him to be on my side.

"It's not normal. It's completely psychopathic for adults to fuck in front of kids," he explodes. "Who does that?"

"It's not really in front of us," I say. "They wait until the lights are out. I don't know if the kids would even notice."

"Stop justifying their behavior. It's abuse."

We hang up and my head feels wobbly, like I've had too much to drink. Ian's response is way too extreme, like someone who mistakes a car backfiring for a gunshot. Sure my parents' behaviour is weird and creepy but it's nothing like abuse. What about all the families around the world that share a single room?

That night I lie awake in the cabin. I can't sleep and I'm not sure I should. My parents are snoring, but my eyes pop open every time a bunk creaks.

Early twenties

The summer I turn twenty-one I go on a vacation with my parents, Holly and their two little foster kids. It's not like I have anything better to do. At the hotel, Holly and I get one bed, my parents take the other and the foster kids are on the floor. When the little ones are asleep, Mom tells me it's time for bed.

"I'm not tired," I say and lock myself in the bathroom. I know what's going to happen now and I'm going to wait them out. No way am I lying three feet from their bed while my parents perv it up. I run a bath and keep adding hot water. I fall asleep for a second and jolt awake. I heat up the water again and climb out when it gets cold. I shut off the bathroom light before I open the door so I won't disturb anyone.

"Why did you keep us up so long?" Mom's voice asks from the darkness as I'm shuffling to bed.

"I thought you'd be asleep by now."

"We were waiting for you," Dad says. He'd be yelling if he weren't trying to keep his voice down.

I want to bolt but I'm in my pjs and they're going to be pissed if I take off. I lie down and bury myself under the blankets next to Holly. I made her take the far side so she would be further from Mom and Dad, but I regret it now that she's asleep and I'm wide awake and trapped next to my god-awful parents. I shove my hands over my ears and try not to breathe.

Dad smacks his lips like he's eating oranges or chewing Hubba Bubba. A disgusting smell like a thousand Dad farts gets into my sheets. I choke on it. Static fills my head, screeching as loud as a fire alarm. It drowns out everything but the stink of sex.

I barricade myself in the bathroom in the morning. I can barely change into my clothes. I shudder when my skin is exposed and tremble in the cold. I close the toilet and sit on the lid and rock back and forth, my arms wrapped tight around my chest.

I force myself to go up to Mom and Dad. "That wasn't okay," I say. "You knew I was awake."

"You made us wait up for you," Dad says.

"No I didn't. I stayed in the bathroom because I was waiting for you to get it over with so I wouldn't have to hear you again."

"You had better not be criticizing us," Mom says, hard like the time she slapped me and her ring left a white mark on my cheek. "It's your responsibility to honour your parents. Are you doing that right now?"

"But it hurts me," I say. "You have to stop."

"You are unbelievably selfish," Mom says and storms away.

"We're your parents," Dad says. "We have the authority to do whatever we deem right."

I stare him down until he leaves.

All I knew in the tents of my childhood was what I was told: wives submit to your husbands and children obey your parents. But I'm not their see-no-evil monkey any more. I saw it and I said it and they had better fucking stop.

A year or two later my entire family goes to Calgary on a road trip to visit Tenille. Even Bethany, her husband and their kids come along.

We cram into a single hotel room, and I have to sleep on the floor with the kids. My parents are using their orange and blue sleeping bag, the massive one that fits them both, but there's nothing to worry about now. They know I'm onto them, and there are way too many of us in the room for them to try anything.

I'm about to fall asleep when I hear a sloppy sucking noise. Like a dog with a mouthful of peanut butter. I plug my ears and try to smother myself with my pillow. How can I be related to these filthy perverts? They fucked in front of eight of us: four daughters, three nephews and one son-in-law. They don't give a shit about any of us.

Now

My parents are taking Holly and my nephew Noah to meet up with Tenille on her new missions centre in Papua New Guinea.

I ask Dad to stop by before they leave. He does but he won't come past the porch.

"Do you promise the kids will be safe with you?" I ask.

"We are not accountable to you," he spits over his shoulder as he storms away.

A few days later Ian and I are driving to Fernie for an Easter ski trip after my parents and the kids took off. Going to Fernie to visit my old town was Ian's idea, his gift to me.

"I can't stop worrying," I tell Ian.

"You did the best you could," he says.

"But I failed. Those poor kids."

"It's not your fault your parents are dicks."

I sigh and stare out the window. In Fernie we walk along Second Avenue, looking for the coffee shop where I used to work. It's a bagel joint now, but it looks the same. Ian really does love me to bring me here, to want to see this part of my past. As we cross the river on the way to the house where I once lived, he says, "You had a lot of freedom for a nineteen year old."

"True," I say, but I'm not sure that's the right word. I remember all the times I got lost as a kid before Mom bought me a leash, a red bracelet on a length of rope that meant I could wander away and still stay found.

Mom knew she needed help keeping me safe, but maybe she also meant to give me a bigger world, one where I wouldn't notice the edges, like the zoo butterflies that fluttered safe behind soft plastic strips. Maybe freedom only exists when you can see its edges like a picket fence off in the distance.

Ian and I go skiing and it's exhilarating to chase him down the mountainside as he weaves his way in tidy curls, always just beyond my reach.

On Easter morning as I lie in his arms I whisper, "I would marry you right now. I love you all the way."

"I love you too," he says. "But you know what I think about that."

"Yeah, I know marriage doesn't matter to you, but I would if you wanted."

My parents are taking Holly on another trip, this time to some Christian conference in Ohio with a special stop at a creationist museum.

"That's an oxymoron," Ian says. "There's no way they should be allowed to call it a museum. The sign on the front should have to say, 'House of Lies.'"

I smile. "Agreed. But that's not the part I'm worried about. They're going to share a hotel room. Just Holly and my parents. At fifteen, she's more than old enough to get what's going on."

"Gross."

"Yeah," I say. "They're going to wreck her. I don't know what to do other than report them."

"Why don't you send your parents an email?"

"They won't read it."

"What if you copy your sisters? That way your parents won't be able to ignore it."

I draft an email and write about a study I read of 717 mental health and child welfare workers who unanimously agreed that it is unacceptable to engage in sexual activity in the same room as a child after the child is two years old. *I'm sure you didn't know that*, I write, *but I hope your perspective changes now that you do.*

I write that I was sexually assaulted – no details, just a quick hit – and say I believe my parents' behaviour taught me I was powerless to stop things that hurt me. *I know you have always done the best you could, but please keep your private activities to yourselves from now on.*

I show Ian my draft. "You have a hammer," he says. "Why don't you bring it down hard?"

"They don't mean to do wrong," I say.

I save the email and read it again in the morning and think about it all day. I'm sick to my stomach but it needs to be said. I'll never be able to forgive myself if I don't fight to the death to keep Holly safe.

I copy Bethany, Tenille and Jenna and hit send. Then I call Mom. "I sent you an email," I say. "It's important. Can you read it?"

She sounds mad enough to burst a blood vessel. "I'm busy. We're packing. I don't think we'll have time." She slams the phone down.

I call Bethany to ask for help getting Mom and Dad to read my message. "I saw it," she says. "I'm sorry to hear you were hurt. I had no idea." It sounds like she's crying.

"Thank you," I say and I'm crying too.

"You were wrong to include me and the other girls on your email," she continues, her voice hardening like Pharaoh's heart. "This is between you and Mom and Dad. You should have dealt with them directly."

"I've tried," I say. "I've tried like a dozen times, but they won't listen."

"It doesn't matter. Only God can judge. I'm calling Mom to tell her I support them."

It takes a long time to get through to my parents again. When Mom picks up I ask her again to read the email. "Please, this really matters to me."

"Maybe. If I have time," she says.

Mom and Dad take Holly and leave for a week. They don't respond or acknowledge a word I said.

"I have no ideas left other than calling Social Services," I tell Ian. We have a family picnic coming up and he suggests cornering Dad there. "When he told me not to move in with you it seemed like your dad didn't value your opinions. Maybe he's sexist. I wonder if he'll be more prone to listen if we're in a public place and I'm there too."

Ian and I pull Dad aside by a picnic table and I ask him to promise to abstain in front of me and the others.

Dad smirks. "What if you two were sharing a room with another couple? Would you agree not to have sex in the same room as them?"

Fuck off. What kind of person does he think I am? "I promise we will never have sex in the same room as anyone else ever. Guaranteed," I say. "Now, do you?"

"All right," Dad says but he takes it back a second later. "No. You don't get to dictate what I do."

"Can we see a therapist together?" I ask.

"I'm not interested," he says and goes back to his hot dog.

"Why are you only now figuring out that your dad is shit?" Ian asks when we're alone. "You've been making excuses for him for the last three years."

I don't know. I just always wanted him to be better.

After my email backfires, I don't have a clue how to fix my family. Holly isn't safe with my parents, and it's my fault. My brain is too small. I don't know what to do or how to help. I can't save her or anyone else. I can't even save myself.

23

Soot

Now

I always thought I didn't want to have a baby, but for the past few months when I'm wrapped snug in Ian's arms I can't stop imagining us with a little girl.

"Do you want to have a baby someday?" I ask.

"No."

"No? Or just not now?"

"It's not something I've given much thought. I don't see it happening."

"Maybe you might change your mind later on?"

"I suppose that's possible, but I doubt it."

Later I ask him about names. "I like Vanilla," I say. "For a name, I mean."

"Pepper is a better food-related name," he says. "And it's much more lively."

We settle on Ashley Vanilla Pepper, and I have to remind myself that he doesn't want her. Not for a long time and maybe not ever.

I dream Ian and I have a baby. Ian holds me as I cradle Ashley Vanilla Pepper in my arms and her tiny pink lips sigh as she sleeps. I love her and Ian loves us and we are unbelievably happy.

I rest my hand on my belly. I'm not ready to have a baby, but is anyone ever ready? If we started making a tiny person I want to adore her.

When Ian opens his eyes, I tell him about my dream and that I think it means I'm pregnant.

He yawns. "Let's wait until we have more information before worrying."

Worrying? Shit, that means no.

Even though we used protection and my dream might not mean anything, I spend the day Googling things that cause miscarriages – things like vitamin C, energy drinks and trampolines – and try not to bring it up again.

That night Ian's almost asleep when I can't hold it in any more. "I know you don't want to talk about it, but if I'm pregnant can we keep her?"

Ian doesn't answer.

Oh god. "If you don't want her, you need to tell me," I say.

"Your period isn't late, is it?"

"No, but my stomach feels weird."

"Probably psychosomatic because you were looking up symptoms all day. It was just a dream," Ian says. He sees me crying and then he sighs all the air out of the room.

"I get that it sounds crazy, but it matters to me," I say. "I don't want to have an abortion so if that's what you want I need you to tell me when it's early enough for other things to work."

"I don't want a baby," he says. He's crying and gasping for air and these are the first tears to run down his cheeks in twenty years. "I'm sorry, D. I can't imagine being bound to another person for the rest of my life."

He doesn't want our baby. He doesn't love me. And he's never going to marry me. "I won't ruin your life," I say, and I'm sobbing too and kissing his tears. "You're the best thing that's ever happened to me."

Ian turns his back and I shake half a bottle of vitamin C into my palm. He knows what I'm doing as I chew the tabs and as the acid burns through me, but he has nothing left to say.

I give up on our combination of condoms and spermicide, and go back on the Pill. It's like swallowing craziness – that's why I quit it a year ago – and I can feel the hormones spreading through my body like poison.

"It's not the Pill," Ian says. "I know you want an excuse for your moods but there isn't one. This is just how you are."

I switch to an IUD, the kind with no hormones, but Ian's right: it makes no difference.

"Take this," I say, handing Ian a photo book when he's packing for a trip. "For when you miss me." It's full of pictures from a photo shoot I did in my underwear when Ian gave up porn and after I deleted the bare-bum picture he took of me at the lake. I felt awkward doing the boudoir shoot and way too exposed, but I had to in case he needed something to look at when I wasn't around.

"Don't need it," he says. "I already know how you look."

My hands tremble as I put the book back in the night stand. "Come here," he says and pulls me into a hug. "You have nothing to worry about."

When he's gone I watch his Netflix history. There are naked women everywhere. In like every single episode. I bet he'd have taken their pictures with him.

Fine, if he doesn't want to look at mine he doesn't have to. I grab the photo book and rip the pages out. I stomp to the kitchen and throw them into our biggest pot.

I hold his lighter to the pages and watch as my feet burn, as the flames flick up my legs. Goodbye to my purple nightgown and stupid hopeful smile.

My pictures are so fucking amateur. Not even racy enough for his Saturday morning TV. Well, at least I'm not showing anything more if he doesn't care to look.

"Which is your favourite?" I asked Ian when I first gave him the book.

"This one," he said, pointing to a shot of me in a suit jacket and bra.

"Oh yeah? Why's that?" I asked, fishing, starving.

"You have the greatest expression. A cute grin. It's so you."

I light that fucking grin on fire and watch my face and my not-sexy everything melt away.

I hold the lighter low in the pot, against all the loose edges. Ashes fly up. They blow around the kitchen and land on the counter and the stove and my head. They look like trapped moths, smashing against the ceiling and longing to break through.

Maybe I'm being crazy. I am. I have to stop.

I check my phone. Ian still hasn't called or texted or emailed.

I need someone to come over right now. I scroll through my contacts. Some of the girls think porn is unforgivable, others say it's borderline and the rest say it's normal. I get so confused talking to them. They're like a thousand voices yelling at the same time and I just want someone to tell me what's right.

I call Shane. He's on the porn side, on Ian's side, and he's going to tell me to smarten up, to get over it, to pull myself together. Plus he's already seen the worst of me. "Please help me," I beg like a kid lost at the zoo.

"Be right there," he says.

I can't let him see what I've done and besides I'd be cheating on Ian if Shane sees an ashen bra or leg. I carry the smoldering pot to the bathroom, lift the toilet seat and drop the blackness in. I flush. The toilet chokes on the ashes. I flush again.

The doorbell rings.

I put the pot back in the kitchen and go to answer it.

"Smells like a bonfire," Shane says.

"It was."

He pulls a clump of ash from my hair. "Are you okay?"

"No." My voice is dry and hoarse from the smoke and the inferno inside.

"I hate to say it, but maybe your relationship isn't going to work," he says.

I glare at Shane. A year ago he told me I was "the one that got away," which is total bullshit because he's the one who kept tossing me aside.

"I'm rooting for you," Shane says. "I want your relationship to succeed. I know you've had some hard times, and I want you to be happy. You deserve it. But you can't have a relationship without trust. It's the fundamental ingredient. You're going to have to trust that Ian is a good man and that he loves you. Can you do that?"

I gag on the answer. "I don't know." I'm covered in soot and I'll never come clean.

Shane leaves and I'm alone and Ian still hasn't emailed. I get out of bed and turn on all the lights. It's way too scary to be alone in the dark.

I get a glass of water and notice the butcher's block. My hand reaches for Ian's sharpest knife. I press it against my forearm. I want to make myself bleed. To make my body match the pain in my heart.

The blade is hard and cold as I slide it across my skin. It stings and I pull back. I'm not even bleeding. I just made a thin white line.

I fall to the floor clutching the knife in both hands. I'm too weak, too pathetic, to draw even the tiniest drop of blood.

"Where's my book?" Ian asks like ten minutes after he gets home.

"I got rid of it," I say.

His eyes look broken.

"I'm sorry. I didn't think you cared."

We have a long talk and I cry most of the night and by the end he agrees to stop watching shows with naked women for a few weeks so we can work things out in therapy with Nicole.

Even so I'm afraid to leave the house when he's watching the women's ski finals.

He throws his hands up. "I'm not doing anything! It's the fucking ski races. Have you seen how much clothing these women are wearing?"

There's no air in the house. I'm suffocating and my heart is smashing like it's trying to get out of my chest. Like I'm so poisonous it has to escape or it will die.

Ian looks super freaked out and tells me to lie down.

I fall over on the couch. I don't understand why there's air for him and not for me.

He lies next to me and pulls my back against his chest. "Feel my breath," he says.

I feel his lungs rise and fall.

"You're okay. Just breathe with me. In and out."

I do for a second. I get some of his air but spit it back out. I don't want to share anything with him. I'm so afraid of who he is.

Ian flies out for an interview for a job in Toronto and I follow him a week later to spend Thanksgiving with his family.

His mother, an elegant brunette who brought white roses to the airport the first time I visited, is already asleep when Ian flips through her cable channels and comes across a show about making candy. "Let's watch that," I say.

He ignores me.

"I want to see the candy show."

"You won't like it," he says. "It's not about bonbons."

My stomach tightens. Right. It's another show about how I'm not good enough for him.

I'm awake long after he crashes beside me. I slip out and make my way in the moonlight back to his mother's white leather couch. I stare through the window at the black grass, at the skeleton tree and at the rocky barrier that keeps the water at bay. The blackness beyond, Lake Ontario, throbs and beacons.

I lust after the dark ripples. I long to feel them cold against my skin.

I see myself walking barefoot across the lawn and down and down and down into the depths, my white nightgown billowing in the blackness. The water rises over my head and I succumb.

I remember the drowning woman who hangs in our living room at home. Sometimes when I look at her I try to see hope. To imagine her bursting up from the dark, coughing and sputtering and dragging herself to safety.

But that's a fantasy. She's dead and she's so lucky to be free, to hang on the wall suspended in the exact moment her soul was released.

I'll join her right now. I need the water, need the end.

But the alarm will go off when I open the door. Shit. I won't get far enough away before Ian swims out and drags me back.

I sit on the couch for all eternity wishing I could shimmer and disappear like a fleck of moonlight on the black water.

"Sometimes I think about hurting myself," I whisper in the dark when we're back home. "I'm afraid of my mind."

Ian fiddles with the lamp and switches it on. "What do you mean?" he asks. His face is caved in like he's a hundred years old.

Oh shit, I'm scaring him. "It's nothing," I say.

He doesn't believe me. "Promise me something?" he asks and his voice cracks.

I wait. My throat is crying inside.

"Promise we can tell Nicole at our next appointment?"

I nod.

He looks like he sees me out at sea, drowning way beyond his reach.

24

BUBBLE WRAP

Now

The lights are shining through the window when I get home from work. I'm so happy Ian's inside that I flop down in the front yard and make a snow angel for him.

He meets me at the door and ruffles my hair. "It's sweet that you're excited to see me," he says. "Remember the job I interviewed for? They made me an offer."

"Congratulations," I say. "That's great news!"

"I don't need to take it," he says. "I haven't told anyone else. This is a choice we need to make together."

"My vote is yes. It's a good opportunity and I know you want it. We'll figure everything out."

"Thank you," Ian says with a deep sigh.

He accepts the position and makes plans to start in the New Year.

"I'll quit my job and go with you," I say.

"We don't even know if I'll like it. What if it's shit? Just wait."

Later Ian says, "I'm worried about us."

I hug him. "It's going to be fine. I love you. We'll do whatever it takes."

Ian isn't cheering up.

"Hey, do you want to open your Christmas present?" I ask. "It's a good one!" I grab the package I'd set under our tree earlier that day and put it on his lap.

"Shouldn't we wait for Christmas?"

"Nope. Open it now," I say, kissing his cheek. "It's proof we're going to make it."

Ian tears off the snowman wrapping paper and pulls out a photo book. He flips past bike rides, our pie-eating contest, a water-balloon fight and him doing pushups with my nephews on his back. There are shots of Valentine's Days and Jenga towers and our shadows kissing in a field.

It took forever to finish the book, to make such a shiny past, but I'm glad I did. As I laid out each page I saw we were so good together. I watch Ian see that too as he turns the pages. He closes the book and reaches for me.

Ian and I are leaving on New Year's Eve to drive to Toronto, find him an apartment and settle him in. We have two last counseling sessions before he moves and I'm trying to fix us for good.

Ian's been saying he resents how I censor him, so I want to find a compromise, a way we can both be happy. I've been drafting compromises for weeks and we're so close now. I'll give up a little more of myself, Ian will concede something, anything, and everything will be fine.

Still we had a big fight earlier this morning. Last night Ian said I don't get to keep him from watching his TV shows any more. The rapey naked ones he gave up for me a few months ago. I tried not to freak out. I held everything in like a pot with a lid that weighed a thousand pounds. Ian fell asleep, and I lay beside him hating him, hating men.

"What if I wanted to kill someone?" I asked when he woke. "Should I let myself daydream about it? Plot it out? Imagine all the ways to hurt him and watch him die?"

"It's not the same, and you know it," he said, punching the bed.

He's wrong. There's no difference between yearning for blood and lusting after flesh.

But we're going to figure this out.

Once after we argued I ordered a $100 painting I'd wanted for years but had been too cheap to buy. It's a flower with a long, skinny stem. "Love is bigger," it says.

Three years ago Ian and I were on a bench sharing a bag of cinnamon buns at the Farmers' Market when he said, "They don't taste as good as they look." He paused and added, "My parents are splitting up."

"Oh no. What happened?"

"It's been a struggle for a long time. They've started resenting each other, and resentment means it's over."

He was quiet for a while, and I waited for him to continue.

"I expect they'll be happier this way. Sometimes love isn't enough."

"I'm sorry about your parents," I said. "But love is always enough." It is. It has to be.

Ian and I are in Nicole's office, facing each other in our respective leather chairs. I pass him a copy of my list. "What compromises did you come up with?" I ask.

"I don't have any," he says.

"But you agreed. You said you would come back with your own since you didn't like mine last time."

"I tried. I stared at my computer screen for hours and the screen stayed blank."

"Fine. We can start with my sheet. What about picking a few?"

"No," Ian says. "I'm tired of giving things up to make you happy. I can't give you what you want. I need to be able to think my own thoughts and make my own choices."

"Oh," I say sadly. "Then why are you here?"

"I've been coming to therapy to help you. I know you're having a hard time and I want to make it easier for you."

"Is there anything else you need to say?" Nicole asks Ian.

He shakes his head.

She waits and asks again. "Is there anything you need to say?"

Ian stays quiet. He looks far away. He looks like he did earlier that morning when we argued and the light hit half his face, leaving the other side lost in darkness.

I'm cold then hot then cold. "Let's talk about my list," I say. "I only need you to pick one or two things. And we can change them if you want."

Nicole interrupts. "Let's give Ian a chance to speak."

The room falls silent again.

Hesitantly, sorrowfully, Ian raises his eyes to mine. "We need to split up."

I stare at him, shake my head, knock his words down.

"Oh Sweetie. I don't need you to agree to any of these compromises," I say, folding my sheet to hide all the things I'd been asking of him. "I'll stop wanting you to change. I love you. We're so good together."

Ian doesn't say anything.

"Why are our chairs so far apart?" I ask and drag mine closer to his. I reach out and take his hands. "We can fix this. We'll make it work." I want to fling myself at his feet, to wrap my arms around his ankles and beg him not to leave.

Nicole speaks from far off in the distance. "D, stop. You need to respect what he told you."

Ian says miserably, resolutely, "I'm so sorry."

Our time is up and we walk out side by side, slow and silent. We cross the icy road toward his SUV.

"What do you want to do now?" he asks after he turns on my heated seat. "I can find a place to stay. Should I drop you off?"

I shake my head again, shaking everything out. "I want you to come home. You live there too."

"Are you sure?"

"Yes. I love you."

"How should we do this?" he asks.

I pause a long while, like I have to pull out the Jenga block that will send the tower crashing.

But if I let him go, if I'm perfect now, will he see that he wants to keep me?

"I love you, Sweetie," I say. "I want you to stay for Christmas like we planned, but it's probably better for us if you move as soon as you can. How long do you need?"

"Maybe a day or two."

We get home and he takes his paintings off the walls. Naked gashes in the plaster show where once a grey winter storm had swirled above a tiny city, acrylic on wood, worth a month of his salary.

The drowning lady comes down too and I miss her. I wish I hadn't wrecked everything. Imagine if I could have liked her, if I could have let Ian be who he is.

Ian and I pack his things in short bursts punctuated with crying. We lie down and I press my skin so closely to his it's like I'm trying to wedge myself into him, to embed myself so deeply that he can't leave.

"Why?" I whisper.

"You want me to be someone I'm not. My whole world view is based on critical thinking, on discovery, on being open to new ideas. I can't filter my mind for you."

"I'm sorry," I say. "I take it all back. Please, please let's try again." I beg and whimper and beg and cry.

Stop it, I tell myself. This won't work. Show him why he loves you. I stand and help him up. "I'm sorry. Let's keep packing."

I hold the bubble wrap as he shrouds the drowning woman in plastic and packing tape. We put the TV back in its box and tape it closed. Soon the house is a stack of boxes.

"Let's go to bed," he says. "We've already got so much done. Thank you. You're a phenomenal woman."

Good, it's working. More love and I'm sure he'll change his mind.

"I want to keep everything exactly the same until you leave," I say, and when we kiss goodnight I taste his tears and mine.

We wake early, before my alarm goes off. "Let's have sex," I say.

"Are you sure?" he asks.

I pull him toward me. Our bodies know each other, know we belong together. Maybe they can stitch us back up.

He still loves me, his eyes say so, and I feel the thread drawing us close.

Ian leaves to wrap everything up at his office. I go to work and they tell me to go home because I can't stop crying. Someone in the elevator said, "Hey, how are you?" and I lost it.

I call Mom. "I need you. Can you come over right now? You might as well bring Ian's Christmas present."

Mom sits on the couch, in Ian's spot, and I lay my head on her lap and weep. She strokes my back and it feels familiar, like her comforting me when Bethany left us for kindergarten.

"Jesus loves you," Mom says. "He's the Great Comforter and wants you to come back to Him."

"Please stop evangelizing me," I say. "I'm too tired and sad. Can you just listen? I was going to help Ian find a place and maybe buy him some furniture. I want to give him a thousand bucks so I can still help him move. Is that crazy?"

"Maybe a little," Mom says. "But I understand." She drives me to the bank and the teller hands me a pile of bills.

Back in the car, I cry again. "It's not enough. Should I get more? Would $2,000 be better?"

"This is enough. Any more and he might not take it."

"Oh," I sigh. She takes me to the drug store where I buy Ian's favorite snacks for his long drive. I get him a theatre gift card too, a peace offering so he can watch a few movies, anything he wants, without me censoring him.

Mom drops me off and I tuck the stack of $50s into a card and lick it shut.

Ian comes home and we work for hours. We're both sweating by the time he's satisfied he'll be ready to leave in the morning.

"I need to take a shower," he says. I kiss his salty lips and pull him close. "Me too."

We get into the shower, kissing and lathering each other up. He spits a mouthful of water at me. I splash him back. We laugh and I remember the name of an *Iron and Wine* album, one we'd listen to in bed on Saturday mornings: *Kiss Each Other Clean*.

We lie in bed, pressed tight like lovers wearing the same skin.

"Thank you for being so wonderful today," Ian says. "You never stop surprising me."

"I have something for you. I want to give it to you now but you have to promise to keep it. If not, I'm tucking it into the SUV so you have to take it."

Ian nods and I hand him the card. "Remember you agreed."

"Whoa, how much is this?" he asks, fanning out the bills.

"It's some."

"I can't keep this."

"Please Sweetie. I want to help you start your new life. Plus you have to buy all new furniture since you're leaving everything for me."

Ian looks at me, at the stack in his hands, and back at me.

"You agreed and I want you to have it."

"Okay," he says slowly and we kiss and stitch more love, more promise, into each other.

I can't sleep but I stay in bed to lie beside the man I love. If only I hadn't fought so hard against what he was watching, what he was thinking, who he was.

I get up and start on a drawing for him, all twisty lines and hearts. I write William Blake's words on the page: "He who binds to himself a joy does the winged life destroy, but he who kisses the joy as it flies lives in eternity's sunrise."

The poem is about how I destroyed our relationship and how I can fix us – with love and letting go and giving Ian all the space he needs.

I hear Ian stirring and keep drawing as quickly as I can. I have to finish it so Ian can hang the promise of a better us on the walls off his new life.

"Hey, where are you?" Ian calls. "Come back to bed."

I crawl in with him and we hold onto each other, mushed against each other's skin. We kiss and say, "I love you" over and over again. "We'll take a break," he says, "But I promise to keep my heart open to our relationship."

When Ian finishes loading the SUV, I hand him my drawing. "I love it," he says, voice wobbling. "My own original artwork. Thank you."

He hugs me. "You're the strongest person I know. You're going to be okay."

He goes outside and puts his key in the ignition and keeps his boots and jacket on when he comes in again. "I'm all set," he says. "I can't fit one more thing in there."

Then he steps toward me and hugs me tight.

I squeeze back just as hard, willing him to change his mind.

He pulls me even closer.

We feel each other breathe, and I slow my breath to match his so our chests rise and fall like our lungs are in the same body.

Time stops and I wish it wouldn't start again, that the world would end here and now.

We keep hugging and then I feel it. An almost imperceptible loosening of his grip. His arms are still locked around me, still secure and tight, but he's starting to let go.

I have to let him leave.

I drop my arms like they're dead. As they fall to my sides I feel my heart crack. There's a splitting, a ripping in my chest so painful, so shocking.

"It hurts," I gasp.

Tears are rolling down my cheeks. "I love you and you are free."

"I love you too," Ian says.

He turns and walks out our door and down our sidewalk and gets into his SUV.

"I love you," he mouths back at me, and then closes his door and drives down the street and away.

Apart

25

MISSING ORGANS

Now

I stare at the empty road, clutching my heart. I'm crying so hard I'm screaming. I fall to my knees and wail until my throat aches.

I wrecked everything. He wanted to love me and I drove him away.

I look at the couch and scream again. He's gone and this is all that's left.

I collapse on the hardwood floor. My body feels vacant, like a shell that's left after a soul moves on. It's like I'm missing organs, like there had once been an octopus woven through me and now there are tentacle holes everywhere.

I pat my stomach, my legs, my chest. How can I be so hollow and yet made of skin?

Forever passes.

I'm lying on the floor with my life smashed down and some other me says, I'm sorry you're so sad.

Weird, it's like my heart is talking.

I touch my heart and it keeps beating kindness: Yes, it hurts. I'm sorry you lost everything.

I see myself with my new broken heart and my old still-broken heart that hasn't been whole since youth group when I sang hymns with my hands raised high.

I want to pick myself up and kiss my forehead and tuck me into bed. My fingers caress my arms, my throat, my face. I love you, Sweetie, they seem to say.

Jenna and the kids come over. Sophia, my three-year-old niece, heads straight for Ian's candy bowl. It's not there.

"Where's Ian?" she asks.

"He's gone," I say. It's all I can do to force the words out.
She's quiet for a while. "When is he coming back?"

"He got a job far away and moved there," I say. "He isn't coming back."

Her little face scrunches up, and I cry at her expression. "It's sad, isn't it?" I ask, and kiss the top of her head. "It's okay to be sad. I miss him too."

As she snuggles into my arms and drifts off to sleep I wish I had a grownup, some kind auntie, standing guard over me.

I'm self-medicating with social media, scrolling through Facebook day and night.

Wendy, a work acquaintance I haven't seen in years, posts a link to her blog. My arm hairs spike out as I read her history. It's full of incest and violence and shame. I don't know why I keep reading or why I don't despise her for her wretchedness.

Once I told a friend who worked in a youth home a tiny bit about The Terrible Night. Then we had a blowout and she accused me of pushing her away. "I see this all the time," she said as she left. "It's what the kids do when a worker gets too close."

I thought I had to hide my darkness, that no one could love me if they saw it. But I see Wendy's and I cry for her pain.

I shiver. How brave and strong she is. How amazing she's able to let her past exist. She went to the centre of her suffering and sat in it. She opened her heart to it and told the truth and somehow I read it and loved her for it.

What was it Rumi said? "The cure for the pain is in the pain." I hate the thought, but what if he's right?

Maybe I can let my secrets out too. Can I tell them without drowning, without hating myself? I don't know, but I have to try.

I sit still for a long time. I'm rubbing my arms as if they're frightened puppies.

I open my laptop. Words fall from my fingers and fill the screen. It's like a writing quote I once read about words just bleeding out.

I fill a few pages with the bad things that happened to me and read it out loud. It's awful. But true. I go to bed hugging myself tight as my pillow absorbs my tears.

The next morning, Christmas Eve, I turn my computer on before brushing my teeth. I read my words again. "I'm sharing this to shine some light into my dark and sad corners," I wrote. "I hope to heal, to love more fully and to have the capacity to trust those who deserve it. I hope also to be brave enough to let the world be real around me in its beauty and chaos."

I do want that, more than anything. I message Wendy and ask if she would be willing to read my story. She agrees. I send her my pages and shiver like a hypothermic as I wait for her judgment, for the gavel to come crashing down.

Seventeen minutes pass as slow as years before she responds. I'm afraid to read her words. I close one eye and squint at them. "I'm so sorry D. That is horrible and nobody should be treated that way."

We exchange a few more messages and she says, "There's a lot of ugliness in the world. Sometimes it's hard to see past it. But there's also a lot of beauty if you look in the right places. And thanks. I'm really glad you shared that with me."

I'm bawling. Somehow she felt for me the same kindness I felt towards her, the same desire to scoop me onto her lap and promise that it won't always hurt.

I wonder if I'll ever be able to extend that grace to myself, to forgive my soul for its shame.

Holly has been floundering in school for years. She's in grade eleven now but she still has a hard time reading. I bet it's because Mom doesn't let her choose books she likes.

Last week before my heart fell out, I took Holly to Chapters and we spent an hour cruising the aisles to find her a Christmas present. She picked *The Hunger Games*.

"Will you be allowed to read it?" I asked.

"Yeah, I had a copy for a while and Mom didn't say anything when I started it," she said.

"Did she know you had it?"

"I think so."

I bought Holly the book and made her a promise: as soon as she finished it, she could pick another. If she kept on reading, I'd give her a book of her choice every month for the whole year. I was proud of my strategy, of the incentive for her to read.

But as Holly opens her gift on Christmas morning, I know I made a mistake. Bethany asks to look at it. She reads the back and pulls Mom aside. "It's glorifying death," I hear her say. "Kids murdering kids."

"It's a dystopian society," I call over to them. "I've read it myself. The point is that people shouldn't kill each other, that it's important to take care of one another."

Mom says Holly can't have it.

"Okay, I'll take it back and get her a different book," I say.

"Not from Chapters. She can't have anything unless it's from the Christian book store."

I protest but it's futile, all seeds on infertile soil, all pearls before swine.

I wonder if this is what Ian was trying to tell me all along: that you need an open brain to be able to think.

I declined an invitation to fly to Vancouver for my cousin's New Year's Eve wedding because I was planning to be in Toronto with Ian. When I message my cousin, he says there's still room for me, that they'd love it if I could join in.

Fat tears roll down my cheeks as the flight attendant points out the emergency exits. Ian went east and I should be running after him, not going west. The plane taxis toward the runway and I'm yelling inside: Stop, you're going the wrong way!

My flight is late getting in so I miss the ceremony and get to the reception in time for the speeches. The bride's father takes the microphone. "The best advice I have to give is this: Always, always dare to trust."

Of course. That's how I blew it. How can you love if you don't trust?

My old best friend Jody lives in Chilliwack now. We fell out of each other's lives when we were seventeen but sometimes love never stops. I stay with her and she makes space for my tears and we bathe her babies and wash them clean.

I'm sobbing myself to sleep when I notice a warm glow inside. I put my hand on my heart, on the centre of the heat. A voice from within booms: Magnificent.

Maybe I am. Look how much love I gave Ian as he left. Look how kind I'm being to myself. Look at me doing my best.

My parents leave me their car when I get back and say I can borrow it on the weekends. I pull up at my place. It's so dark inside that it takes me an hour to go to the door. It's dreadful in here, packed with the leftovers of a happier life. I need to get a roommate or a lover or take a trip or find something, anything, that will distract me from my wreckage. But no. I have to face myself straight on. I need to get used to being alone, need to stay here in my house until it becomes bearable. Some days I cry so hard that I take selfies with tears dripping off my chin. It's the only way I can think of to bear witness to my pain, to have it exist somewhere other than inside me. The silence squeezes my heart like a pop can. I weep so much I give up on wiping my eyes, and salt crystalizes on my eyelashes. I let myself feel everything, my sadness and aching and longing. I watch them as they rise and fall and knock me to my knees. I tell them that they're allowed to be here, that they're part of me, that I will take care of them.

I'm still seeing the couples therapist, but now Nicole sits in Ian's old chair. She tells me to eat and sleep. I've forgotten how.

I've been writing compulsively ever since Wendy held my words so gently. I get home from work and start typing and somehow it's two in the morning and I forgot to have supper. I'm weary to the bone but my words insist on flooding out, on splattering all over the screen. I take all my vacation time and stay home and more words write themselves.

Ian calls in March. He says he's thought it through, that we're over for good, that he's never coming back.

I stop breathing. The other women in the broken-hearts support group I joined thought I was in denial, but I shrugged it off like a hopeless idiot.

I pause. I'm still going to love Ian the best I can, still going to let him go with grace.

"Okay," I say and repeat the words I learned in meditation: No matter how much I want things to be different, things are as they are.

I'm bawling in our chair, the one we bought together, as I say the words over and again, as I prepare myself for Ian to hang up, to leave me forever.

He does.

I slip to the floor and I'm scream crying. I hate it, but this is how it is: he's gone.

26

PIERCED

I'm in the middle of a meditation retreat when Gary crosses my mind. My throat closes over. It's like there's a metal band clamped tight around my neck. I try to force it loose but it squeezes tighter.

I scream but nothing comes out. My mouth is stretched open as far it goes, a dark and gaping morgue.

My larynx rips open. It hurts like being pierced through with a sword. Tears ooze out like blood from a wound.

"My throat split open," I tell Nicole, when I'm back in her office. "It wasn't real but it also was."

She nods like she knows. She tells me to keep breathing and to feel everything. She says that's called Somatic Experiencing, and it's all I need to do.

I haven't even agreed to try it before my throat constricts again. Thick fingers – Gary's – are strangling me. I reach up but I can't make him let go. The edges of my throat collapse. My trachea shrinks and disappears. I'm not breathing, just rocking back and forth, my mouth open in a silent scream.

"It won't kill you," says a voice from far away.

I struggle for air. A breath finally comes and I suck it in.

"Are you sure?" I ask a long time later. "It feels like it will."

"I'm sure," Nicole says kindly. "Now, can you find a place in your body that feels okay?"

I search past the steely grey tightness in my stomach. My shoulders are clenched, my legs contracted. My head throbs. "No."

"That's all right," she says. "Keep looking."

My face is scrunched up like eyes avoiding the sun. My fingers claw into my legs. "My chest is warm."

"Curious. How does the warmth feel?"

I put my hand on my heart. It's peaceful. Still. Like it's breathing compassion in and out, like my pulse is beating a reminder through me: You're okay, you're okay and you're okay.

My heart grows. It's bigger than my body. It stretches out to the white office walls.

I sneak into the boardroom on my breaks and curl up tight in the window well, tucking my head onto my knees. I'm down to a hundred and seventeen pounds, and everyone tells me I'm too skinny. Even I agree. I'm eating full-fat everything and as much as I can, but my cheeks are sunken and my underwear sags.

I follow my boss into her office. "I can't keep working so much. I'm cracking."

"Oh D," she says and pats my arm. "You're a great worker. We'll do whatever we can to keep you around."

We cut my hours in half and I go home and sleep. I'm fine on half my salary. It's not like I buy anything, and I paid my house off two long years ago, a few months after Ian moved in.

Nicole tells me about how people who have been traumatized can get paralyzed by fear. Literally, she says. Like how an animal in the wild will collapse when a predator gets too close.

"Does that sound familiar?" she asks.

My head tilts to the side. Part of my face disappears. I remember the time with Cameron the con when I wasn't there. The time Kyle and I were in the shower and my wrists couldn't push him away no matter how hard I tried.

I head over to yoga. We're halfway through class when the instructor talks about pigeon pose. I hate pigeon. I'll skip it and go to the washroom instead.

I'm about to stand when the instructor says, "Sometimes if you've been afraid – not an ordinary fear but something that really makes you go 'Whoa!' – it gets stored in your legs. This pose can wake it up. Don't worry if you get angry or scared or sad or whatever. That's normal. All your feelings want is to be felt."

I guess I'll try it. I bend one knee forward and slide my other leg behind me. My body quivers and tears drip down.

After class I pull the instructor aside. "What did you mean about people storing things in their legs?"

"When something really bad – like really, really awful – happens and you can't make it stop, sometimes the experience moves into the body and gets stuck there," he says.

"So I should quit doing pigeon."

"No. I'd keep doing it and noticing how it feels. If you keep stretching, whatever's been locked away in your body can come out. I know it sounds weird, but bodies can heal themselves if we let them."

"Do bodies remember what's happened to them?" I ask Nicole.

"Yes, our minds might not remember but our bodies do. Your trauma from the sexual assault is stored within you, and our work will be to help your body release it."

Weird. It reminds me of Harry Potter with his horcrux, the nightmare that got shot into him. The only way for Harry to get better was to die. I shudder. "How do we do that?"

"For your trauma to heal we need to knit your feelings, actions, memories and any images from that night together into one cohesive piece," Nicole says. "You need to build a clear picture of what happened and how it affected you."

It sounds horrible. My throat tingles, and my whole body vibrates.

"What's happening for you right now?" she asks.

There's an egg wedged in my throat. It's choking me. My stomach burns with fury. I imagine crushing the shell and making the viscous yolk ooze down my throat.

I flex my throat to crack the egg. Nothing happens. I clench tighter. A fragment of the tip splinters off. A jolt of pain, of fire, runs through my entire body. My god, it hurts.

"Any memories?" Nicole asks.

I'm lying on Amber's carpet. Gary is behind me. His thick, hairy arms are wrapped around me like pythons. He's trying to unbutton my jeans.

I hate him so much I'm shaking. My arms tense. I push my hands against my chair and imagine shoving him away, forcing him to stop.

A bonfire rages in my gut. The flames burn through me, shooting up past my chest and to the top of my head. I exhale and the fireball retreats to my belly. I inhale and it burns. Exhale, cool off. Inhale, and heat flares everywhere. I keep breathing fire until it fades to embers.

I strain to remember what happened after Gary forced his stubby finger inside me. I see that black door again. It's open a sliver, with a blinding white light behind it. That's as far as my memories go. Black door. White light. The end.

I'm in Nicole's office with my eyes closed. The light beyond the door is searing my eyelids. I go to the door and slide it open. My stomach drops out. I see myself tinged in sepia and lying on the carpet. I'm naked except for my beige bra, a hand-me-down Mom gave me from Grandma. My knees are bent out to the sides.

Gary is above me. Smashing himself into me. A drop of his sweat splatters against my cheek. His hands around my throat. Squeezing. Me dying.

My head is floating, like it's full of helium that's trying to carry me up and away. Once I died in a dream. I heard that was supposed to be impossible, that if you die in a dream you die in real life.

I can't see Gary any more but I feel his hands choking me. His grip is so tight.

I watch from the ceiling as my old self gives up, as her life slips away. I follow her out. He's killing us and this is the end.

Nicole's voice breaks in. "You're here," she says. "You're alive."

I gulp in a breath and it feels like my throat blows up from the inside. I looked dead lying there beneath him, like a body that had been frozen and left behind.

"Do you feel an impulse to move?" Nicole asks.

I nod.

"Let your body move if it wants to but go as slowly as you can."

My shoulders clench. My wrists and fingers are tensed and tight.

"Can you find where the impulse to move begins in your body?"

I slap my left shoulder. "Here. In the middle of the joint."

"How curious," she says. "And now what's happening?"

My shoulder is burning with rage. My palms are pushing against the sides of the chair.

"Good, slow it down," she says.

My shoulders contract. They pull in and push out like they're screaming for a fight. It's like the Hulk is about to erupt from my skin.

My elbows roll inward as I shove against the chair. My fingers tense into claws shredding prey. My stomach clenches and my body holds the contraction. My legs cramp.

An electrical current jolts through me. Like when I had tendonitis and my physiotherapist attached sticky pads to my skin and shot a current into my cells.

I keep pushing against the chair. My body quivers, seizes up, quakes and explodes.

Then there's nothing. A void.

"I'm exhausted," I say when my heart slows.

"I'm not surprised. That was a lot of hard work. Your body is fighting back and doing all the things it couldn't do the night Gary assaulted you."

"But it's not real," I say. "He didn't actually choke me."

"Okay," she says but she doesn't sound convinced. "Your experience is consistent with someone who has been strangled."

No way. My ears ring and cover over her words.

Ian and I talk once a month. I want to stay best friends, to talk every day, but the schedule was his idea. This way we can move on and still stay in touch, he said.

When he calls and tells me about his yoga class or the bachelor party he went to in Montreal, all I hear is that he's surrounded by women – women who are not me. I try not to let him hear me cry but I'm sure he does because he says, "Sorry, I have to go."

Even though I'm only working two or three days a week, I don't get less tired. I sleep and write and go back to bed.

One day I write about Gary. The whole story. Even what happens beyond the black door. I slam my diary shut when I'm done but the words are burned onto my eyelids. I rip out the pages. I want to destroy them but I won't let myself. Not this time. I won't burn them or flush them or try to erase them.

Instead I tear the pages into one-word scraps. I divide them between my garbage cans, separating the words but letting them exist.

My body shakes. I lie down and my legs jolt like I'm a puppet on a string.

27

Horton Hears a Who

My niece, Sophia, and I are playing in my parents' living room after a family dinner where Dad sat too close and ate too loud and I tried not to hear him chew.

I give Sophia an airplane ride and plop her down. We're giggling and lying on the floor when my parents' poodle wanders over and steps on my throat. My arms lock at my sides. I can't breathe.

I watch the dog standing over me and feel her terrible weight crushing me, her paw pressing down against my flesh. I hold as still as death. The dog shifts and puts more pressure on my dying spot.

Then she's over me and gone.

My breathing goes wild. Somewhere far in the distance, I hear voices reassuring me, telling me to breathe deep. I can't listen. I'm too far away, lost in a long dark tunnel.

Slow down. I turn my attention to the tunnel and the suffocating fear. I listen to my breath and feel it, erratic, flicking in and out. I don't try to stop it or change it, just notice it and let it be.

Tears slip onto the carpet. My breath slows. I reach up and pat my throat. It didn't cave in or rupture or rip open. You're okay, I tell myself. I sit up and wipe my tears.

I have my parents' car again, and as I drive home my body tenses up like it wants to move, like it wants to fling the dog off my throat. I grip the steering wheel tight as my body jolts.

That night I'm brushing my teeth when it feels like Kyle, the guy who pushed me up against the shower wall, is next to me, forcing himself on me.

My hands drop to the edge of the porcelain sink. My toothbrush dangles from my lips while I push down hard. I lift my feet so all my weight, every last ounce, is shoving him away from me.

My body spasms like I'm being swarmed by wasps. My toothbrush falls out of my mouth, and I drop to the floor shaking and twitching.

My body stills and my jaw gapes open. I'm sitting in a ball, pressed against the wall.

I feel a muffled no somewhere deep inside. I will it to come out. I gag and strain to bring it forth. My mouth is moving in the shape of a no, my tongue pressing against the roof of my mouth and dropping down like it's trying to flick out a sound. Nothing.

I fling my head back and forth to build momentum. I'm dry heaving, nearly vomiting. A voiceless breath of air puffs out.

I bawl and drop my head to my knees. I try again. A tiny no comes forth, so faint it's a hint of a whisper like the sound of a *Horton Hears a Who* villager whimpering in her room.

I stay curled up on the bathroom tiles, encouraging my nos to come out and be heard. They're soft and blurred, but they grow like the voices on a speck of dust on an elephant's clover, banging pots and yelling and banding together. They crescendo and merge into one solid long scream.

"Noooo!"

I find Kyle on Facebook and send him a message. "I don't expect to hear back from you, but I'd like an apology," I say. "I froze and didn't say anything and didn't push you away, but I didn't want that. You knew, and it wasn't okay that you took it from me."

Eight hours later he responds. "Not how I remember it," he says. "But I know I was a dick, and I'm sorry."

"Thank you," I say, and he asks for my number and calls to tell me that he wishes he could make it up to me, that he could use someone like me in his life.

I tell Nicole about Kyle's apology and how he wants to be friends. "I miss him, and I'm so lonely."

"Stop using your mind," she says. "What is your body saying?"

I'm hot and angry. I feel Kyle pinning me against the shower wall. I hear myself screaming inside: Stop. I said I don't want to! As he continues, so do the words that never came out: Fuck you. Stop it, Asshole. I said no.

"What's happening?" Nicole asks.

"I'm yelling inside. Swearing."

My wrists are pushing against the chair. I'm back in the shower, palms against Kyle's chest, forcing him off me. I push and grunt and shove until my fury is spent.

I cry and shake. My throat quivers and my teeth clatter against each other. I'm wheezing. My body rocks like epilepsy on speed.

"Are you sure you're okay?" Nicole asks.

I don't know. My whole body is jolting and spasming and out of control.

Nicole keeps saying I don't have to poke around in my past. "Our work together is about the present," she told me. "It's about what's happening for you right now."

Nicole is normally wonderful, but that was a total lie – at least for someone with a body like mine, where the past is always alive in the present, alive and happening right now. And right now. And right now.

My body goes crazy at home too. It throws me against doors, walls, the back of my chair, the kitchen sink.

"Why aren't I better yet?" I snap next time I walk into Nicole's office. I'm furious that I'm still so broken after six months of convulsions and ripping out my guts and staring them down.

"We can stop our sessions any time you want," she says.

"I just want to be fixed. How much longer will it take?"

"Unfortunately I can't tell you that," she says. "It's going to take as long as it takes."

I'm crying but I nod. I'll keep going even if I'm in therapy forever. I have to. "Fine. But why is my body so psychotic? Are we making me worse?"

"No, you're getting better. Your reactions are a normal part of the healing process," she says. "When you froze, all the energy your body would have used to help you fight or run away was locked up inside you. Now that you're letting some of that trapped old energy out it's like lifting the lid on a boiling pot."

I'm driving home from Jenna's place out in the country with the Top 40 blaring from the speakers. I'm singing along when instead of the lyrics I'm singing a chorus of nos. Yelling them. I shut off the radio and shout until my throat is raw.

I have to go back to the police station. I get a block away but can't go any closer. I turn and speed home.

The next morning, Friday, I'm sitting very still on the couch. Do you want to talk to the police? I ask my throat. It doesn't go tight. My breathing doesn't change either. It surprises me. My words must want to come out.

I lace up my runners and walk to the police station. My legs are speeding like they've been waiting forever for me to catch up. I hesitate when I get close. I wrap my arms around my ribs. I promise to take good care of you, Sweetie. I march through the front doors, take a ticket and wait for my turn.

"Forty-three," calls a big bald officer. It's me. I stand and go to the counter. "I want to reopen an old sexual assault case from when I was eighteen," I say, looking him in the eye.

He takes me to an interview room and we sit down. "Last time I reported my assault the officers thought I should wait until I remembered the entire night. I don't. Well I do, but not with solid memories, the kind that would hold up in court."

I take a big breath and keep going. "Here's what I do remember," I say, and tell him how I woke up when Gary lay behind me and that he ran his hands over me as I kept saying no and trying to push him away. I tell him that Gary unzipped my pants while I was saying stop and trying to fight him off and that Gary forced his finger inside me as I struggled against him.

"That's as far as my solid memories go," I say. "But I know now that what I just told you was a crime on its own."

"You're right," he says. "What you described is definitely sexual assault."

"There might be a videotape in my file. Can you check?"

He clicks away on his computer. "No, there's nothing here."

Shit, Tonya never sent it.

"I don't know Gary's last name," I say. "It was more than a decade ago."

"That's going to be tough. Do you have evidence or witnesses?"

"No."

"Even if we had his last name it's pretty unlikely we could lay a charge. He could just say he wasn't there."

I nod and wipe my eyes. What did I expect?

"But I can see this has had a major impact on your life. I want to help you," the officer says. "If you can get me his last name, I'll track this guy down. We won't be able to prosecute, but I want to knock on his door and say, 'I know what you did to that girl all those years ago.'"

"Please," I say. His offer is not enough and yet it's everything. He believes me. And cares.

I take the officer's card and go straight to the university. When I first tried to get Gary's last name, I had asked over the phone. This time I'm showing up as a real person, one whose eyes are rimmed with red.

I go to Campus Security. The man at the desk takes my information down in capital letters. "We'll get his name and share it with the cops," he says.

I shiver. We're going to find him.

The security guard calls later that day. "We haven't found him yet, but I think we're getting close. I hope you can try to have a good weekend."

My phone rings on Monday morning. It's the security guard. I sit in the corner at the front door, steeling myself for the battle that's to come. I've been planning it all weekend. How I'll follow the officer to Gary's door, how I'll trick him into confessing, how I'll stare into his snake eyes as I testify and destroy him with his own fucking venom.

"Gary isn't on the class list," the security guard says.

"What?"

"No one named Gary was registered for the University 100 course that semester. We found the other names you listed so we know we have the right class."

I slump against the wall. "That's not possible. Can you check again?"

"I'm sorry. We've been through the list a dozen times. He's not there."

Sounds fall out of me. I'm heavy like a boulder loose at the top of a mountain.

"I'm so sorry," the security guard says. "I wish I could have found him for you."

I feel numb. Dead. I was so close. Campus Security and the police were helping me this time. They were on my side. And I was ready to stand up and fight back and knock Gary down.

I don't know why he isn't on the list. Maybe he was only in the girls' computer lab and not their class. Or maybe he dropped out?

I look for Tonya online. I can't find her.

I can't remember Amber's last name but I Google her anyway.

I find an obituary. The black and white photo isn't clear and the young woman isn't looking at the camera. It can't be her. She's way too alive to be dead.

Gary is gone. I can't get his name and I can't find the girls and there's nothing else I can do. Fuck him for winning, for stealing everything from me, for making me collapse once again under the goddamn weight of his arm.

Fine, there's one last thing I could do: I could tell everyone I know and ask them to help me track him down.

I draft a post to share on Facebook. I work on it for hours, adding and deleting and changing words.

My throat closes when I go to post it. I'm pouring sweat. I can't do it.

I go to bed and I'm being electrocuted. I'm all rabies and leprosy and foaming at the mouth. I tap my chest, slapping hard to make myself calm down.

I try to slow the current running through me, to isolate the points where the convulsions originate. My thigh tightens, the centre of my quad, deep inside. I feel it squeezing in as I concentrate on it. Then it shoots out and flings my leg into the air.

My stomach contracts beneath my belly button. It pulls in and turns solid, like Olympic abs. Then my stomach erupts and arches my spine off the bed. My shoulder goes too. There's a crushing inside, a gathering in. A pause. A landmine explodes.

There are so many convulsions I lose track of what's happening. There's an onslaught, rapid and wild.

There's a stabbing in my vagina. It's sharp and piercing. A scalpel. I scream and writhe but there's no escape.

It's gone.

It's back.

It's gone and back. And back and I'll die.

I'm shaking, a leaf being torn from its branch.

I see Gary above me. I tense and coil, ready to strike. He reaches for me. I kick and punch and scream. I'm attacking the air, my pillow, my bed and the wall. I know I'm insane but I can't stop.

He's choking me. I throw him off me and crush his throat and jab my fingers through his eyes. I scream into my pillow. "No. Stop. Fuck you!"

My voice grows hoarse, then silent. I lie still.

I have to escape. I have to get as far away as my legs will carry me.

I'm on my back in the tangled sheets and running. I kick and elbow the mattress as I sprint as hard and fast as I can. I run forever.

My arms and legs drop back to the bed. I pant and gasp for air. All is still. Eerily quiet.

Then the demons rush back in, throwing me everywhere. My body jolts as the numbers on my alarm clock keep pace through the night.

The next day I share my post on Facebook.

I'm afraid to lie down, afraid of being left alone to face the wildness in my body. I want to invite some guy, any guy, maybe even my old ex Shane over to tuck my hair back and hold me until I fall asleep in his arms.

But I won't. I can't. I have to do this on my own.

Instead I hold myself gently, like a baby, as my body thrashes alone through the night.

Nothing happens with my Facebook post. One girl shares it, a few people ask if I'm okay and that's the end. My words slip down the newsfeed and disappear.

28

DROUGHT

I'm in San Francisco, walking around Fisherman's Warf in a stupor. I signed up for an eighteen-day silent meditation retreat thinking it would be good medicine but that's stupid. It's going to be awful. It's more than twice as long as any retreat I've ever done, and I'm terrified to spend so much time alone with my mind.

I catch a shuttle to Spirit Rock Meditation Centre, passing through yellow hillsides thirsty from California's worst drought in two hundred years. Even the land is parched and dying.

I'm early so I walk the grounds and find the meditation hall. It's a rounded room, two-stories tall, and wooden except for the windows that fill it with sun and sky and space. I choose a cushion that faces a low platform where the teachers will sit.

Later that evening a bell chimes out over the valley and a hush settles in. I join a hundred others as we slip off our shoes and pad to our seats in the hall.

The teachers enter, and I stare at them in awe. They don't look like regular people, not like anyone you would see in line at a movie. They look different. Radiant. Like they're made of love and air, like you would slide right through them if you hugged them.

I know one of the teachers already. She comes to Regina a few times a year to lead retreats. She smiles at me from her cushion, and my heart stills. I'm ready.

The retreat begins with a series of vows: to do our best to not harm any living creature, to take only that which is freely offered, to practice celibacy, and to keep silent except for when asking questions of the teachers.

How to describe what happens when the gong chimes and silence descends? Waves of emotion. Every feeling ever known arises in me and passes away and rises again.

Grief turns me cold and wrings me out like a dish cloth.

Gary crosses my mind. A burning glare.

Later I follow my tears back to their source and feel sorrow's icy hands pawing at me. My god I miss Ian. I wish I didn't have to do this alone.

It's awful but I do what the teachers advise: I ask myself, "Can this be okay in this moment? Can I accept my experience just as it is?"

I nod and my heart continues bleeding. I place my hand on it and welcome my tears. I remember my niece, Sophia, saying, "I wish we were twins, Auntie D. I wish you were little like me." It melts my heart and the puddles drip from my eyes.

Days pass. We sit. Then walk. Then listen to the teachers. Then sit. That's the whole agenda. There's nothing to do but turn inwards.

One day the teachers say suffering happens when we want what we don't have and when we don't want what we do have. I cry on the path by the dried-up stream where the drought is killing off so much life.

Ever since our second date, I'd been setting goals for Ian and me. I wanted to see him again. I asked him to be exclusive and to spend more time with me. I counted the days and weeks, then the months and years we'd been together.

I asked him for compliments and when he didn't know what to say I gave him lists to recite. A thousand times I told him I loved him just to hear him say it back.

I told him he had to be who I wanted instead of who he was, and he tried. He really did. But no matter what I convinced him to give, I kept wanting more. I was a mouth attached to an endless stomach, devouring all the love I could force out of him.

Once I caught a frog and wanted to keep him so badly that I clasped him tight in my palms. I felt him pinging between my hands, struggling to escape.

That's what I did to Ian too. He had to leave to save himself.

I forgive you, I tell him and fall to my knees.

My tears dry and the storm inside grows calm. I ruined us but I don't blame myself for it. Not any more. I did the best I could.

I'm on a bench absorbing the sun at the end of a walking meditation when I hear a soft chirping in the leaves below. I hop off the bench, crouch down in the dirt and follow the chirps until I see a lizard the size of my pinkie. I smile at him and his adorable calls.

Weird, his skin is moving. I look closer. He's covered in a pulsing carpet of miniature ants. They're eating him alive. His chirps are the screams of his death.

I recoil, then sweep in to save him. I'm going to make the ants stop. I'll keep him and care for him and love him back to life.

Yet as my fingers hover over him, I know I can't help. He's too far gone and this is his end. As dreadful as it is, all I can do is let it be. This suffering and dying are part of the trade we give for breath.

The lizard's chirps continue. I stay with him, giving him the only thing I have: my witness. I share his pain and hold his suffering in my heart as he passes over.

I cry as his chirps fade, as he slips away. I weep for all the agony that exists in the world, for the cruelty of this life and for the tiny, insignificant best I have to offer.

I've been twitching every night for months now but it's way worse on retreat. My spasms are lasting for hours and keeping me up long into the night. The electric shocks follow me everywhere: into the meditation hall, into the shower, during meals and even on the hills where I run to escape them.

I try meditating through my tremors and sit at the back to keep from disturbing the others. It doesn't work. I can't stop my legs from rising and slapping down hard against the floor. I go to my room and lie on the carpet and let my legs fling themselves in the air.

Later, during forgiveness practice, I replay everything I've done wrong: I failed Holly; I raged at my family; I broke Ian's tooth; I drove him away; I slept with men who didn't care about me; I picked on Jenna and Tenille; and on and on.

I'm wracked with shame. I'm sorry, I say to everyone I harmed.

I'm sorry, so sorry, I say to myself too.

I feel lighter, unbound, as if I'm Christian in *Pilgrim's Progress* setting down his pack. I can't take back my mistakes, but I can forgive my long-ago selves. They didn't know how to do better.

Tears are still rolling down my cheeks when I realize my parents never meant to hurt me. I forgive them too.

My heart is so big it stretches out of my chest and fills the whole world.

What about Gary? I feel him reach his arm around me. I forgive him.

An electrical storm blasts through my body and sears me to the core. Fuck Gary.

I run upstairs to a vast empty room. I lie on the floor, limbs stretched out, and surrender to the violence. It's like I'm in an electric chair, like I'm a marionette on fire. My whole body tenses up. My stomach contracts hard, pulling my legs and shoulders in tight like I'm doing crunches. There's an explosion and my body shoots out long. It's still for a second. Then my legs go wild, shaking like clotheslines in a storm.

It's time for lunch and I'm starving but there's no way I can make myself stand. I lie on my back and feel my body descend into the depths.

It's my birthday. I'm thirty two. It's gratitude day and it's sunny and warm.

On our way to the last meditation of the night, a woman I'd met on the shuttle hands me a tiny gift. It's wrapped in tissue and tied with a delicate dental-floss bow. I open it and find a purple lozenge, the best gift she could scrounge. I bow to her and we laugh like a movie on mute, mouths open, cheeks flushed.

I pop the lozenge in and head to my cushion. The hall is different at night: quieter, darker and full of a haunting stillness as candles flicker like stars. The teacher leads us in a chant, the metta sutta, the Buddha's instructions on radiating kindness over the entire world.

When the chant fades into silence, I close my eyes. I'm savouring the purple lozenge and the pleasure of such an unexpected gift.

My leg jolts. My shoulder joins in. I welcome the twitching. I allow it and remind myself that I'm safe.

Suddenly Gary is standing there, life-sized, before me. We stare each other down. I feel both hatred and its absence.

I forgive you, I tell him. You must have been at a terrible place in your own life to have been able to do what you did. It's not okay and it will never be okay, but I forgive you for my own sake.

We keep staring at each other and a voice booms through me, a lion waking up inside: You can't hurt me ever again.

I sit up tall and heat shoots up my spine like flames. My body expands, inflating like a hot air balloon. Gary shrinks as I grow. He withers down to the size of a toy G. I. Joe, then to a speck and then disappears. I'm still here, a giant lion roaring away the man who once tried to steal me from myself.

My neck wants to move. It flings my head back, leaving my throat bare, open, exposed. A blanket of blue flowers springs up, covering me from toe to chest. My throat changes into a thick green stem. A huge flower erupts from the top of my throat where my face had been. I'm a lion's garden, filled with ferocious love.

I wake in tears. There's a deep crack in my labia, my old wound split open again. My ghost is back, and she spent the night clawing away at me.

I beg one of the teachers to meet with me. "Do you need medical care?" she asks.

"No," I say. "But I'm afraid. Why did I attack myself?"

We talk more and I tell her how I tried to forgive Gary and then roared him away.

"Oh D," she says. "You need to be careful with forgiveness when you're dealing with trauma. Sometimes the body isn't ready to forgive."

I'm sobbing. "But I thought I would be better by now. I've been working so hard for so long and I just want to be done."

"That's a pretty big expectation," she says. "Can you let go of that and let your experience be whatever it is?"

I nod but the disappointment is crushing me. I'm so tired of being broken. Will I ever be okay?

I try to hold still in the meditation hall. My cheek is incredibly itchy. I resist the urge to scratch and just pay attention to the sensation. It turns into burning. It flames for a moment and fades, leaving no evidence that it ever existed.

Then a memory. Gary. A flash of anger. It ignites and burns in my belly. My face tenses. Jaw tightens. Brows furrow. Rage grows inside and fills my body with heat.

I ask myself, Can this be okay? I open to the fire and let it move on its own without chasing it or scolding it away. The flames take over, and I worry they'll consume me, burn me at the stake.

But what about this moment? Can it be okay? I draw my attention back to the heat. It fades and passes away while I sit still and watch it leave.

It passes away like the end of a day, like a toddler's first goldfish, like a leaf in the autumn, like grandparents, like fruit flies, like memories, like a flower that's been picked, like childhood and youth, like Ozymandias, like a worm that gets eaten by a bird that gets caught by a cat that gets hit by a car, like starving children across the world, like everything.

The days weave together, a million tiny moments that I despise or savour or simply notice one at a time as I fall deeper and deeper into silence and into God, which is just another word for Love.

29

PIÑATA

I call Ian when I get home but his number isn't in service. He must have changed it without telling me. Maybe it's because I tried calling him before the retreat. When he didn't answer, I left a message saying I was terrified and lost and alone. Or maybe I just cried and cried and filled his voicemail with tears.

I email Ian, but he doesn't respond, not for forever. "I can't say anything without you getting upset," he writes.

I hate to admit it but he's right. There's nothing he could say that wouldn't hurt me, nothing besides, "I love you and I miss you and I'm giving up half of myself and coming straight home."

A few years earlier when Jenna and Brad found out that they were going to become parents, we invited the whole family to my place for dinner so she could tell them.

Jenna barely spoke as Brad sat next to her, his hand on her knee. As the evening wore on, Bethany and the kids got up to leave.

"Just a minute," Jenna said, her voice quivering. "There's a reason I called you over." She paused. "We're having a baby."

Long seconds passed with everyone on mute. Then Mom's voice came out strangled, "Congratulations."

There was no fight, no yelling, but later Dad told me, "It's nonsense that he isn't marrying her."

"You don't want them to get married," I said. "You want them to break up."

"Technically yes. But now she's stuck with him."

Brad didn't stand a chance with my parents, not since he told them he was a part-time magician, that he performed at birthday parties and fairs.

"It's witchcraft," Dad insisted. "He's bad news."

I could never convince Dad that Brad was just hiding tricks in his sleeves.

Jenna and I take her kids, Sophia and Max, swimming. We're setting our towels beside the pool when I notice her ring. It's on her middle finger, a silver band with blue stones.

"Why are you wearing a ring?" I ask. Jenna never wears jewellery, and who wears a ring in the pool?

She blushes.

"You're engaged!"

For their engagement announcement, Jenna draws a caricature of herself in a white dress and Brad in a suit, and tucks it inside a piñata full of Ring Pops.

We invite the whole family to our parents' place and everyone crowds into the family room. Even Tenille and her husband and son beam in via Skype.

My nieces and nephews take turns striking the piñata with a broomstick. Nothing happens until Dad takes the stick. He clobbers the piñata and Ring Pops fall to the floor like confetti.

Jenna's drawing flutters out and she gives it to Sophia. "What's the picture?" Jenna asks her.

"It's you and Daddy."

"What are we doing?"

"Getting married."

"They're engaged!" I say and it's loud and happy, a piñata of cheers.

Everyone hugs, except Dad who goes around shaking hands. "Thank you," he says to the groom.

At a wedding planning meeting with all the parents, Jenna and Brad say they're going to have a cash bar during the dance. "It will be a good fundraiser for the happy couple," Brad's father says, and my parents avert their eyes.

When the others leave, Dad mutters, "What are they doing having alcohol there?"

"It's a normal thing to have at a wedding," I say.

I am Jenna's maid of honour. All the sisters are in the wedding party, even Tenille since she and her family are home for a year to promote their missionary work.

The sun shines bright and beautiful on Jenna and her lacy dress. The seats are full beyond the hedges. Bethany, Tenille and Holly take their places next to the archway, and Sophia sprinkles flower petals on the grass.

I carry Max to deliver the rings, hand him to Mom, and join the row of sisters as Jenna walks in. She's glowing, radiant, a sun herself.

Brad's eyes redden as she comes toward him. He's beaming and she is too. They promise to love each other forever, and then they're scooping up the kids for the walk down the aisle.

After the reception and pictures, Mom takes the kids home and puts them down for their naps. Hours later when we get to the dance, Jenna texts Mom and asks when she's bringing the kids. Mom says something about giving them snacks. Jenna asks again. Mom doesn't answer, just texts about her day.

Jenna is agitated, her face flushed and pinched. I follow her out to the parking lot. "She's not bringing my kids, is she?" Jenna asks.

"I'm not sure but it doesn't look good."

Jenna turns her back to the guests who are arriving. Her hands shake as she dials. "Do you want me to do it?" I ask.

"Please. Can you remind her she promised to bring them?"

Mom picks up. "Jenna wants to know what time you're bringing the kids," I say. Mom doesn't answer, just rambles on: They're tired. Max has a dirty diaper. They need to eat. They want to watch TV instead.

"Okay, but they need to be here," I say. "It's what Jenna wants."

"Let me talk to her," Mom says. Jenna takes the phone but Mom won't let her speak. "Please Mom," Jenna says, but that's as far as she gets. Her voice cracks.

I take the phone back. "Look Mom," I say, talking over her. "Your opinions don't matter and neither do mine. All that matters is that Jenna wants her kids and you agreed to bring them."

"It's dangerous," Mom says.

"Because there's going to be alcohol?"

"Yes."

Jenna's eyes are welling up with tears.

"Mom, it's fine," I say. "I'll take care of the kids. Jenna is getting upset. Are you going to bring them or do I need to pick them up?"

"You can't take them," Mom says. "You don't know the roads and it's getting dark. They don't want to go. They're already in their pyjamas."

"It sounds like you're not bringing the kids, so I'm coming to get them."

Mom continues protesting. "It's not your call," I say. "I'm hanging up now. I'll see you in a few minutes."

I hug Jenna and send her back into her party. I get Brad's keys. Then I find Tenille. "Will you go with me?" I ask.

"No way," she says. "I'm not getting in the middle of that."

"Please?"

"You know Mom's just going to yell at you. Why don't you make Jenna do it?"

"Because it's her wedding," I say.

"Good luck, but it's going to be bad."

When I get to my parents' place, two of my aunts form a buffer between Mom and me, keeping me in the living room and Mom in the kitchen. One aunt wags her finger at me. "You're such a bully," she says. "You're behaving like a total spoiled brat."

Her words land like fists. "I don't think that's true," I say.

"Yes it is," my other aunt says with her hands on her hips. "We heard everything you said. Your mother had you on speakerphone. It's unacceptable to talk to her like that."

Mom is wiping her hands on a dishtowel. "I'm sorry for raising my voice," I call to her. "I didn't mean to be disrespectful." Mom doesn't react, just keeps wiping her hands.

"How dare you choose to endanger those kids?" asks my finger-wagging aunt.

"What? I haven't had anything to drink if that's what you mean."

She rolls her eyes.

"There's nothing dangerous about me taking the kids to be with their parents," I say.

"We can't stop you from kidnapping them but if you do, your mother says they aren't allowed back here tonight. We aren't helping with anything, not even the car seats."

"I'm sure you don't see it," I say, trying to hold my voice steady, "but I'm making what I believe is the kindest choice."

Mom says nothing as the tirade continues, just stands there silently endorsing the sticks and stones.

I take the car seats and buckle them in. I go back for Sophia and Max. They're crying from all the commotion. I pick them up and kiss their heads and take them away.

Back at the dance, their kids in their arms, Jenna and Brad thank me for saving their wedding. Someone calls me a hero. It doesn't make me feel any better. Mom's eyes are haunting me. She looks betrayed, like I'm a fox in her coop, eating her babies.

At my place Sophia falls asleep in the crook of my arm, while I lie awake. I remember the time Dad told me I wasn't good enough and the hundred nights I lay awake in my childhood bedroom as my parents' voices complained about me through the vents.

I was perfect tonight. A martyr. I walked directly into a fight to protect Jenna. I've been doing that for as long as I can remember: taking on the weight of the world to save everyone else.

Why won't anyone do that for me?

Wait a minute, someone will: Me.

I take Mom aside after the gift-opening the next day. "Last night wasn't okay," I say. "It wasn't fair that you didn't defend me, that you stood there and let your sisters attack me on your behalf."

I ask for an apology, but Mom says that I was wrong to defy her.

"Your mother is right," Dad says, barging in. "Get over it. You're causing a scene."

"I will not get over it. I need an apology. Probably Jenna does too."

Mom makes a choking sound and darts upstairs.

"Look what you've done to your mother," Dad says.

"What she's done to herself," I say.

A few minutes later Mom comes back. "I was wrong," she says in the tiniest of voices.

"Thank you," I say.

Mom leans, crying, into my arms like a child waking up from a nightmare.

30

REWRITE

I try to calculate how much time my body has spent in convulsions. They come every single day and have for months, sometimes lasting most of the night. Maybe a hundred hours. No, that can't be high enough. Two hundred?

"How much more twitching can there be?" I ask Nicole.

"It's different for everyone. Your twitching will subside once we put your whole story together in a way your body can process, when all the pieces connect."

"Why hasn't that happened yet? Shouldn't I be done by now?"

"There could be another piece, something you haven't been able to feel," she says. "From now on when your body starts shaking ask yourself, 'What else is happening?' "

I glance at the Feelings chart tacked to her wall, showing cartoon faces that run the gamut of emotions. A tiny flicker of dread pricks the centre of my chest with its cold sharpness. I follow it inside. There's a mass expanding like cancer, like black ice crystallizing through me.

Someone grabs me and pushes me down. He wraps his hands around my throat and I will surely die.

Can I stay here in this moment and let myself feel it? I stare into the darkness and feel the pressure closing around my throat. The edges of my body disappear. The ice crystals freeze through me and beyond, stretching off into the distance.

Gary runs his greedy hands over my torso. I'm pushing him away as hard as I can, but I know what's coming. I'm going to lose.

I breathe deep and remind myself it's not real. Not any more. I stay in my eighteen-year-old body and feel everything.

I'm shoving against him, trying to force his arm away. He laughs. I push harder. My left shoulder, the one that cost me everything that long-ago night, tightens up. My muscles pulse and throb. I want to fight. To throw him off me. To fucking kill him. I push against the edge of my leather chair. I fight and shove until he's gone. Gone. I fucking made him stop.

My breathing is shallow, erratic. I can't get any air. He's back. I struggle but nothing. I use my last breath to say, "He's strangling me."

I flex my throat hard, raise my hands and squeeze them beneath the choking grip. I push like mad, like a mother lifting a car off her child. Gary's fingers loosen.

I kick him in the gut, like in my last self-defence class when I smashed my foot through a board. He flies across the room and crumples to the floor. I punch and kick and gouge out his eyes.

He stops moving.

When I'm convinced he's dead, I stop moving too.

"What happened for you?" Nicole asks.

I'm too ashamed to meet her eyes. "Something awful. Psychotic."

"There's no judgment here," she says.

"I imagined hurting him," I whisper. "Killing him."

"That's perfectly normal. It's actually a necessary part in healing from post-traumatic stress. "

"I don't get it."

"You have to stop being the victim. Anger can help with that if you let yourself feel it."

"How?"

"It can allow you to reimagine the ending in a way where you save yourself."

"But that's not what happened."

"Right, but you need to know that you could handle it differently now. That's what will keep you from being retraumatized whenever you relive that night. We need to rewrite your old memory so that you know you're safe now."

But I don't want to fight Gary, not even in my head. What about guarding my thoughts and loving my neighbour and turning the other cheek? "Won't it make me hurt somebody?" I ask, remembering the gashes I'd clawed into Ian's flesh.

"It's not dangerous. Your body knows the difference between fantasy and reality."

That is not true. That's what Nicole said about porn too. A mind is a wild territory that needs to be controlled. Thoughts become actions, and they grow when we feed them. Don't they? Everyone from Buddha to Jesus to Gandhi said so.

I'm wiped out for days after I murder Gary.

I'm lying on the couch surrounded by banana peels and apple cores.
I reach for my laptop. I have to write about it.

I'm only a few words in when my left arm – elbow, shoulder and
wrist – clench tight. Not now, I tell my body. I'm busy.

My arm sucks in like a spring pulling back, getting ready to explode.
I slide my laptop to safety.

My arm swings madly. I smash Gary – my red cushion – in the face.
I pin him to the couch. I punch and slap him hard. I throw him to the
floor and stomp on him, my legs pumping like I'm running on him,
trampling him into the ground. "Fuck you. I said no!"

I'm punching him again. Spit foams out of my mouth and lands on
him. The cushion slides under the couch. I yank it back and stomp on it.
"No. Stop!"

I drop to my knees and pummel him. "Die," I yell with each punch.
I slap him across the face. I squeeze the cushion between my hands and
I'm strangling him. I whip my belt off and cinch it around his throat and
feel the fucker die.

Holy shit, am I ever crazy. My body shakes and quivers.

I can't stand having the murdered cushion next to me. I take it, still
bound in my belt, and hide it in a cabinet in the spare room.

I open my laptop and try again. I write about how I'm a maniac,
how I ache for blood.

I walk to Home Depot to get a new anode rod for my water heater to
keep my showers warm through the winter. It's dark when I leave the
store carrying the five-foot metal rod that's as thick as a quarter.

Traffic thunders down the road. Headlights flash like cougar eyes. I
grip my spear tight and snarl at the SUVs that barrel toward me. Come
closer, I dare them, and my mouth tastes like blood. I imagine striking
out, bashing someone's hood, stabbing my rod through a window.

At the underpass where the sidewalk winds down through the darkness, I wish for a shadowy figure to appear. Usually I'm afraid when I
hike this stretch but now my hands are dripping sweat.

I see a man in the distance coming toward me. There are no cars.
No witnesses. Just concrete pillars holding the highway over our heads.
No one would hear him.

The man draws near. Scenes from *The Walking Dead* play in my mind. Spearing a zombie in the chest. Stabbing through its eyes into its brain. The main character, Rick, ripping some guy's throat out with his fucking teeth. Blood and sweat and screams.

The man is just steps away. I clench my weapon. I'm starving for him. I want to tear him apart, to paint the underpass with his goddamn entrails. One word, one look, one move on his part and I'll spit him out of this fucking world.

He passes me. Does nothing. Says nothing. Keeps going.

Fuck you! Why couldn't you give me the slightest provocation?

I wish he would come back and give me a reason to rip him apart but he keeps going, blending back into the darkness.

I'm putting the rod in the storage room when my body clenches tight. I lean against the wall. I'm burning inside, broiling, frothing. My god, I wanted to hurt that guy.

The rod is in my hands like a baseball bat and I'm striking the wall. I swing it again and again, making pockmarks in the plaster. I sweat and pant and smash away. The wall cracks. I ream into the weak place. A chunk the size of my fist breaks off.

I beat the wall until it's hideous, riddled with gouges and holes. Then I run my fingers over its wounds, eyes glittering as if stroking a lover's chest.

My twitches still shudder through me every night but now they're multiplying like mad, like a nightmare I once had where I pulled a wart out of my foot and found it attached to a clump of warts, each one attached to vast colonies of its own. I tugged them out like Hemingway's old man reeling his marlin up from the depths, and as I piled the mess next to me I realized I was nothing more than a hollowed-out skin.

I wake up sweating. I see Gary above me. I'm too weak and exhausted to fight back. Please, I'm so tired.

I know there's only one shortcut, one way to make him leave without tormenting me all night: to give in, to agree now to whatever he did then, and have it all be okay.

Why is it such a big deal anyway? It's just a thing that bodies do. I'll give myself an orgasm so I can go to sleep.

My eyes snap open. No. I refuse to play this game, even if I never sleep again. I don't consent. No matter how painful the truth is, I will not fucking erase it.

Would I have slept with Gary on purpose if he hadn't disappeared after The Terrible Night? No! What a crazy thought!

But I went back and fucked all the other guys who forced their way inside me.

That can't be right.

I list the guys on my fingers: Kool-Aid Dave, Mr. New Year, Cameron the con, shower-wall Kyle and snowplow Thomas. I tracked down every one of the guys – across provinces, even – to throw myself on their beds. To forgive and forget and turn the other goddamn cheek. Anything for a do-over, for a retroactive yes.

31

HIGHER THAN GOD

My parents are convinced the End Times are upon us, that the Christians will be pulled up to heaven in a flash, leaving their cars running, microwaves beeping and clothes, still warm from their bodies, crumpled on the floor. Whenever a blood-moon eclipse draws near, Dad emails me links to his prophesy magazines.

"Stop sending these," I write back.

He sends another.

"Quit it," I write. "Also I'm pretty sure I'd notice if you and Mom vanished in the twinkling of an eye."

I go to my parents' place for dinner with Jenna and the kids, and we end up staying the night. Dad's the last one up. He's in the dark, staring at the computer as if he's going to be beamed into the glowing screen instead of up into the sky.

He must have crept around like the Tooth Fairy because when Jenna wakes up there's a Rapture survival guide on her diaper bag. I laugh when she shows me the book. "Great, you'll need that when Mom and Dad get magnetted out of the world."

I'm almost home when I notice another black book with a cross on the cover tucked in with my things. Shit, he Raptured me too.

Later my parents take me to the hardware store. I wait until they're dropping me off before I give Dad his Rapture book. "You have to stop propaganda-ing me," I say.

"I'm trying to keep my girls safe," he says. "We're living in the End Times. All the signs are here."

"That's a risk I'll take."

"Keep the book. Please."

"No."

"I hate to leave you on your own."

"You have no other choice."

Mom pipes up. "D, honour your father."

"You know I don't believe the same things you guys do. You have to respect that."

"No, it's your responsibility to submit to his authority."

"It is not," I say and we keep arguing until I get out of the car and slam the door.

Jenna and the kids are hanging out at my place when Mom and Dad stop by with a frozen pizza. "The sermon this morning was about family," Dad says. "I took some notes."

He puts on his glasses. "Your mother and I want to have a good relationship with you girls," he reads. "We should get along and try to communicate better, even though you're on a different path."

Sounds good but I bet he doesn't mean it. I slice the pizza and pass everyone a plate.

Dad bows his head. "Dear Je——," he says.

"No thank you," I say. "Since we're going to respect each other and you know we don't share the same beliefs, I'd rather not be involved in your prayer."

Mom and Dad gape at me.

"Thanks for the pizza, though," I say.

Jenna blusters over the kids, blowing on their slices to make the moment pass.

Mom and Dad silently bend their heads.

"You stole Jenna's faith," Dad says when he's finished praying.

"No I didn't."

"You yanked it right out of her."

"That's not fair to D or to me," Jenna says in her soft little peacemaker voice. "I made my own choices."

"Under duress," Mom says.

"Enough," I say and slap my pizza onto my plate. "I'm done being your scapegoat. You have to stop blaming me for what other people do."

Mom hangs her head. "It's been easy to blame you because you've always been strong enough to take it."

"That's a horrible reason! I'm not some monster trying to destroy everyone," I say. "I am a good person."

"Your mother and I agree," Dad says, leaning forward earnestly. "You're a good person on the human level. But everyone is pathetic without God."

"I am not pathetic!" I yell, and my glare burns the old fanatics up and out of my house.

My parents can't stop thinking I'm a sinner. Their world doesn't exist without good and evil, without repentance and a burning lake of fire.

I can't change them, but I don't have to take it any more. I call Mom. "I'm done hearing how you and Dad think I'm bad. If I feel attacked, I'm going to ask you to stop. If you continue, I will leave."

Mom says she understands but her voice sounds like a puppy's whimper.

I'm painting the spare room, the one that used to be Ian's office. I pick a vibrant slobbery pink, the shade of freshly-chewed Hubba Bubba.

The spare bed looks junky lying on the floor so I buy a metal frame for it. I put the sides on the floor to screw them together. I can't figure out the slots or how to line up the bars. I pinch my finger and try again.

Finally it's a rectangle. I ease the box spring onto the frame. It falls through. I fix the frame but now it's too small.

I give up and call Dad. "I'll be there tonight after my run," he says.

When he comes in, rain pours off his jacket and pools on the floor. He smells musty, like sweat, like our tent when I was a kid.

I try not to breathe. "You ran in the rain?"

"Rain or shine. I can't break my routine," he says.

We yank the bed frame apart, line it up and twist the screws in. The room is too small. The frame takes up too much space.

Dad is too close. His arm brushes my back.

I shudder and my nose fills with that awful smell.

Rain drips off his face like sweat.

I'm dizzy.

A flash of sweat running down. Gary's sweat splattering on my cheek.

Dad touching my hand when he takes a bolt.

Fuck, I hate him.

I duck my head so he won't see the rage flaring through me. I run out of the room. "Leave it," I call from the kitchen.

He doesn't. Of course he doesn't. He never fucking listens. He clatters around in that small stinky room until the frame will hold the bed. "There, I think that will do," he says.

"Thanks," I say through my teeth. Get out!

I tuck myself in and put my hands over my heart like I do every night as I brace for the twitches that are sure to come.

My left leg jumps. Then again. My shoulders join in. The convulsions come so hard my body folds in on itself, legs and shoulders rising like I'm doing the boat yoga pose. My twitches continue.

There's a prick of dread deep in my belly.

I'm eighteen on the carpet, helpless beneath Gary's weight.

I'm ten in the tent.

I pull myself back. No, I'm thirty-two and safe in my bed.

I let the twitches come and go. I pay close attention to my whole body, looking for any sign of a fight in me, any impulse to strike out and save myself.

There's nothing. I'm frozen. Weak. Locked inside myself. It's terrifying. Like when I'm falling in a dream and about to crash and can't force myself to wake up. Like a brain trapped behind glassy eyes.

I go to my parents' place for a night of board games but Tenille and her husband had an argument and no one wants to play.

Tenille is trying to leave, but Mom corners her at the door. "We have to talk."

"Not now."

"Yes now."

"I don't want to," Tenille says, sitting on the bench to tie her shoes.

Mom keeps insisting until Tenille goes quiet like a preschooler who knows there's no escape.

"Mom, she told you to leave her alone," I say.

Mom turns to me. "Who appointed you higher than God?"

"Please don't talk to me like that."

Tenille slips out and she's home free.

"You think you're better than me?" Mom asks, leaning so close that her breath hits my skin.

"That's enough," I say. "Remember you agreed to stop yelling when I asked you to or I would have to leave."

"Right, I forgot you were the mom."

"Goodnight," I say and open the door.

Mom grabs my elbow and pins me to the wall.

"You have to let me go," I say. I yank myself free and get outside. She chases me and shoves me against the picnic table. We scuffle as I pry her hands off me.

I run to the car, and she goes back into the house and slams the door.

I have a voicemail from Mom when I get home: "I'm sorry for pushing you," she says.

I don't call back. I'm not risking another fight. I write a note instead: *It's not okay but I still love you. It's clear we can't have a productive discussion on our own so I am only willing to discuss our issues with a therapist.*

The next day I track her down in her church sanctuary a minute before the service. I pass her the note and she reaches for it, for me, like food for the starving. I shrink from her grasp and race away through the crowded hall.

Later I find a note in my mailbox. Mom's tiny blue printing says: *If you desire to meet with a therapist with us, we can arrange a meeting.*

Dad answers the phone when I call. He and Mom have someone in mind: their pastor.

"Does he have any qualifications?" I ask.

Dad checks with the pastor and calls me back. "No, but he's met with a lot of people to talk about their problems. Your mother and I would prefer talking with a Christian."

I'd rather see a pro but I agree. Best not to push my luck. Not when I've been asking for this for years.

32

ALL THE WORST WORDS

I'm regressing. I keep shutting down now when my twitches come. Nicole doesn't think it's a major issue but she's wrong. I have to do something big.

I've been working half time for six months but I can barely drag myself to the office on Monday, Tuesday and every second Wednesday. I'm way too tired.

Maybe I should walk away. I'm desperate for more time to sleep and write and go to therapy. It's not like money is a huge issue. I've been so cautious with my paychecks that I have ten thousand dollars banked up. I don't have a mortgage, a car or any big expenses. I don't even have internet or a TV. My bills and groceries only cost six hundred a month, basically the same as a roommate would pay if I needed one. But it would be crazy to give up my career. Wouldn't it?

On the one hand, I want to leave. I have to if I want to get better. There is no other hand. Sitting on the couch in the afternoon sun with my laptop perched on a stack of pillows, my fingers share what my insides know: I need out.

I give my notice the next day.

I go for coffee with a friend who is working on his psychology PhD. He tells me about a type of therapy where people who are afraid of spiders are exposed to them so much that eventually their fear runs out. "If you hold a spider for long enough and nothing happens, eventually you realize it's not so bad," he says.

Haven't I already done something like that? I did. With Brenda, the first therapist Ian and I saw together.

Brenda asked me about The Terrible Night and repeated my words back to me a thousand times. She held her fingers in front of my face and had me follow her hand movements with my eyes as she said all the worst words. The treatment was supposed to stimulate different parts of my brain, allowing me to access the memories and feelings stored there.

The words Brenda repeated that day stopped where my mind used to turn off. Now I know more: that Gary raped me. I know because I saw it, because I watched it happen when I looked down from the ceiling of the sepia-stained room. I felt it too. Remembered it in my body.

What if I try that therapy again, this time with everything I know now? I have to do it, have to bury myself in spiders. I can't let myself freeze ever again, can't let myself get trapped beyond my reach.

"I want to do the weird eye-movement treatment I tried years ago with my other therapist," I tell Nicole. "Actually I don't want to, but I think I should."

"Eye Movement Integration. Why do you think that's a good idea?"

"It seems efficient. Let's bomb the rest of my memories out of hiding."

"We're not going to do any bombing," she says. "You need to be gentle with yourself. Are you sure you want to do this?"

"Yes. I need it."

"All right." She pulls out her notepad and asks me to summarize what happened that night.

I tell her and she writes down the scariest words I can think: Rape. Can't breathe. Collapse. Die. Words that set off my twitching as they come out of my mouth.

"Stay in touch with your experience of being raped by Gary," Nicole says as she moves her fingers from above the top of my glasses down in a straight line as far as my peripheral vision goes.

"Saying 'no' and 'stop' and pushing him away. Collapsing. Gary above you, raping you. Throat hurts. Thinking, 'I can't breathe. I'm going to die.'"

She draws her fingers into a fist. "Are you having any thoughts, any feelings, any physical sensations?"

I'm okay. Not afraid. Maybe this won't be so bad.

She moves her fingers back above my glasses and draws them across my line of vision as she repeats the scenario.

My body explodes in twitches. My throat closes over. I can barely squeeze out the words to tell her what's happening.

When I'm breathing again, she holds her fingers up and recites the words.

Nothing happens this time. I'm numb.

We go again. I'm furious, full of screams. No and stop and fuck you. Then I'm pinned beneath him. My body feels floppy, weak, helpless.

Next time I'm angry and ready to fight.

Then I'm neutral, totally fine.

We go again and I'm being strangled.

"Are you seeing any images?" Nicole asks. I see Gary's sweat dripping off his face. I strain for a closer look. Is it stubble or a beard? I stare deep into my brain. Too far. I feel a hollowness, a white fog, around my left ear. My head tilts to the side. The cloud slips up and out through my ear, and I feel it separating from me.

"Any thoughts, any feelings?" a voice asks, as jarring as though I'd been asleep.

My voice comes down from the ceiling, slow and strained. Sounds drugged. "I'm far away."

We continue. Or she continues along with whatever of me is left behind.

"Is anything happening for you?" she asks.

Her voice makes me nauseated, exhausted, like Piglet floating through the clouds on a blustery day, attached to the earth by only a thread of his unravelled scarf. How hard it must have been to hang on when the winds came for him.

"Huh?" My voice comes out small, like part of me has been erased. I wish I was solid enough to ask for help, that Pooh could spool me back in.

"Let's check in," she says. "How are you feeling?"

Floaty.

"Can you feel your feet on the floor?" she asks.

I can't. All I feel is this thick fog in my face. My head tilts like it's trying to suction a ghost back in through my ear.

"Feel your feet in your shoes," she says.

Ah, heels. Toes. Clammy.

"We're almost out of time," Nicole says. "We're going to have to continue the treatment at your next session." She goes through the words one last time, and I whimper when her hand closes into a fist.

We book the next time she has available but it's a whole week away. "How am I supposed to make it until then?"

She tells me to close my eyes and imagine the tiniest box in the world. I put everything scary in the box and bury it deep in my yard and then our time is up. "Leave the box in the ground," she says. "It's too much for you to process on your own."

That night my body roils like a ship in a storm, wilder than ever. Gary's hands are all over me. His sweat splashes against my face. Stop, get away. I shove The Terrible Night back into the box. Terror sneaks out of the box and seeps in through my pores like vapour.

I dig up the box. I need somewhere else for it to go, somewhere it can't reach me. It rattles and thumps and threatens to explode.

I see myself putting it in safest place I can imagine – down deep in Nicole's pocket.

My family gets together for Thanksgiving dinner and when I go to the table there's only one spot left: beside Dad. Mom points to it, "There's your place."

No way I'm spending a whole meal listening to him chew. "No thanks," I say. My nephews, Bethany's kids, are on a bench. "Squish over," I tell them, "I'm sitting with you guys."

"No," Bethany says. "Do not let her in. D, Mom told you where to sit."

I turn and slip down the hallway into the dark family room. I hide behind the couch. My heart is pounding out drumbeats. I don't know why I'm being so petty or why I have this huge lump in my throat. All I know is I cannot go back.

People are calling me but I don't answer. Someone flicks on the light but I clench my legs in tighter, trying not to be found. Mom and Bethany pass by in rounds and then give up the search. Almost an hour passes by the time I coax myself out of my spot and onto the couch.

Bethany catches me before I can disappear again. "I'm sorry," she says. "I didn't want my kids to help you disobey but I shouldn't have bossed you around like that."

I'm sobbing. How embarrassing that I'm being so dramatic. "I get that. I just can't sit next to Dad. I can't explain it but I can't hear him eat."

"I'm sorry," she says again. "I made you miss dinner but I can't make you miss pumpkin pie."

I manage a smile and she says, "Please come back. You can have my chair."

So we go to the dining room but I don't sit. I stand in the doorway eating my pie, knees bent and ready to run.

It's my last day at City Hall and I'm too tired to care. I pack up my folders, carry my boxes home and go straight back to bed.

Thursday comes. Appointment day. I walk to Nicole's office, my feet reluctantly pushing on. My body is all tingles and chills, then terror and sweat.

I brought a rock with me. A polished amber stone that fits in my fist. I clutch it as if its weight will anchor me in place.

Nicole holds her hand up and begins. "Staying in touch with your experience of being raped..."

The first time we go through the story I feel nothing.

The next time my head fills with swears. Fuck her. I hate her. Why is she doing this to me?

"Any thoughts?" she asks.

"Cursing," I say.

She goes again.

I rage at Gary, imagine forcing him off me.

Next time he's across a crowded table at the campus bar, drinking a pint and mocking my haircut. Everyone laughs. Even Amber, who I thought was my friend.

Nicole repeats the words from her sheet, and my head goes floppy. I'm weak and losing. A bunch of cotton balls gather above my ear, trying to make their escape. I cut them off. "I'm starting to disappear," I say.

"Can you feel your back against the chair?"

I concentrate on the sensation of my spine pressing into the leather. Sit, stay, I tell myself like I'm my own pet. Stay. Good girl. I'm here and dizzy but mostly solid. "Okay, I'm ready."

Nicole raises her hand.

I hated Gary, and he knew it. Whenever he turned to Amber and me in the computer lab I ignored him or got up to leave or hid out in the bathroom down the hall.

Nicole goes again.

Gary's sweat. It runs in rivets off his face. Dad's sweat. Dad eating an orange and slurping the juice from the rind. Gary's sweat. That rancid hockey-bag smell.

I'm drifting away. "Help," I call, "I'm leaving again."

"Feel your feet on the floor," Nicole says.

They're clenching, seized up tight. I feel my palms curled around my rock. My hands are boiling. The rock is slick and smooth in my clammy hands.

We continue. Nicole moves her fingers and repeats the terrible things.

I see Dad drenched from the rain screwing my bed frame together as droplets trickle down his face. My parents and their double sleeping bag. Gary choking me. No, stop! Fuck you!

Floating away. Pulling myself back. My feet, my brown shoes, the rock damp in my hands.

Nicole starts again.

Wanting to leave the party when Gary shows up but Dad said I can't ask for a ride if it's after 10. I'm stuck. "You're too wet to mean it," Gary says when I tell him to stop. "Why didn't you yell?" the cop asks. "You would have yelled for help if you didn't want it."

We go again.

I throw Gary into the corner. "'Vengeance is mine,' saith the Lord. 'I will repay.'" I rain fire and brimstone down on Sodom.

Next time Nicole closes her hand into a fist, I'm so tired I could sleep through eternity.

She starts up again.

I'm crying. I'm sorry, Sweetie. I'm so sorry you didn't know how to keep yourself safe.

Nicole wraps up our appointment with a few more motions, and I follow her finger with my eyes. I held my spiders and made it to the end.

We're booking our next appointment when I ask, "Why did my parents show up in all that?"

"We call it a gift when a surprise like this pops up. It's a clue telling us what we need to work on next."

My parents, huh? My parents who taught me how to float up above myself, who taught me I wasn't allowed to say no. My parents who just agreed to see their pastor with me.

33

Speed Cleaning

The pastor hands around mugs of tea and we take our seats in his living room, he and I in chairs flanking the fireplace and Mom and Dad on the couch. My chair is so big my feet don't reach the floor. I pull my legs up beside me so I won't look as small as I feel.

"Why are you here?" the pastor asks.

My parents hesitate. "They think I'm bad," I say. "They always have. They blame me for other people's choices, and when I try to defend myself they tell me I'm full of sin."

I sit tall in my seat. It reminds me of a throne now that I'm speaking, like I'm holding a scepter and issuing a decree. "Also my parents have sex when other people – me, my sisters and my nieces and nephews – are in the same room as them. I've asked them to stop a dozen times but they refuse."

"Whoa," the pastor says, peering at me through his round glasses.

"I know," I say.

"You are way out of line," he says to me.

What the fuck?

"She brought it up at a family picnic," Mom says, her eyes glinting hard. "She even got her boyfriend in on the conversation."

"You have no right to confront your parents about their private sex life," the pastor says. "And involving third parties?" He shakes his head.

Dad smirks.

I'm sweating and my belly churns like I have the flu. There's a book on the coffee table, *The Busy Girl's Guide to Speed Cleaning*. Who cares if it's three against one. They're all wrong, and there's no oven in which to hide the dirty dishes. There's no short cut, no escape.

"No," I say, like a king on his horse committing his army to war. "Their sex life is not private. I wish it was but they made it my business when they involved me."

"Oh boy," the pastor says and all the air comes out of him.

Mom and Dad deflate like old balloons.

"Far be it from me to question parents in front of their child, but we can talk about you," the pastor says.

What, I'm the only person who can be held to account?

"I don't know why you're constantly bringing this up," Dad says to me. "We stopped but you keep hounding us about it. Your mother and —"

"Wait, you stopped?"

"Yes."

"So you'll never have sex in front of me or the girls or any kids ever again?"

"That's what I said."

Oh my god, what a relief. They're done forever, and all the kids I love are safe.

"I didn't know you stopped. Thank you. Why didn't you just tell me?"

"It's none of your concern. It has nothing to do with you," Dad says.

I stare at my parents. My enormous chair swallows me. I'm Alice in Wonderland, shrinking again. I'm not even a person to them.

"There's a whole lot of broken in this room," the pastor says. "I'm appalled and, frankly, I'm not your guy. You need to find a registered therapist immediately. Do it this week."

Mom takes down his instructions like Moses on the mountain transcribing the words of the Lord.

We're sitting in a cramped circle in Nicole's office, me in my regular chair, Mom next to me in the chair where Ian dumped me a year ago, Dad next to her and Nicole between Dad and me.

I'd asked Nicole if I could bring my parents and she'd said it was fine as long as they knew I'd been seeing her on my own and as long as I understood that she would be neutral, that she wouldn't lobby for me.

"Frank and Irene, what would you like to get out of our session?" Nicole asks.

"Beats me," Mom says. "I didn't know anything was wrong."

Dad has nothing to say either.

"Okay, D, why don't you start?" Nicole says.

"I don't know who you are," I say to my parents. "Sometimes you're kind and we have fun together but other times it seems like you hate me."

"We love you," Mom says like I've stabbed her. "I was so happy when you were born."

My ears ring, blocking out her words. If you let in the nice things, the bombs hurt more.

"Frank, what do you have to say?" Nicole asks.

"Her mother and I love her," he says like a robot.

Oh yeah? "I'm furious I had to fight so hard for you guys to stop fooling around in front of the family," I say. "And Mom, you suggested what happened at Amber's place was my fault because I had been drinking."

She starts to nod and I look away so I won't see her head betray me.

"Believe that if you want, but I was sexually assaulted a bunch of times, even when I was sober."

Mom gasps, like more stabbing, like I'm riddling her with holes.

"That night you guys said I wasn't allowed to call for a ride after ten or if I had been drinking. I wanted to go home when Gary showed up but I couldn't call you and then I was assaulted."

"No," Mom says. "We said you could call any time and we would come and get you."

"Sometimes you said that but other nights you and Dad told me not to call."

Mom and Dad are shaking their heads.

"Maybe you were tired. Maybe you were frustrated. Maybe you didn't want the other girls to know I was drinking."

Still their heads keep shaking.

A fire flares inside. My voice shoots out loud. "If I was allowed to call, why did I look at the phone and then at the clock and then not call even though I was afraid and wanted to get away?"

Mom is crying thick tears that dangle from her chin before pooling on her sweater. "I'm sorry. I'm so sorry," she chokes out. Dad's eyes are red too.

"It's not your fault," I say, "but you refused to help. Remember how many times I asked you not to have sex in front of me? You spent all these years training me that I couldn't say no."

"We only ever did that when everyone was asleep," Dad says.

"Not true," I say, slapping him with my voice. "You knew I was awake the time in the tent when Mom told me to lie still and go to sleep. And you deliberately did it in front of me when I was twenty-two. We were sharing a hotel room, remember? I hid in the bathroom for hours that night, hoping you'd be asleep when I came out, but you were awake and angry and started as soon as I lay down."

Dad's faces contorts like he's trying to cannibalize himself.

I turn to Mom. "And you said you thought I had been abused by a babysitter when I was three. I don't think that's true, but I wonder why you never thought, 'Oh maybe we should stop having sex in front of her because it seems to upset her. I wonder if it reminds her of anything.'"

It's another mortal wound. She might die from my words. So what? It's not my fault she never once listened. I keep lambasting her: "All those nights I kept plugging my ears and there was nothing I could do to save myself from you. So no wonder I couldn't protect myself later on. Do you know I even dated some of the guys who hurt me?

"The first time I ever fought back was with you. It was the day after the night in the hotel. I told you it wasn't okay. I told you that you were breaking me.

"Mom what did you do? You said it was none of my business. You said I was selfish and inconsiderate." I don't care that I'm yelling, that I'm a freight train of fury.

I turn to Dad. "And then you came over and said the same things. You told me I wasn't allowed to question my parents, that I wasn't allowed to say no.

"And then, surprise, I was sexually assaulted again. But you were wrong: I GET TO SAY NO!"

I'm screaming and crying so hard I'm gasping for air. "AND YOU DO NOT GET TO TELL ANYONE ELSE THAT THEY DON'T GET TO SAY NO. YOU DO NOT GET TO HURT THEM TOO."

"Do you understand what she's saying?" Nicole asks.

"Yes," Mom says, her head hanging low, dragged down by remorse and sorrow.

"I don't know why she's still talking about this," Dad says, his voice tight and sharp. "It isn't an issue any more. She got what she wanted."

"It doesn't seem like it's resolved for her. No one can decide for someone else when an issue is over," Nicole says. "We have five minutes left but it sounds like you all want to improve your relationship."

My parents agree.

"I don't know," I say. "I'm so tired of this and of them telling me I'm a bad person."

Dad looks old. He is old. Grey hair. Old-man pants. "I will stop any time you don't want to continue a conversation," he says.

"Thank you," I say. "And do you promise not to call me a bad person ever again?"

"It depends on the context. You're not a bad person in this world, but everyone is a sinner until they've been redeemed."

"Ah," Nicole says. "Do you see how that might be confusing?"

Dad squirms in his chair. "I suppose."

"I want you to promise never to call me bad again, no matter the context," I say, staring him down.

Dad's eyes dart around the room, pinging off Mom, the walls, the bookshelf.

I'm seven again, trying to push him off the couch.

"Okay," he says reluctantly, but he hasn't changed his mind, he's just agreed not to speak it. I can't shove him off the couch, and there's no use trying. This shitty nothing is all he has to offer.

34

BLUE MITTEN

My old ex, Shane, and I are watching *The Walking Dead*. I put the popcorn bowl between us as a dividing line to keep him locked on his side.

But do I want him to stay over there? I haven't kissed anyone in the year and a half since Ian left, haven't felt anyone's hands warm on my skin, and god I miss it.

I set the popcorn bowl on the floor and lean against Shane. We kiss as the good guys kill zombies, and Shane's mouth is greedy. He pulls me close and presses his body hard against me.

I shudder. My body shakes and jolts and throws him off.

We try again. My body spasms and kicks and won't let him near. I'm sweating and heaving and can't catch my breath.

"What's wrong with me?" I ask Nicole.

"Nothing's wrong. Now that you've started listening to your body, you won't be able to override it any more."

I'm walking home from a coffee shop around ten on a Tuesday night and the streets are empty in all directions. I'm two blocks from home when a man, maybe in his early twenties, rounds a corner and stumbles up the sidewalk toward me.

"Hey," he slurs and reaches for me.

"Sorry," I say, speeding up to get past him.

"Please, I'm lost."

He isn't wearing a jacket, just a burgundy sweater, even though it's January. I guess I could help. It would be mean not to, and he looks harmless enough with his enormous Bambi eyes. I get the address from him and check the numbers on the buildings near us. "It's that way," I say, pointing toward downtown. "But it's pretty far to go without a coat."

"Thanks," he says and swoops in for a hug. He's so close I can't dodge it without being rude.

His arms close around me. I pat him on the back and then try to pull away. He won't let go. Shit, he's going to kiss me. I duck my head but he forces his lips against mine.

Bam!

He shoots back a few feet. He's on the other side of my blue mitten. He's rubbing his Adam's apple.

I stare at my outstretched arm, trying to figure out what happened. I punched him. Hard. In the throat. My arm moved by itself, like Grandma's doll that animated when I pulled a cord on its back.

"That wasn't okay," my voice is yelling. "Never do that to anyone else ever again!"

"Sorry, sorry," he mutters and scuttles away.

I run home, wrists and arms shaking, jaw quivering. I'm bawling by the time I unlock my front door.

I flop onto the couch and let my body move as it pleases. I'm twitching like crazy but I can handle it. The realization surprises me.

Yes, but I should ask for help. It's the kindest thing I could do for myself.

I reach out to Shane – the stoic who isn't even rattled about the other night – and to another friend, then to Mom and to Jenna. "Something bad happened," I say, and they listen and let it be and still love me.

The next day I'm in my living room staring out at the street. Everyone says I did the right thing, but isn't it my fault? I let that man hug me.

A cop car stops in front of the neighbour's house. I run outside and the cop rolls his window down.

"I did something that might have been bad," I say, and tell him what happened.

He's smiling. "Nice work. I'm glad you did that. I wish more women had that kind of instinct."

"Are you sure I didn't do anything wrong?"

"You're in the clear," he says. "He was assaulting you and you protected yourself. I tell my wife if anything like that happens to her that she should jab her thumb into the guy's eye socket. You did the right thing."

I go back inside.

If it was okay for me to punch that guy, I wonder how bloody I'd have been allowed to leave Gary. I wish he was the asshole I'd punched in the throat.

Isn't there anything else I can do to find Gary?

What if Tonya still has the tape from The Terrible Night? What if I make it worth her while to look for it? I'd pay hundreds. Thousands. I'd give anything for it.

I search for Tonya online. It takes weeks and tonnes of digging before I find a number. When she picks up, I ask if she tracked down the tape.

"Sorry, no," she says.

"Is there any chance you still have it, any chance at all?"

"No," she says. "I cleared everything out."

Shit. "I'd pay you," I say. "Whatever you want. Please?"

"Sorry, I don't have it."

"Do you remember Gary, the old guy?"

"No."

"What's Amber's last name?"

"I don't know."

"What about Teron, the guy Amber liked, do you know his last name?"

"I don't remember anything."

"Nothing? What about Amber's daughter?"

"Sierra?"

"That's her name?"

"Yeah, but that's all I know."

I type Amber and Sierra's names into my search bar. A funeral home listing comes up. That can't be right. I click on it and see a black and white photo of a woman crouching down with her elbows on her knees, surrounded by long silky hair. She's not smiling, not looking at the camera.

It's not Amber. It can't be.

I read the obituary: Amber is survived by her daughter Sierra.

I shriek and click away on my laptop, trying to prove that this is some other Amber. I find an old court case. A child custody ruling over Sierra.

I know the court file is private and should never have been posted online, but I read it anyway. I didn't know Amber left home when she was twelve. I didn't know she was a drug addict or that she once spent fifty-eight days in rehab only to fall back down. I didn't know our semester together was one of the highlights of her life, a flash of momentum that burned out before finals and shot her lower than she'd ever been. Exactly a year after The Terrible Night, the court papers say she suffered a breakdown.

I had no idea anything was wrong. I didn't know her at all.

I click back to the obituary. It is her. "Passed away suddenly," it says. I cry and cry, for her and for me.

I Google Amber's mom. Maybe she knows something. I find another obit. Fucking shit. Everyone is dead.

Everyone except Tonya, who knows nothing. Tonya, who threw the evidence into a goddamn landfill.

I find a private investigator in the phone book. He's a retired cop so he must be good. "I'm looking for a man named Gary," I tell him. "He was forty and married and a student at the University of Regina. I know the semester he was there. That's all I have. Can you do anything with that?"

"Was his name Gary or is that what he told you?"

His question is so jarring that my head snaps back. What kind of jerk investigator is this? "I think his name was Gary. That's what everyone called him."

"Was he a student, or is that what he said?"

I stammer. "He was on campus a lot. I thought he was a student, but he wasn't on the class list. I guess I don't know."

"I don't turn away cases where I can be of use," he says, "but even if this Gary was telling the truth that's not a lot to go on. We could go through piles of your money and still come up with nothing. I'm sorry."

I cry for days. I've waited too long and now I'll never find him. It's over. I failed. And it's my fault if he hurts someone else.

No, that's not true. I did everything I could, even if that black door with the white light behind it is closed now once and for all.

My parents' house is in chaos the night before Tenille and her family are scheduled to fly back to their mission assignment in Papua New Guinea.

The main bathroom is occupied so I go to my parents' room to use theirs. Their door is open. The bathroom door is open too and fuck: There's naked Dad, scrubbing himself in the shower. I whirl around and away through the door he couldn't be bothered to close.

I go to the basement where Tenille has her luggage spread all over the floor. My three-year-old nephew is hiding surprises in the suitcases.

I'll take auntie duty. I'll get the crayons and take him upstairs to colour. Dad is dressed now and sitting at the computer desk. I reach past him for the pencil holder that's full of crayons. "Just take two or three," he says.

I grab the container. "We need more."

"Put them back."

"Are you using them?"

"No."

"Then I'm taking them."

"Why can't you do what you're told?" Dad asks, knocking a stack of papers to the floor.

"I get to disagree with you."

Dad's eyes go cold. "I'm your father. You need to obey me."

"I will never obey you again. You can say what you think, but I get to choose how to behave."

We glare at each other. "Do you think we're equals?" I ask.

"You're my child."

"How old am I?"

"I guess you're an adult."

"So we're equals?"

"Yes," he says reluctantly.

"I went to use your bathroom."

Dad jumps like I caught him. Good, he should be ashamed. "Too much work to close a single door?"

"Look, you can't see it but your mother and I are trying to accommodate you." He sighs. "Like that sex thing. We decided we won't do it when you're here in the house."

"I know we've talked about this a billion times, but why did it take you twenty years to listen to me?"

"Maybe we thought you were trying to control us. Maybe we thought you were being ornery." Dad's eyes glimmer. "But we were destroying you."

I take the crayons and bolt. His words are like coming in from the cold, when inside feels worse than outside, when the ice crystals in my fingers burn as they melt.

I go to a lazy yin yoga class in a studio I haven't visited since Ian left. I unroll my mat and remember being here years earlier. Ian was in a handstand, sweating through his light blue t-shirt and smiling upside-down at me. I'm on my back with my legs up the wall when the instructor's voice breaks in: "Lower your right leg and place the ankle over your left knee."

I do and seconds later I'm crying, tears slipping over my ears and into my headband. It breaks my heart that Ian won't return my emails any more, that he doesn't have a shred of love left for me.

My legs burn and quiver against the wall. My jaw clenches tight. Fuck him. He tricked me and made me love him and threw me away.

The fire goes out. In its place, only tears. Ian wasn't a villain. He was simply who he was: kind, exhausted and wretchedly human, just like me.

"This is an inverted pigeon pose," the instructor says as we switch legs. "It can bring up strong emotions. Whatever happens for you, be open to it."

Fucking pigeon. I didn't recognize it this way. My hamstring feels pinched, afraid. I remember how tortured I felt when Ian watched TV shows packed with naked women. My body squeezes in on itself now as it did then, flooding me with dread. Maybe his shows were as innocuous as he thought, but my body knew only what it felt: racing pulse, shallow breath and that infernal ringing in my ears.

Finally pigeon pose ends. I stretch out on my mat for the resting period. Yes, I kicked Ian so hard I broke his tooth. Yes, I bit and clawed at him until he bled. I'm sorry I hurt him. But I'm sorry for myself too. I wasn't so crazy after all. I was lost and afraid and fighting to survive.

That night I'm in bed staring up at the ceiling. If even my worst deeds don't make me bad, were there any villains in my life? My parents certainly weren't out to get me. Ian loved me as well as he could. So did Shane.

And the other guys? They stole from me and left heaps of wreckage in their wake. But aren't they also the product of their own unresolved wounds? In elementary school didn't they learn, as I did, that the strong are allowed to take from the weak? And what of this culture that says women's bodies exist for the enjoyment of others, where TV shows hire porn stars and where Ian's cousin comes home from his grade twelve grad to an adult who says, mocking, "So? Did you get laid?"

But what about Gary? He's a monster.

Yes.

But is he? Or is it that his venom was all I saw and so all I knew?

There must be more to him than the time he unleashed his rage on my long-ago self. No one can be that hateful without also being broken.

"We're all the walking wounded," Mom used to say. We are, aren't we? All riddled with holes. And if we aren't brave enough to turn ourselves inside out, to find the goodness within from which we are made, how can we keep from causing harm?

My body gives a gigantic puppet-show jolt.

My skin hums inside and grows still. I watch the night darken and close my eyes.

What if there are no villains at all?

35

JAGGED HEART

I scrape together the last of my savings and go on another meditation retreat in California.

The days dawn foggy and cool. My mind is quiet. I'm not crying much, and it surprises me. Three days in I meet with a teacher. "Should I do something to make it harder?"

He laughs. "No, be kind to yourself, but remember why you're here. Really commit to it. We're planting redwood seeds, and there's no limit on how big a heart can grow."

In the hall that evening I see myself carrying a wooden box. I lift the lid. Inside are a dozen troll dolls – miniature versions of all the people I've been trying to forgive: Dad, Gary, a coworker I argued with at City Hall, the rest of the guys who hurt me. And Amber. Weird, why is she here? My stomach churns and my chest is hard like it's full of concrete. I close the lid tight and twitch through the night.

The next day I race up a dusty path into the hills until I reach the top. I run along the crest until I see San Francisco in the distance resting against the bay.

"Gary says hi," Amber said when I saw her in the hall a few days after The Terrible Night. It was the last time I saw her. She laughed when I frowned. "Yeah, he thought you'd be like that."

"I was wet when I woke up," I told her. "Cold."

"You puked so I threw water on you."

I keep walking and Amber is everywhere, her sunglasses, her K-car, her snug yellow shirt, her laughter tinkling out over the hills.

On the video the guy Amber liked asked Gary, "Don't you just want to fuck her in the ass?" when I was passed out on the carpet. Amber must have been pissed.

What did you do to me? I scream at her ghost.

I run to escape her. The sun blazes down, and I sprint over the rocks until I'm spent.

I bend forward to catch my breath. A rock sparkles on the ground. I pick it up. It's a jagged white heart, streaked with dirt.

I tuck it into my sports bra, heart against stony heart.

I hurry to the meditation hall in my pjs. The morning practice opens with a few minutes of yoga, and the teacher invites us to pat ourselves down to help our bodies wake up. I tap my arms, legs and belly as the room fills with a gentle fluttering. Good morning body, I tell myself.

The movements in the room come to an end, and the silence returns.

What did Amber do? I replay The Terrible Night. My red shirt. Amber and Tonya jostling for the mirror. Gary coming in the front door carrying a case of beer.

The meditation ends and the hall empties. It's time for breakfast but I'm not ready. I lie down and spread a blanket over my legs. I feel Gary pressed against my back. His python arm slides around me. "You know you want it."

I'm losing. Throat hurts. Can't breathe. Black door. White light.

Wait, the hallway light wouldn't be that bright. It's blinding, like looking straight into the sun. Why is it like that?

I reach for the handle. I pull the door open and slip through.

I stand in the endless white glow. There's no floor but I'm not falling. I feel sleepy. Dizzy. Lightheaded.

COME BACK! YOU'RE GOING TO DIE!

A black shape, me, lingers beyond the door.

My body jolts. It's violent, electric. Can't breathe. Mouth open in a scream that won't come.

My hands slap against my face a thousand times. They move on their own, drumming madly like a beheaded chicken running for her life.

HOLY SHIT. I ALMOST DIED!

I keep slapping my face, softer now. You're alive.

My breathing slows, speeds up, slows again. You're alive. See, you're breathing. My heart thunders like it's going to explode. Shh. I love you.

I think he almost killed me. No, I know.

Shh. You're okay. Come, eat.

I meet with one of the teachers. "How are you doing?" she asks.

I can barely speak. Tears stream out slow and thick like honey. "I remembered something terrible."

"Oh D," she says, and her warm gaze bubbles through me like hydrogen peroxide in a wound. "Be really gentle with yourself. You do whatever it is that you need. Maybe tea? Or a nap? It's a beautiful day. Why not lie out in the sun and feel it melting you?"

I splash cold water on my face. I'm weak, exhausted, but I go back to the hill. I climb in the afternoon heat, higher and higher like Icarus flying toward the sun. I'm oozing sweat. I mop it up with my tank top and keep climbing.

At the top I scramble up a boulder that stands in a small clearing. I spread my arms like Columbus bold on the deck. I didn't die. I'm alive, and I have been for fourteen years since The Terrible Night. The breeze dances across my skin. I'm alive in the sky, which is also alive.

I race down the hill, slip, fall on my hands, get up and keep going. Breathe in. Out. In. Alive.

I take a shower, feeling the too-hot drops ping against my back. I rub lotion into my shoulders. I feel my hands and the coolness spreading across my skin. See, alive.

I lie on my tangle of blankets. My legs jolt. Then my shoulder.

The girl who's sharing my room comes in and fusses on her side of the divider. She lies down too, bed creaking.

My legs twitch. Back. Legs.

Someone rings a bell. It's time to go to the hall. My roommate gets up. My legs shake as she closes the door. One more minute, I think. Or should I stay?

"Your twitching could be a disorganized reaction to your trauma," Nicole said at our last appointment. "If so, it won't stop until your body can organize and execute its response."

Body, what do you want? My legs twitch. My shoulder joins in. Please, what do you need? I'll do it, whatever it is.

My heart beats fast, booming like a grandfather clock inside my chest.

I see myself at my first-aid training course. That plastic torso and head. My wrists stacked, fingers intertwined. I'm pushing down hard on the dummy's chest, panting as I pump life into him.

"Harder," the instructor calls. "Harder or you'll lose him."

My legs twitch. Heart races. Am I trying to jolt myself back to life?

My body hums. Twitches as if to agree. How to organize the response?

My back jolts. Then shoulder. Legs a moment later. Maybe if my twitches happen at the same time?

My breathing goes wild. I slow it down. You're okay. You're safe.

My legs jump. Then my shoulder. Come on, I invite, all together.

My legs and shoulder jolt at the same time.

There's a pause.

My back goes.

Legs and back.

My ears ring.

Back jumps.

Back. Legs. Back.

Ears.

Shoulder, legs, ears and back.

A mad convulsing. Spine arches off the bed. My back rises so far only my shoulders and feet are left on the bed. I hang half suspended in the air, all dark arts and black magic, all Voldemort blasting Harry Potter with an unforgiveable curse.

My spine unclenches. I drop back onto the bed.

My whole body thrashes. Neck, fingers, everything.

Finally the furies release. I raise my hands to my heart. It beats hard, as if I've shocked it with electric paddles.

Well that's certainly enough to bring someone back to life!

I smile.

It freezes on my lips. Chills run down my spine. Did I die? Did my twitching bring me back to life?

My legs jolt. I'm tingling, vibrating from within. It's my body saying yes.

Thank you, I say, rubbing my heart. My legs tremble. Arms join in. Everything quivering, tingling, warm.

Beyond my window a bell rings. Forty-five minutes have passed since my roommate left. But fourteen years slipped by too, backwards and forwards, in this body that saved me, that was always on my side.

It's my birthday on the retreat. I had my birthday here last year too. I'm thirty-three today. There's ice cream at lunch, bittersweet chocolate. I lick out my bowl. Happy birthday to me. Then I take a bite of a warm California peach, and the juice drips down my arm as sticky and decadent as life itself.

A few days later I'm back in Regina and sitting across from Dad at a picnic table. My palms are sweating. "You mentioned having good memories of me," I say. "For my birthday could you give me a list?" His eyes rest on my face and wait until I raise mine. He nods. "I'll try. I have good memories but a bad memory."

I dart away then, over to the playground, where my parents' foster baby giggles at the top of the slide. He hesitates and then lets go, plunging down into Mom's outstretched arms, into the love that's always been there waiting for him.

When Grandma died, Mom adopted a thousand of her dolls, all the orphans left behind after my aunts and cousins helped themselves. Mom brought them home like children and gave the house over to them, posing dolls everywhere, on couches and chairs and one on each stair.

"Don't you think you have too many dolls?" I asked, moving an armful to clear a place to sit.

Mom's voice broke. "Yes, but they each deserve a good home."

I go back to Nicole for a final round of eye-movement treatment. "Staying in touch with your experience of the night you almost died," she says with her fingers raised.

My eyes follow her hand as she moves it across my line of vision.

She speaks the words I'd written out: "Throat hurts. Can't breathe. Thinking, 'I'm going to die.' Reaching for the door. White light." Her hand closes into a fist.

My body shudders. My shoulder rises up, trying to swallow me. I reach for the door, and white light floods in. It's warm and bottomless, stretching on forever. I step into the glow.

My ears are sirens. My legs jolt. Wrists flap. I feel my feet tensing hard against the floor.

We go again and I disappear, my insides slipping out through my ear.

I shake my head and suction myself back.

"Any images?" she asks.

My eyes are closed but I'm squinting at a coffee-stained scene. "Yes, but it's not something I could have seen."

"No need to rationalize. What is it?"

"I see myself lying on my back. I'm looking down from the ceiling. Gary's above me."

"And?"

"He's kneeling over me. Crushing my throat. Oh my god, why am I just lying there?! Why am I letting him do that? Holy shit, I'm dead."

GO BACK!

It takes forever to catch my breath. When I do, my horrible therapist raises her fingers and begins again.

I'm at the black door, pulling it open.

"Any thoughts?"

My ghost answers. Her voice is tinny and slow. It echoes as it comes out of my mouth. "The light isn't scary. I thought it was but it's warm. Soft. Like in a sun room."

My body jolts. My hand flaps against my chest, knocks me back into myself.

Nicole raises her hand again. "Thinking, 'I'm going to die.' Reaching for the door. White light," she says.

Fear rises in my chest and turns to sorrow, which melts out of my eyes and gives way to compassion, to me rubbing my heart and saying, I'm so sorry Sweetie.

She raises her fingers, and it happens again: fear, sadness, kindness. Next time it's sorrow, followed by love.

"Do you recognize a pattern?" she asks.

I nod. I knew that pain acknowledged begets compassion, but I didn't know it could extend even and especially to a broken piece of self.

"How are you doing?" she asks.

"I'm all right. The Terrible Night feels further away like it's not happening now, like it's back in its place fourteen years ago."

"Good," she says, and draws a diamond with her fingers to close our session. It's been three grueling years of therapy, but I did it and I lived.

Gary nearly killed me, nearly strangled me to death. I don't remember it in my brain like a normal memory but I know it in my body.

I wanted to say I wasn't sure but my throat closed over and wouldn't let me breathe.

It's true, and this body that saved me deserves my trust.

I've been daydreaming about climbing a mountain but I can't find anyone to go with me. I Google adventures and come across Outward Bound's backpacking trips. There's a free one for women who've experienced abuse and want to find freedom at the top of the world.

I apply and soon I'm getting off the bus in Canmore and looking for the Hostel Bear. Inside there's a picture of a grizzly.

"There are only black bears around here, right?" I ask the worker.

"And grizzlies."

Shit. I heard there were no grizzlies left in Saskatchewan or Alberta because humans had driven them away. I should have double-checked, but what kind of province allows campgrounds in grizzly country? And what kind of psychopaths would lead a group into such danger? No wonder I had to sign a waiver.

Grizzlies are monsters, the worst bear of all. They'll rip you apart for the sheer joy of watching you die.

I shudder and go to meet the seven other women who make up the rest of the team.

Our guides pick us up in the morning and show us how to load our packs with our borrowed tents, sleeping bags and cooking pots. "A few last things," one of the guides says, passing out whistles and holsters of bear spray when we're in the parking lot at the base of the trail.

I hold my can in my palm, flicking the safety off and on. It's my last chance to escape but I need to do this. I'll stay in the middle of the pack, the smartest place for prey.

It's August but it's freezing as we trudge along the trail. It's beautiful, probably, but I'm watching the path ahead of me, looking out for rocks, roots, danger. We pass rockslides where the mountain, beaten, crumbled into dust.

It's drizzling. We trudge along, slow and clumsy under our packs, going zero kilometres an hour. The drizzle turns to rain. Cold drops hit my face and splatter against my glasses.

"At least it's not snow," someone says. Then, a minute later: "Oh would you look at that? It's snowing."

The snow is thick and piling up on our packs, and it's hours before we reach camp. That night I lie awake shivering and think about turning back.

It's nicer in the morning. Warmer. It's only going to be a week, I remind myself.

We're cruising along and I edge up near the front of the group. My legs are solid and stronger than ever as they carry me up the mountainside on the way to Turbine Canyon.

We break for lunch halfway up one of the steepest parts of the trail. There's nowhere to sit so I move off to the side behind a scraggly clump of bushes. I reach for my water bottle. A flicker of sunrise orange catches my eye. A butterfly. She flits over to a blade of grass. Then rests on a branch. Then flies straight toward me.

I hold still, hushed with awe. Her wings flutter, and she alights on my hip as if she's anointing me. Her wings – spread wide and trembling – are covered in tiny black freckles, in specks of deepest darkness.

She's standing on my tattoo, on Isaiah 30:21: "Whether you turn to the right or to the left, your ears will hear a voice behind you, saying, 'This is the way; walk in it.'"

Her wings pulse. Up she rises and away.

The next day we're hiking to a glacier. We get to a ridge across from it and stop to take pictures. No one else wants to keep going, to make it to the top of the mountain, to stand at the entrance to the sky.

I beg one of the guides to let me go up on my own, and we wander away from the group while she decides.

Someone yells over to us. I can't make it out. More yelling. "Bear. There's a bear!"

We hurry to join the rest of the group and stand together at the top of the ridge, ten women against a beast. The leaders are waving their hands in the air and chanting, "Hey bear, we're over here."

I raise my arms too, remembering what they told us in the parking lot the first day: band together, take up as much space as possible and try to look like a many-headed monster. As if a bear would fall for that.

I scan the mountainside. Two hundred meters below, I see him.

A grizzly.

He's huge and brown and lumbering. He could tear me apart with a stroke of his paw.

I give up on my stupid jazz hands and reach for my bear spray.

The grizzly glances toward me and I drop the can to my side. I can't tell who is human and who is bear.

He dives into a pond of glacier melt and splashes around, reveling in his afternoon dip. After a while he hauls himself out and shakes off like a dog, sprinkling water like blessings all over the rocks.

He turns away and climbs slowly, steadily up the opposite ridge. His great bulk gets smaller and smaller as he shrinks into the mountainside.

The butterfly with her darkness.

The bear with his light.

Me with my stains and this wide open heart.

EPILOGUE

After two years of therapy and singleness, I fall for a beautiful man named Kyle, a single dad who does shift work in Estevan.

Months ago I shared my secrets with him and recognized the tenderness in his voice like I'd only given him more to love. Like a diamond that's been cut and now all its edges gleam.

"Look at me," Kyle says gently. He is gazing down at me on my bright pink sheets, the ones I bought when Ian left.

I love you, he says or I say or our bodies say as they move together. My hands glide across his chest, caressing him.

They freeze. It's too much. I'm fragile as frost, as glass about to shatter.

I concentrate hard. My wrists tighten and push against him. My mouth drops open: "No." It's a whisper, faint like a voice coming up from the dust of a clover. But it's enough.

He blasts across the bed like I shot him from a cannon. He's silent and still like we practiced.

My wrists tremble. Jaw quakes. Legs quiver.

A warm humming runs through me. It tingles like an orchestra strumming life through my veins.

"I did good," I say as the music fades, and my tears are holy: silver, glitter and gold. This body is back, and she is mine.

I wonder again why Gary came in Amber's living-room door when the kitchen door was next to the parking lot. Why would he have walked any further than necessary on that cold March night? He seemed the type to drive a truck with tires squealing and park himself wherever he pleased. Did he live around here? What if he lived just down the sidewalk from Amber?

I'll call the private investigator again in the morning and ask him to check if Gary lived in the apartment complex. They must be able to track down records of previous tenants.

I'm so close. It's like my birthday parties when I was a kid and my sisters hid my gifts, yelling "hot" or "cold" as I ransacked the living room. I find Tonya on Facebook and message her again. "I know you said you don't have the tape but if you ever come across it in a corner of your basement I'd pay thousands for it."

Tonya answers immediately. She doesn't have it. We message back and forth and she says she threw her class notes out a few years ago.

"For your University 100 course?" I ask.

"And 110."

"Wait, there were two classes? You and Amber were in both University 100 and 110 that semester?"

"Yeah."

Holy shit. Everything is buzzing. I'm back in the Campus Security office. I must have driven myself here. I'm rambling as the 24-hour security guard takes notes. Sweat drips down the back of my legs. I'm afraid I'm going to fall. I'm gripping his desk with both hands but my nails won't catch on the polished surface.

"Two years ago you guys searched the University 100 class list and didn't find his name. There's another class list I'd forgotten about. He has to be on it."

Campus Security calls me at work the next day to ask for my testimony. I give it and wait for them to call back.

They email a few days later. They found Gary and gave a stack of information to the police. By the afternoon the officer I spoke with two years ago is on my case. He remembers me and still wants to help. We hang up, and sobs of relief shake through me.

But what happens next doesn't matter. Not any more. Gary could be a murderer or serial rapist who's never been caught. He could be in jail. He could be dead. Or he could be a better person with a garden and a dog he allows up on the couch.

Whoever he is now, I passed him out of my hands and into the law's. After fifteen years, I finally heaved his weight up and off of me.

At the grocery store a few blocks from Amber's place I find a bouquet of lilies: yellow, pink and white with petals stretched wide like stars.

The white lily, the largest one in the centre of the bouquet, is dusted with pollen shaken loose from her stamen, the rusty flecks marring her splendour. I go to brush the specks and stop myself. The mess is true.

Even these flowers, these heady bursts of life, are cut off at the stem and doomed to die. That's why I chose them over the orchids and all the other potted plants. These lilies are a sacrifice, a savagery, another death needed to memorialize that which is no more.

I carry the lilies to Amber's place and knock on the door like it's fifteen years ago and she's about to answer.

She's not here. No one is.

I leave the flowers with a young woman who lives next door whose coral blouse makes me think she's getting home from church. "Do you want me to pass on a message?" she asks.

I shake my head but my mouth opens. "I knew a girl who lived there once," I say. "She passed away. I want to leave the flowers to brighten their home and remember what was lost."

I shiver as I speak and tingles run through me. The flowers aren't only for Amber. They're for me too, for the parts of myself that died that night.

Four years after Ian left – my secrets aired out, my shaking stilled – I climbed out of the past and into right now.

The End

ACKNOWLEDGEMENTS

Deepest thanks to Merilyn Simonds, my insightful, talented and kind writing coach, for believing in my story and my ability to tell it. Thank you to Coteau Books, especially John Agnew, Susan Buck and Dave Margoshes, for your steadfast support and for bringing my book to life. Thank you to my editor Janice Zawerbny for your deft but gentle cuts.

Thank you to Sage Hill Writing Experience, the Saskatchewan Writers' Guild and the Regina Public Library Writer-in-Residence program for the myriad ways you support writers in Saskatchewan and for allowing me to learn from such gifted instructors as Merilyn Simonds, Wayne Grady, Alison Pick, Reg Silvester and Gail Bowen.

Thank you to my therapists and meditation teachers, to the Regina Insight Meditation Community, to Spirit Rock Meditation Centre and to Outward Bound Canada for teaching me how to make peace with myself.

Thank you to the team at the University of Regina that works to keep students safe and to the police officer who believed me. May you continue your vital work with the same compassion you showed me.

Thank you to all my darlings who kept picking me up and dusting me off. Thank you to Ian for having loved me so well and for handling my unravelling with such grace. Lastly, thank you to my parents for encouraging me to do whatever I needed in order to heal, including telling this story. I can't fathom how much love that must have taken.

Citations for quoted works:

Blake, William. *Songs of Innocence and Experience, with Other Poems.* Basil Montagu Pickering, London, 1866. Digitized by Google Books.

Damrosch, Leo. *Eternity's Sunrise: The Imaginative World of William Blake.* Yale University Press, New Haven, 2015.

Faulkner, William. *Requiem for a Nun.* Random House of Canada Limited, Toronto, 2011.

Rumi, Jalal al-Din. *The Essential Rumi.* Translated by Coleman Barks. Castle Books, New Jersey, 1995.

Rowling, J. K.. *Harry Potter and the Deathly Hallows.* Raincoast Books, Vancouver, 2017.

Shakespeare, William. *Hamlet.* Global Grey, 2018.

Shakespeare, William. *Romeo and Juliet.* Global Grey, 2018.

Scripture quotations taken from *The Holy Bible*, New International Version®, NIV®. Copyright © 1973, 1978, 1984, 2011 by Biblica, Inc.® Used by permission. All rights reserved worldwide.

ABOUT THE AUTHOR

D. M. Ditson is obsessed with telling the truth. She has been writing for over a decade as a journalist and communications consultant. She shares her life story to show that healing is possible and maps out her trauma recovery with hopes of helping others free themselves.

Wide Open is her first book. Before it was published, her memoir won the John V. Hicks prize, awarded by the Saskatchewan Writers' Guild. Wide Open also won a 2020 Saskatchewan Book Award and a Columbia Basin Trust artist grant.

Ditson recently moved from Regina, Saskatchewan to Nelson, British Columbia, where she can be found enjoying the mountains. She is happy.

Manufactured by Amazon.ca
Bolton, ON

22182729R00138